THE VICTORIAN GARDEN

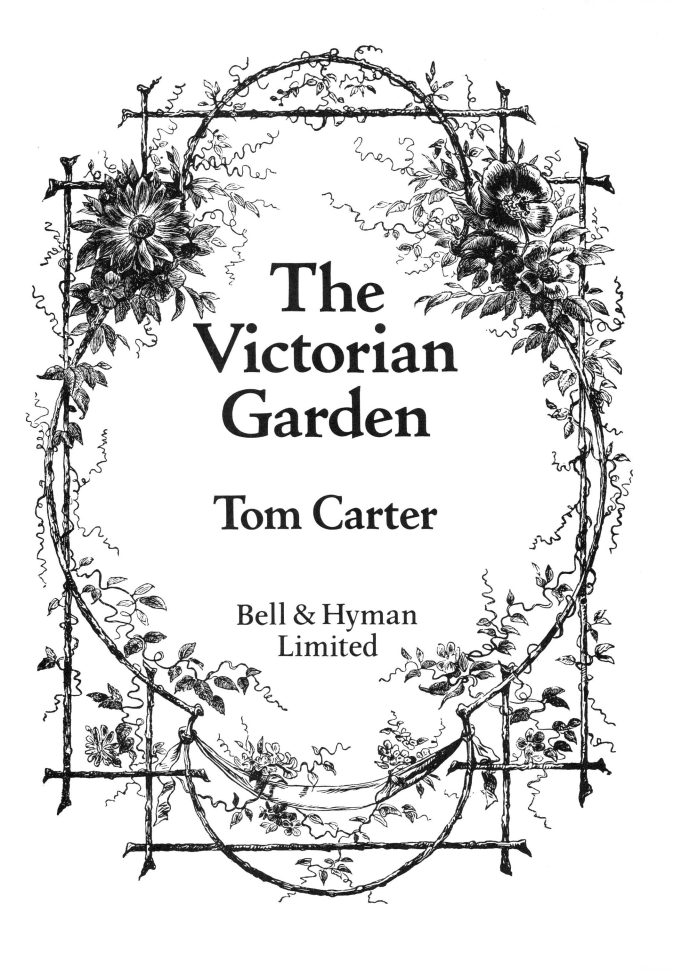

The Victorian Garden

Tom Carter

Bell & Hyman
Limited

Published in 1984 by
BELL & HYMAN LIMITED
Denmark House
37-39 Queen Elizabeth Street
London SE1 2QB

ISBN 0 7135 1440 X

Produced by Cameron Books,
    2a Roman Way, London N7 8XG
Designed by Tom Carter
Managing editor: Jill Hollis
Editor: Elisabeth Cameron

Monochrome printing and binding by
    R.J. Acford, Chichester, Sussex
Monochrome reproduction by Tenreck Ltd,
    172a Brent Crescent, London NW10
Colour printing by Chromocraft Ltd,
    Shepperton Studio Centre, Middlesex
Colour reproduction by Thames Colour
    Scanning, Roslin Road, London W3

Contents

Author's note

The material in this book is largely derived from published works of the nineteenth century. The spellings of the original texts, though often inconsistent, and the contemporary names of plants, some of which have since been reclassified, have been retained, but obvious typographical mistakes have been corrected.

Dates in attributions are those of the editions quoted, not always those of first publication. The titles cited in picture captions are those of the works from which the illustrations have been taken: in many cases the same woodcut or engraving appeared in a number of different books and periodicals.

The photographs on pages 13, 118 and 121 are reproduced by kind permission of the Marquess of Londonderry, and are from the collection published in *The Londonderry Album* (Blond & Briggs, 1978). The cartoon on page 161 has been supplied by the Mansell Collection. The front jacket picture is 'The Oaks' by Joseph Kirkpatrick, from the Christopher Wood Gallery, reproduced by permission of The Bridgeman Art Library. The 'Portrait of Adelaide Maria, Countess of Iveagh' (1885) by George Elgar Hicks, opposite page 16, is reproduced by permission of Christie, Manson & Woods, and the Rockery at the Royal Horticultural Society's Gardens, Chiswick, opposite page 161, by permission of the Mary Evans Picture Library.

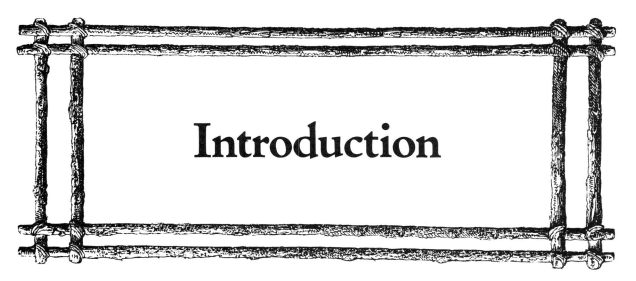

Introduction

'The love of gardening is natural to man' proclaimed John Claudius Loudon, in the introduction to the first volume of *The Gardener's Magazine*, which appeared in 1826. Loudon himself died in 1843, only six years after Queen Victoria's accession, but his works, complemented by those of his wife, Jane, made a major contribution to the development of the Victorian garden. He was, like many eminent gardeners, a Scotsman, but in 1803 travelled to London, which he made his home for the rest of his life—the last twenty years of it in a house built to his own plans in Porchester Terrace. His interests covered every aspect of the arts and sciences of gardening, from the grand vistas of landscape design to the smallest detail of microscopic botany, while his skill at gathering, assimilating and passing on knowledge made him a model for horticultural writers of the whole age. His ability to inform without being patronising and to be critical without being abusive was, however, not shared by all of his successors.

With the founding of *The Gardener's Magazine*, Loudon could claim to be the first horticultural journalist. He hoped that it would be 'an acceptable addition to the periodical works already before the public'. Other journals then in existence, most notably the *Botanical Magazine* produced by William Curtis since 1787, had little to offer to the practical gardener. Loudon also inaugurated, in 1829, a *Magazine of Natural History*, which included the first published articles of the great art-historian and critic, John Ruskin. Loudon practised as a landscape gardener and was an accomplished painter, but it was for his books that he was chiefly remembered. *The Encyclopaedia of Gardening*, in which he assembled a vast body of information on the state of horticulture in Britain and throughout the world, together with a comprehensive study of horticultural history, first appeared in 1822 and quickly became established as a standard work. The monumental *Arboretum et Fruticetum Britannicum* of 1838, with four volumes of text and four of plates—the list of contents alone fills 140 pages—is still, after a century and a

John Loudon as landscape gardener: discussing improvements with clients on a Lincolnshire estate. 'Nothing could ever make up to us for the pain and slavery of ten days spent in this way, but the pecuniary compensation'. A sketch by a travelling companion in *The Gardener's Magazine,* 1826.

half, an absorbing and impressive guide to 'The Trees and Shrubs of Britain, Native and Foreign, Hardy and Half-Hardy'. Underlying all his works was the assumption, again expressed in his 1826 introduction, that the 'agreeableness and utility' of gardening were universally accepted. For John Loudon, as for many authorities of the time, the utility was more important than the agreeableness: the pleasure garden was a luxury, while the kitchen garden, like the farm, the plantation and the orchard, was an essential economic resource. It was not until the end of the century that 'The Garden Beautiful' took undisputed precedence over 'The Garden Useful'.

Gardening in the Victorian world was an activity in which the rules of a rigid society could be relaxed a little—where men and women, labourers and intellectuals, poor and rich could mix with comparative freedom. Professional gardeners, although often badly paid, were generally respected, and their art appreciated. The significance of the garden itself lay not only in its practical and aesthetic value, but also in its potent symbolism. The processes of growth, renewal and decay provided countless moral lessons, with examples drawn as much from the humblest root as from the most exotic blossom. Man's reliance on the fruits of his labour, which had been taken for granted in previous ages, was a common theme for moralists and educators in the nineteenth century, as they observed an increasingly urban population losing its sense of dependence on the soil. The pre-Victorian *Vegetable Substances used for the Food of Man,* produced by the Society for the Diffusion of Useful Knowledge in 1832, considered that the culture of the earth served as the key distinction not only between mankind and the 'inferior orders of animate creation', but between savage and civilized humanity. *The Juvenile Rambler* of 1838 said of Van

Diemen's Land, or Tasmania: 'The natives of the country are so completely ignorant, that before the arrival of the European settlers, they had scarcely any notion that the soil could be cultivated.'

The religious, as always, discovered apt parallels between mankind and the flowers of the field and garden. In 1846 William Jones wrote in the tract *The Book of Nature*: 'To-day the flower bloweth, and spreadeth forth its leaves, and we admire its beauty, but its glory is short; for it soon fadeth, and falleth away to the ground. I am like this flower, frail and mortal.' 'Such as I am at my death,' he confessed, 'such shall I be at my resurrection. If I am the seed of a thorn or a thistle, there will be no hope that I shall be found a rose or a lily, when I am risen again.' The view that man was near to God in a garden was a popular one, reflecting the importance in Christian teaching of the two great gardens of the Bible, Eden and Gethsemane. Shirley Hibberd, the author of many practical works, exclaimed in the contemplative *Brambles and Bay Leaves* (1855): 'O heaven and O earth! In the garden is your meeting-place, for there God talked with Adam, and there the Saviour wept in agony for all... A garden is a Divine institution, a Biblical reminiscence, a present solace, a refuge, a retreat.' John Keble, the Oxford divine and poet, addressed the flowers in similar style:

> Relics ye are in Eden's bowers,
>   As pure, as fragrant, and as fair,
> As when ye crowned the sunshine house
>   Of happy wanderers there;
> Ye dwell beside our paths and homes,
>   Our paths of sin, and homes of sorrow,
> And guilty man, where'er he roams,
>   Your innocent mirth may borrow.

Gardening was an occupation for which not even the most pious and puritanical had a bad word. For the rich it was, in Loudon's words, 'a source of agreeable domestic recreation', while it was constantly recommended to the poor as beneficial to physical, mental and spiritual well-being. Not every Victorian gardener would have fitted Shirley Hibberd's description of 'a healthy, jovial fellow, with a hearty word for everybody'—many were bad-tempered, argumentative and jealous of their privacy—but the garden offered plenty of opportunities for exercising patience, diligence and all the other virtues.

'Contact with the brown earth cures all diseases,' wrote Hibberd in 1877, and the prescription was often applied to what were thought of as moral and social ailments. Men and women labouring in their gardens were safe from the dangers of political agitation and from the temptations of vice. In his preface to the 1838 edition of *The Manse Garden*, the Scottish minister Nathaniel Paterson encouraged his parishioners to grow vegetables and to ornament their cottages with 'roses, ivy, and fruit trees, which at once hide the deformity of naked walls and suggest the idea of comfort within... When home is rendered more attractive, the market-gill [tavern] will be forsaken for charms more enduring.'

'Furnishing the Garden' - a chapter heading from *Beeton's Book of Garden Management,* 1872.

The same attitude was exported to distant parts of the British Empire. The Horticultural Society of Sydney, Australia, noted in 1863:

> Love for a garden has a powerful influence in attracting men to their homes, and saves them from many temptations; and on this account a taste for gardening is an additional security for domestic happiness and comfort. It is also a recreation which adds materially to health, promotes civilization and softens the manners and tempers of men.

The desire to improve the fortunes of the lower class, though in part a mere conventional duty, often arose from genuine concern. The rural poor had suffered badly from the enclosure of common lands in the late eighteenth and early nineteenth centuries. The provision of land to give the labourer recreation as well as food was a constant demand of radical politicians, and horticulturalists were generally sympathetic to the cause. Loudon's *The Cottager's Manual* of 1838, a collection of articles originally published in *The Gardener's Magazine*, was one of a number of works designed to guide estate-owners towards a more enlightened treatment of their tenantry. In it he dealt with husbandry, cottage architecture and domestic economy, and with the right of working people to a degree of relaxation: 'Nor do we object to tea because it often occasions gossiping among the cottagers' wives. Why should not the cottager's wife have her gossip as well as the wife of the landlord?'

Social reformers recognised the value of gardening for profit and for pleasure. Charles Kingsley, advocate of what came to be called 'muscular Christianity' was an enthusiastic gardener at his Surrey rectory. Visiting luminaries were drafted into his work-force, and his daughter Rose recalled in *Eversley Gardens* the sight of a future bishop 'toiling away in his shirt-sleeves as earnestly as any day-labourer working for his bread.' In the Study Garden which Kingsley created out of a chicken-yard he would 'pace bare-headed, composing sermon or novel, lecture or poem.'

The associations of flowers provided material for poets and versifiers throughout the nineteenth century. In the early years it was the wild flowers, like William Wordsworth's celandine, which stirred the romantic imagination:

Pansies, Lilies, King-cups, Daisies,
Let them live upon their praises;
Long as there's a sun that sets,
   Primroses will have their glory;
Long as there are Violets,
   They will have a place in story;
There's a flower that shall be mine,
'Tis the little Celandine.

But by the 1890s the jaded taste of the aesthete Theodore Wratislaw could respond only to the heady scents and colours of hothouse blooms:

I hate the flower of wood or common field.
I cannot love the primrose nor regret
The death of any shrinking violet,
Nor even the cultured garden's banal yield.

The silver lips of lilies virginal,
The full deep bosom of the enchanted rose
Please less than flowers glass-hid from frosts and snows
For whom an alien heat makes festival.

Between these extremes was an entire range of Victorian poetry, from the simple appeal of Mrs Hemans's verses, to the pedestrian sonorities of Alfred Austin.

The strain of sentimentality which was a feature of nineteenth-century writing owed much to the floral world, Henry Kirke White's lines on the rosemary, written in the early 1800s, illustrate its morbid side:

Come, funeral flower! who lov'st to dwell
With the pale corse in lonely tomb,
And throw across the desert gloom
   A sweet decaying smell;
Come, press my lips, and lie with me,
Beneath the lowly alder tree...

This tendency also emerged in devotional works, like the *Chapters on Flowers* published in 1836 by 'Charlotte Elizabeth', This was the pen-name of Charlotte Elizabeth Tonna, previously Mrs Phelan, who became famous for her anthems written in the cause of Irish Protestantism. Despite its title, the book has more to do with the spiritual than with the floricultural world, and Mrs Tonna used the flowers and shrubs of the garden to introduce a series of reflections on mortality, all treated with a funereal relish characteristic of the age:

There are many flowers that speak to me of early happy death. The lily of the valley is one: but the fairest is the white moss-rose... The pall may spread its velvet folds, and the sable plumes bow in stately gloom over the dead; but a single white rose, drooping amid its dark

foliage, tells the story more touchingly, and with more eloquent sympathy, than all that the art of man may contrive, to invest sorrow in a deeper shade of woe.

These gleefully sombre musings were remote from the world of the real garden, and, while Charlotte Elizabeth saw the changing seasons as occasions for yet more mourning —'each returning summer bears witness to some additional bereavement... companions long-loved have gone into the grave'—practical gardeners measured the year by a calendar not of sentiment but of unrelenting hard work. In *The Glory of the Garden* Kipling spoke for them all:

> Our England is a garden, and such gardens are not made
> By singing:- 'Oh, how beautiful!' and sitting in the shade,
> While better men than we go out and start their working lives
> At grubbing weeds from gravel paths with broken dinner-knives.

The skills of nineteenth-century horticulture were the culmination of a long tradition. Up to the end of the seventeenth century techniques had been crude and the processes of nature poorly understood; till then, wrote Loudon, 'Those superstitious observances attendant on a rude state of society retained their ground.' Even so, 'Englishmen had for many centuries attained a very fair proficiency' in the practical management of a garden, as Carew Hazlitt, grandson of the essayist William, reminded his readers in *Gleanings in Old Garden Literature* (1887). Francis Bacon had written *Of*

Left: Frontispiece of Mrs Loudon's *Practical Instructions in Gardening for Ladies,* 1841.
Above: Frontispiece of *Chapters on Flowers,* by 'Charlotte Elizabeth', 1836.

Gardens in the early 1600s, while John Evelyn's works on the subject, primarily his 1693 translation from the French of de la Quintinye's *The Complete Gardener*, were seen as marking a turning point. An abridged version of this text was also produced by George London and Henry Wise, whose position as nurserymen and as advisers to the court and the aristocracy gave them an extensive influence in garden design.

In the 'dawn of intellectual day' of the eighteenth century, the evolution of 'modern' gardening was rapid. It closely paralleled the development of scientifically-based agriculture, which was, as *The Gardener's Magazine* later observed, 'so intimately connected with garden culture, that no publication on the one art can wholly separate itself from the other.' The chemistry, physics and 'vegetable physiology' of the 1700s still embraced numerous misconceptions and fallacies that would not be corrected for another hundred years, but they represented an immeasurable advance on the alchemy and astrology of previous ages. The scientific botany introduced by Linnaeus and his followers made possible the proper classification of the plant world, and, led by 'the great encouragers of science, gardeners acquired botanical knowledge, and were excited to greater exertion in their art.' (*Encyclopaedia of Gardening*, 1834.)

> The Swedish sage admires, in yonder bowers,
> His winged insects and his rosy flowers;
> Calls from their savage haunts the woodland train
> With sounding horn, and counts them on the plain:
> So once, at Heaven's command, the wanderers came
> To Eden's shade, and heard their various name.
>
> Thomas Campbell.

The best-known authority of this period was Philip Miller, director of the Society of Apothecaries' Physic Garden in Chelsea. His pioneering *The Gardener's Dictionary*, which was first published in 1731 and ran through a large number of later editions, was followed by several lesser works, among them *The Gardener's Kalendar* of 1732, which was intended as a more manageable guide than the massive *Dictionary*: 'it would not only be portable on all occasions, either in the closet, or in the garden; but it would also be afforded at such a price, as might suit those who could not so well spare money for the larger work.' Other manuals included a series of treatises on husbandry and gardening produced by Richard Bradley, Professor of Botany at Cambridge, from the early 1720s to the late 1750s. These were followed in 1767 by the first appearance of John Abercrombie's *Every Man His Own Gardener*. This compendium of advice and instruction, firmly based on the old tradition of gardening practice, was originally attributed to Thomas Mawe, gardener to the Duke of Leeds, who was paid £20 for the use of his name but made no other contribution. Abercrombie himself—'sixty years a practical gardener'—was too diffident to let his own name be used, and subsequently found it hard to re-establish his authorship. The book, and variants of it under the title *Abercrombie's*

A gardener at Wynyard Park, County Durham, seat of the Marquess of Londonderry, photographed c.1890 by Lord Reginald Stewart, younger son of the sixth Marquess.

Frontispiece of Philip Miller's
The Gardeners Kalendar (1757 edition).

Practical Gardener, stayed in print for nearly a century: as late
as 1857 an edition was brought out with additional material
by George Glenny.

The Horticultural Society was founded in London in 1804
in order to gather together an increasing body of serious
research. Loudon gave its 'enlightened president', Thomas
Andrew Knight, credit for giving the science of horticulture 'its greatest stimulus'. The society encouraged work in
all areas of the subject—with the main emphasis on the productive, rather than the ornamental—but its deliberations,
and the often academic writings of its members were beyond
the level of most gardeners. As the century progressed, a

demand developed for accessible gardening literature. This need was partly met by existing works, such as *Abercrombie*, while a succession of new authors produced books for the swelling numbers of amateur enthusiasts as well as for the professionals. The introduction of cheap printing methods and efficient distribution in the 1840s allowed horticultural journalism to grow from *The Gardener's Magazine*, with a limited though influential readership, into *The Gardeners' Chronicle*, which had a large circulation and popular interests. The public taste for information was satisfied by a wide range of periodicals: *The Gardener's Gazette, The Horticultural Magazine* and *The Cottage Gardener* (later to become *The Journal of Horticulture*) begun in the 1840s, Shirley Hibberd's *The Floral World and Garden Guide*, launched in 1858, David Thomson's *The*

Gardener, two publications started by William Robinson in the 1870s, *The Garden* and *Gardening Illustrated*, and, from 1884, *Amateur Gardening*. The aspirations set out in the introduction of the 1860 *Gardener's Weekly Magazine* were typical:

> We have outlived the days of stage-coaches, and have been for some years reaping the benefits of more rapid and perfect means of communication, interchange of sentiment and thought. In short, we live in the days of *cheap literature*, which is the "order of the day". The benefits attending on this state of things are numerous and unquestionable; to the gardener especially, whose operations are so much dependant on the state of the weather and season, it is a matter of importance to have the assistance of a weekly monitor, and an advantage to be made speedily aware of all matters of interest that transpire in connection with his pursuits, as well as to be able to communicate quickly, and at the lowest possible cost, with his professional brethren and amateurs throughout the length and breadth of the kingdom.

The gardening literature of the nineteenth century, not only the general horticultural books and magazines, but those aimed at the floricultural enthusiasts and other specialists, formed part of the general Victorian movement to educate and improve, whose beliefs were summed up by Cardinal Newman in 1864:

> Virtue is the child of Knowledge: Vice of Ignorance: therefore education, periodical literature, railroad travelling, ventilation, and the art of life, when fully carried out, serve to make a population moral and happy.

The garden was a small reflection of the Victorian world at large. It expressed the self-confident stability which, after an uncertain start, characterised Victoria's long reign. Scientific methods gave growers at least the illusion that they could get the upper hand over nature. Advancing technology allowed the building of effective glasshouses and conservatories, and increasing affluence brought them within economic reach of the new middle class. Britain's position as an imperial power and her command of the trade routes encouraged the continued importation of exotic plants. Professional plant-hunters and amateur naturalists—many of them missionaries of the Church—travelled all over the world in search of unknown species to satisfy a taste for the spectacular.

The high style of Victorian ornamental gardening reached its peak in the 1850s and 1860s in the grounds of the Crystal Palace at Sydenham and of private estates like Trentham and Shrublands. Their opulent formality was attacked and derided by the 'natural' school of gardeners which developed in the third quarter of the century, led by William Robinson. The formal style, with its labour-intensive methods,

Right: Portrait by George Elgar Hicks of Adelaide Maria, Countess of Iveagh, reclining in a conservatory. 1885.

SCARLET-FLESHED ROCK MELON.

'Fruit' - a crayon painting by Monsieur Vidal, engraved for *The Illustrated London News*, 12th April 1851.

Left: A melon from James Anderson's *The New Practical Gardener*, c.1880: 'Among Scarlet-fleshed we have the immense-growing Paterson's Superb Hybrid, a close relation to Scarlet Rock, of which we have given a coloured representation.'

fell out of fashion, although many of its traditions have survived to the present day in public parks and gardens: it was in any case ludicrously inappropriate when imitated on a small scale for the late Victorian villa.

The virulence of its critics in the later years, and a natural reaction against the conventions of the previous generation gave the nineteenth-century garden an image which it has never lost. Its excesses were remembered: its achievements belittled. Many of the finest examples had disappeared, others were in decay. At the beginning of the twentieth century Rose Kingsley visited Eversley, her father's old home, and found the beds and borders, of which even Robinson had approved, choked with a carpet of weeds, and the trim lawns, where Alfred Tennyson had sat, given over to molehills and ants' nests: 'The shrubberies are groves of half-dead Laurel and gloomy Yew.' Her description of the ruined garden recalls Lord Tennyson's lines in *Mariana*, written seventy years earlier:

With blackest moss the flower-plots
   Were thickly crusted, one and all:
The rusted nails fell from the knots
   That held the peach to the garden-wall.
The broken sheds look'd sad and strange:
   Unlifted was the clinking latch;
   Weeded and worn the ancient thatch
Upon the lonely moated grange.
   She only said, 'My life is dreary,
   He cometh not,' she said;
   She said, 'I am aweary, aweary,
   I would that I were dead!'

The Victorian gardener deserves to be celebrated for the prime of his accomplishments, not remembered by the fading remnants of his work. Even where the layout of a garden has been preserved, the style and scale of its planting will inevitably have changed. Some of the great glasshouses have survived, but many have gone—the Crystal Palace destroyed by fire in 1936, Joseph Paxton's Conservatory at Chatsworth, too expensive to run, blown up. Yet, more

The Croquet Ground at Wallington Bridge, Surrey - a plate from Alfred Smee's *My Garden,* 1872.

than any other period in gardening history, the nineteenth century was comprehensively and thoughtfully documented by the writers of the time: if little is left of the garden itself, its pleasures can still be recaptured from their pages.

The last gold has fallen of the last hour of these dear garden days, and only one more word must be said—Farewell! (E.V.B. *Days and House in a Garden*, 1884).

The Kitchen Garden

Jane Loudon wrote *The Lady's Country Companion* (or 'How to Enjoy A Country Life Rationally') in 1845, in the form of letters to Annie, a young wife who has moved to her husband's country estate. In an early letter, she talks of Annie's complaint that 'the kitchen-garden is a mile from the house, and under the care of a cross old gardener, who cannot be displaced.' The grounds of Annie's Manor House had evidently been laid out in the Landscape Style of the eighteenth century, when the kitchen garden was dismissed as unsightly and had to make the best of any position that could be found for it. The still-surviving walled garden and orangery at Ickworth, in Suffolk, built by the 1st Earl of Bristol soon after 1700, were conveniently close to the house until it was demolished a few years later. Plans to rebuild the house on the same spot failed, and when work began on a palatial

'The Manor-House in its original State', with the windows shaded by 'some lofty Scotch pines, which are certainly the most gloomy of all the vegetable race.' From Mrs Loudon's *The Lady's Country Companion*, 1845.

structure for the 4th Earl in 1795, it was on a site suggested by Lancelot 'Capability' Brown, half a mile away, where there was no danger that the menial departments might intrude on the view.

Such an arrangement was impractical enough on a great estate and even less satisfactory when imitated in smaller establishments. William Cobbett, proponent of radicalism and good sense, wrote in *The English Gardener* (1829): 'We must take the best that we can get, never forgetting, however, that it is most miserable taste to seek to poke away the kitchen-garden, in order to get it out of sight. If well managed, nothing is more beautiful than the kitchen-garden... I see no reason for placing the kitchen-garden in some out-of-the-way place, at a distance from the mansion-house, as if it were a mere necessary evil, and unworthy of being viewed by the owner.'

Choice in the siting of a garden was, of course, a luxury. Much of the English population in the nineteenth century had no land, or too little to create a problem in laying it out. Yet formerly most people had had the use of at least a modest area of ground. Under Elizabethan legislation, no cottage could be built with less than four acres around it, and this law stayed in force until 1795, when the Enclosures

> *Cobbett's Nursery, Kensington, Feb. 7.*
> Some of our readers having requested us to give an account of this garden, we called there with a gentleman who was about to purchase some trees. We found the veteran writer sitting in his garden-house, by a wood fire made in one of his cast-iron American stoves, a table beside him covered with newspapers, and a few books behind him on a shelf...
>
> *The Gardener's Magazine*, 1827.

began to deprive countrymen and cottagers of their plots and 'cow-keeps'.

Philanthropists and reformers, including Cobbett, fought to mitigate the effects of the many Enclosure Acts, which had caused widespread destitution through the appropriation of common land and, together with the economic depression following the Napoleonic Wars, led to riots in 1816 and near-insurrection in 1830. The allotment movement, and other schemes, aimed to make small quantities of land available at moderate rents and, although the movement failed to make it a statutory duty, there were landlords who saw wisdom in allowing their tenants this concession.

Where allotments were provided for country labourers, their size varied from ten rods (one-sixteenth of an acre) to two or three acres, with space for some pigs and a cow or two. In 1801, the cottagers of Long Newton, Wiltshire, were offered up to one-and-a-half acres per family at a rent of £1 12s an acre and given a collective loan to establish the scheme. The loan was repaid four years later, and the allotments were still in use in 1868.

In *An Encyclopaedia of Gardening* (1834 edition) Loudon gives the size of a cottage-garden as 'generally something under half an acre,' since 'the extent of the garden of the labourer ought never to be such as to interfere with his regular employment.' He then describes in turn the gardens of artisans, small tradesmen and farmers, which rise to an acre or more and are all assumed to produce only vegetables and fruit. Gardens attached to small suburban houses or tradesmen's villas contained flower beds and lawns which required the attention of a jobbing-gardener, and the grounds of 'suburban or citizen's villas', up to ten acres, needed a 'regularly-bred master gardener'. An extensive staff looked after the thousands of acres that surrounded a 'mansion-residence'.

The typical kitchen garden for a moderately affluent household covered just less than an acre, which was about as much as one gardener could manage, and a family needed to be fairly prosperous to employ professional

...all grasping at the few remaining small patches held by poor labourers, must of course be abandoned as defeating its own end; such a system being hurtful alike to private individuals and the stability of the state. Nay, further, *the right* of the poor must be recognised, and earnest and hearty steps taken to invest them with that right. Governments, indeed, might interfere, and with the force of law compel landowners to appropriate a portion of the land in each parish for the behoof of the labouring population; but this step, it is to be feared, would prove to be of little use, severing the link of good-will between the high and low, and introducing a system of antagonism which would end in the discomfiture of the dependent. *The law of kindness* ought to take the place of legislative enactment, not exercised as a mere piece of charity, but as a moral duty, in the same way that a father provides for, and cares for his children.

Philip Gurdon, 'Field Gardening for the English Labourer' in *The Annals of Horticulture*, 1847.

John Loudon's plan for the cottager's year, from articles in *The Gardener's Magazine*, 1830, reprinted in 1840 as *The Cottager's Manual*.

COTTAGER'S GARDEN CALENDAR.

Catalogue of Vegetables.	January. work.	h.	February. work.	h.	March. work.	h.	April. work.	h.	May. work.	h.	June. wk.	h.	July. work.	h.	August. work.	h.	Sept. wk.	h.	October. work.	h.	Nov. wk.	h.	Dec. wk.	h.	Expense of seed s. d.	Produce	Number of days to serve the family, &c.
Potatoes	- -	-	dig plant	6	- -	-	- -	-	hoe and earth up twice	1½	rea.	-	—	-	- -	-	-	-	- -	-	-	-	-	-	0 6	4½ bush.	26. Small for hogs, &c.
Radishes	- -	-	sow	-	- -	-	ready	-	- -	-	-	-	- -	-	- -	-	-	-	- -	-	-	-	-	-	0 1	20 l. bd.	For breakfasts, &c.
Peas and beans	dig sow	4½	earth up	¼	ear.up	¼	stck	½	ready	-	—	-	—	-	- -	-	-	-	- -	-	-	-	-	-	1 0	7 pecks	7. Pods for hogs.
							-	-	do.	-	—	-	- -	-	- -	-	-	-	- -	-	-	-	-	-	0 6	8 pecks	8.
Early Barnes cabbage	- -	-	earth up	½	- -	-	ready	-	—	-	—	-	- -	-	sow	¼	trsp.	½	man. dg.plt.	3½	-	-	-	-	0 6	200 cab.	40. Leaves for hogs.
Dwarf marrow peas	- -	-	dig sow	1½	ear.up	½	stick	½	- -	-	-	-	ready	-	—	-	-	-	- -	-	-	-	-	-	1 2	8 pecks	8. Pods for hogs
Windsor beans					- -	-	- -	-	- -	-	-	-	do.	-	—	-	-	.	- -	-	-	-	-	-	0 8	6 pecks	6.
Onions	- -	-	digging	4	sow	1	- -	-	- -	-	-	-	- -	-	rea.	-	-	-	- -	-	-	-	-	-	0 6	2 bush.	6. Slice to cold pork.
Spinage					do.	½	- -	-	- -	-	rea.	-	- -	-	- -	-	-	-	- -	-	-	-	-	-	0 2	- -	6. Refuse for hogs.
Early turnip					do.	¼	- -	-	ready	-	-	-	- -	-	- -	-	-	-	- -	-	-	.	-	-	0 1	- -	5.
Lettuce					do.	¼	- -	-	- -	-	rea.	-	- -	-	- -	-	-	-	- -	-	-	-	-	-	0 2	- -	6.
Scarlet runners					- -	-	- -	-	sow	1	stk.	⅓	—	-	rea.	-	—	-	—	-	-	-	-	-	0 9	- -	60. A profitable crop.
Parsneps	dig	10	sow	1	—	-	- -	-	- -	-	-	-	- -	-	- -	-	-	-	tk. up	1	—	-	—	-	0 2	4 bush.	8. 3bush. for hogs, &c.
Carrots			do.	2	- -	-	- -	1	- -	-	-	-	—	-	- -	-	—	-	do.	2	—	-	—	-	0 4	12 bush.	40. 7bush. for hogs, &c.
Barley	- -	-	- -	-	dg. so.	6	roll	1	roll	1	hoe	1	- -	-	reap	2	-	-	thres.	5	dig	12	-	-	0 9	4 bush.	For hogs and hens.
Potatoes	- -	-	- -	-	- -	-	dg.plt.	7	hoe	2	ear.	1	earth	1	- -	-	-	-	tk. up	8	-	-	dig	10	1 6	25 bush.	130. 8 bsh. for hogs, &c.
Sugarloaf cabbage	- -	-	- -	-	dg. plt.	3	earth	¾	earth	¼	rea.	-	—	-	sow	¼	-	-	trsplt.	½	-	-	dig	2	0 6	220 cab.	40. Plenty for hogs.
Savoy cabbage	- -	-	sow	¼	- -	-	- -	-	- -	-	-	-	dg.plt.	1	- -	-	-	-	- -	-	-	-	rea.	-	0 3	160 cab.	30.
Green curled borecole	- -	-	ready	-	sow	¼	- -	-	- -	-	-	-	-	-	dg.plt.	1	-	-	- -	-	-	-	-	-	0 3	100	20.
Cucumbers	- -	-	- -	-	- -	-	- -	-	sow	½	-	-	- -	-	ready	-	—	-	- -	-	-	-	-	-	0 2	90 cuc.	30.
Leeks	- -	-	- -	-	sow	½	-	-	- -	-	-	-	- -	-	dg.plt.	1	-	-	- -	-	-	-	-	-	0 2	- -	Useful as potherbs.
Potherbs, &c.	dig	4	- -	-	- -	-	plant	3	—	-	—	-	—	-	—	-	—	-	- -	-	-	-	-	-	1 0	- -	Mint and balm dried
Mercury	- -	-	- -	-	—	-	—	-	—	-	—	-	- -	-	- -	-	plt.	1	- -	-	-	-	-	-	-	- -	for tea in winter.
Hours monthly		18½		15½		12¼		13¾		6¼		2½		2		4½		1½		20		12		12	11 2		446 days.

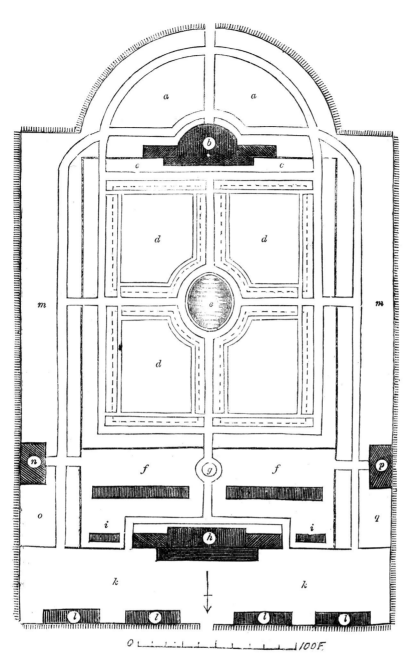

Design for a kitchen garden in *The Gardener's Weekly Magazine*, 1860. An elaborate arrangement – in addition to the 'culinary departments' (d) there is space for fruit at the top (a) and in the slips at the sides (m). The area for forcing melons and cucumbers is at (f), while (k) is for compost and dung. (n) is the gardener's house, (p) storage for fruit and onions, with 'lodging room for under-gardener'.

labour. The tables of expenditure set out in *A New System of Practical Domestic Economy* in 1825 suggested £2,000 as the lowest annual income that would cover employment of a permanent gardener, allowing a wage of seven shillings out of a total weekly outlay of fifteen on garden produce. A couple with three children on an income of 24 shillings a week—more than double a labourer's wage—were expected to spend 1s 2d per week on vegetables, including five pounds of potatoes a day.

The design given by Cobbett can be taken as an example of an early nineteenth-century gentleman's kitchen garden. It measures 215 feet by 132, the longer sides facing north and south. The ground is enclosed by a twelve-foot wall

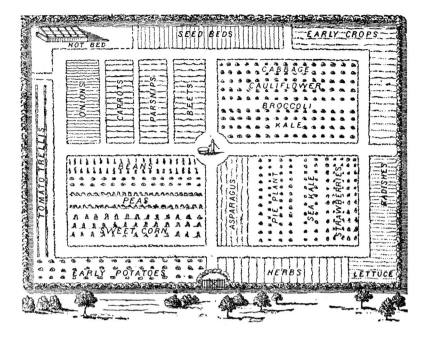

Layout of a hedged kitchen garden of 1879, evidently taken from a transatlantic original. Pie Plant is an American term for rhubarb.

surrounded by a thorn hedge, a bank and a ditch to deter predatory children and pilferers. (The wall is exceptionally high—they were often about eight feet, and stout fencing was sometimes used instead.) Inside, there are borders all round the garden under the walls and six plots, roughly equal in size, at the centre, separated by gravel walks. Five of the plots are cultivated, the sixth is a space for frames and hot-beds—the 'melon-ground'.

There were many variations on this plan to suit particular conditions or individual whims—Loudon's *Encyclopaedia* illustrates oval, circular and irregular forms—but all conform to the principle of a distinct walled garden divided into easily managed areas. By the 1880s, the separation of kitchen garden from 'pleasure ground' had become less definite. An increase in population (by a factor of four during the century) and the general movement into towns and suburbs meant a reduction in the space available to all except the most affluent. A very small garden described in *Gardening Illustrated* (1879) contains a grass walk and flower borders, as well as fruit trees and a few vegetables, in a total area of only 40 by 16 feet.

The most striking feature of kitchen gardens in the early nineteenth century is the wide range of vegetables that they could produce. The 1813 edition of Abercrombie's *Every Man His Own Gardener* lists 41 types, excluding herbs, many divided into several forms and varieties. This compares respectably with the 44 similar headings in Sutton's seed catalogue for 1983. Much the same list is given in Main's revised *Every Man* in 1839, and in the version annotated and extended by George Glenny in 1857. It was only in the later years of the century that the range of produce began to decline. Delicacies which twentieth-century growers and cooks have until fairly recently found unfamiliar or exotic, such as capsicums, globe artichokes and garlic, were not at all unusual.

Cottage gardeners were comparatively unambitious, but normally ensured a good supply of crops by saving their own seed and exchanging it with neighbours and friends, even if they could not afford to buy from seedsmen. Allotment clubs and benevolent societies tried to promote variety by making free seeds available. Regarding the twenty-three headings in one society's list, the editor of *The Gardener and Practical Florist* in 1843 commented: 'We might not have noticed this, except that the seedsmen ought to know how their retail trade is invaded by the wholesale distribution. The list is excellent; and where people desire to set cottage gardeners up they cannot have a much better list, but it is a pity any society, supported by hundreds, should be giving such packets away to spoil the trade of seedsmen.' The same publication is critical of the rather narrow range suggested by a Mr Brady, 'whose advice was chiefly intended for the cottagers of Ireland', and remarks of his plan, 'From this we are to infer, that cottagers are not to presume so far as to grow cauliflowers or brocoli [also spelled brocolli and broccoli], sea-kale nor asparagus, French nor scarlet beans, nor peas: cabbage, cabbage, cabbage is the staple.'

Brady's plan was certainly not typical of his time, and most of his contemporaries keenly recommended highly ambitious garden regimes even to their humblest readers. Gardeners were, no doubt, selective in their growing schemes, but many early to mid-Victorian vegetable gardens were constructed on the same general plan.

Some of the ground was set aside for perennial crops—at their most modest a few roots of horseradish in an odd corner, but often including much-prized asparagus in a carefully tended bed. The preparation and maintenance of asparagus beds was a laborious business, since they needed deep trenching, frequent hoeing, and repeated applications of manure, but their produce was much in demand.

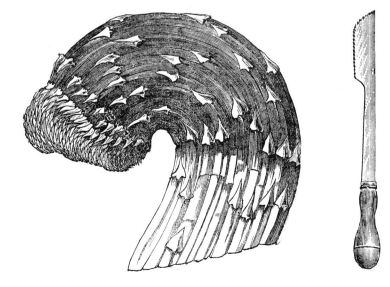

List of seeds applied for to a horticultural society

BEANS. – Early Mazagan; Early Long-pod.
BORECOLE. – Tall Green, or Scotch Kale; Dwarf Green, or Canada Kale.
BRUSSELS SPROUTS.
BROCOLLI. – Early Purple Sprouting; Dwarf Late Purple; Knight's Protecting; Late Dwarf Tartan.
CABBAGE. – Early York; Vanack; Early Brompton; Early Battersea; Nonpareil; Red Dutch for pickling.
CARROT. – Early Horn; Altringham, or Long Grange.
CAULIFLOWER.
CELERY. – Red Solid or Manchester; White Solid.
CRESS. – Curled-leaved. Lasts longer in perfection than the plain-leaved.
CUCUMBER. – Southgate, or Long Green prickly.
KIDNEY BEANS. – Negro; Fulmer's Early; Cream-coloured; Scarlet-Runner Bean.
LEEK. – Broad-leaved London.
LETTUCE. – Black-seeded Green Cos; Bath Cos; Brown Dutch Cabbage; Grand Admiral; Hammersmith Hardy Green.
MUSTARD. – White.
ONION. – New White Globe; White Spanish; Brown Portugal.
PARSLEY.
PARSNEP.
PEA. – Double-blossomed Frame or Charlton; Dwarf Blue Imperial; Dwarf Blue Prussian; Knight's Dwarf Green Marrowfat.
POTATO. – Ash-leaved Kidney; Early Manley; Early Shaw; Bread-Fruit; Lancashire Pink-eyed.
RADISH. – Early Scarlet Short-top; Scarlet Turnip; White Turnip.
RHUBARB. – Elford; Hybrid.
SPINACH. – Round-seeded Spinach; Flanders.
TURNIP. – Early Dutch; White Stone; Scotch Yellow; Swedish.

The Gardener and Practical Florist, 1843.

Left: 'Giant Asparagus' from a garden in Woodstock, Oxfordshire reported by *The Illustrated London News* in 1851. The twelve-heads-in-one measured three inches across.
Right: Knife for cutting asparagus, from *The Illustrated Dictionary of Gardening.*

Seedsmen's advertising of the 1880s.

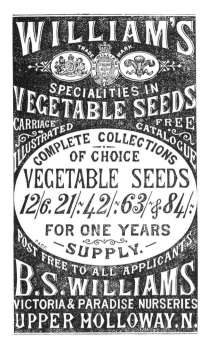

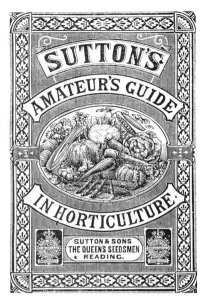

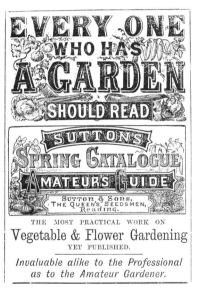

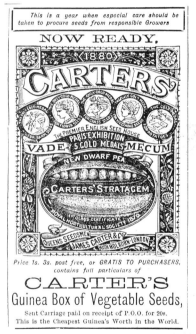

After the cropping season, lettuces and other salads were sometimes raised between the crowns. Asparagus growing declined in the 1860s, partly because of French imports and partly, perhaps, as a result of infestation by the asparagus beetle, which Mrs Loudon mentioned as a serious pest as early as 1840. William Robinson began a campaign to encourage asparagus growers in 1881, with prizes at shows in London and the provinces in succeeding years.

Horticultural shows had, of course, offered awards before then. In 1857, for instance, the Horticultural Society of London had offered prizes of ten, seven and five shillings at their Chiswick exhibition for 'fifty heads not exceeding eight inches in length'. Robinson's competition, however,

was on a different scale, since it was worth an initial hundred guineas, which was later increased. His generosity was not altogether altruistic—his aim must have been to encourage sales of his *Asparagus Culture*, published at the same time.

Permanent beds were also made up for artichokes, if there was space for them. The plants were renewed from offsets every five or six years, and needed little care apart from top-dressing in the spring and protection from the severest frosts in the winter. Two types were grown: the French, with light green heads and outward-spreading scales, and the more popular Globe, with a compact, purplish head. The Jerusalem artichoke, introduced from South America in 1716, was sometimes treated as an annual, 'planted in February or March, by sets, like the potatoe,' according to Mrs Loudon; generally it was allowed to grow on from year to year. 'Plant these in any back slip of ground,' says *The Annals of Horticulture*, in 1847. 'Usually a plot of these, like horseradish, will plant themselves, and the piece may be forked over every autumn, and the largest taken out for use, the smaller only being allowed to remain in the ground.' Enthusiasm for Jerusalem artichokes has always been qualified, because of their marked effect on the human digestion. Cobbett certainly disliked 'this poor insipid vegetable'.

Proper use of the different parts of the kitchen garden was of great importance. The value of an enclosure with high boundaries was not only that it made provision for the training of fruit trees and deterred marauders—the walls or fences created specific conditions in the borders beside them. In Cobbett's scheme, the south-facing border was used for tender subjects and for 'such things as Lettuce, Endive, and Cauliflowers, which stand the winter,' the east

Right: Varieties of beet, from *Hooper's Gardening Guide*, 1883.

Left: Trophy offered in 1872 by James Carter & Co., to be competed for 'by *bona fide* gentlemen's gardeners or gentlemen amateurs' at the Royal Horticultural Society's provincial shows. 24 dishes of specified vegetables were to be exhibited. The cup went to the employer, not the gardener.

and west borders were suitable places for herbs, for seedling celery and cabbage before they were planted out, and for 'small crops, seldom cultivated to such an extent as to come into the general square.' The cool shade of the north border was ideal for striking cuttings in summer and for prolonging the cropping season of plants which would fail or run to seed in a more open position. North-facing borders were often planted with strawberries, 'in order to prolong the season of that much-esteemed fruit by having some as late as possible.'

The bulk of the garden's produce came from the central beds, where a strict rotation of crops was practised. Even before the real reasons were known, it was well understood that plants would not flourish in the same ground in successive years. 'The roots of plants,' wrote Mrs Loudon in 1840, 'every year throw out a quantity of excrementitious matter that they either will not reimbibe, or that is injurious to them.' Thomas Bridgeman, in *The Young Gardener's Assistant* (1847), was more colourful: 'It is a curious fact, that a plant may be killed by the poison which it has itself secreted, as a viper may be destroyed by its own venom.'

Over most of the British Isles and certainly in the southern regions, produce of some kind was available during most of the year, and work was nearly always called for in some part of the kitchen garden. Roots and green vegetables were taken from the open ground, even in January when the weather was favourable, though some were lifted and stored as a precaution against severe frost. Abercrombie had written of beetroot: 'They will acquire a large full growth in the root by Sept. or Oct. to take up for use as wanted, and in continuance all winter and spring following: or in Nov. it may be proper to dig up a quantity, cut off the leaves, and deposit the roots in dry sand, under cover.' The first shoots of the new season from the overwintered roots

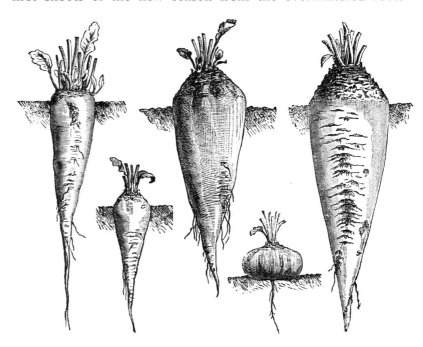

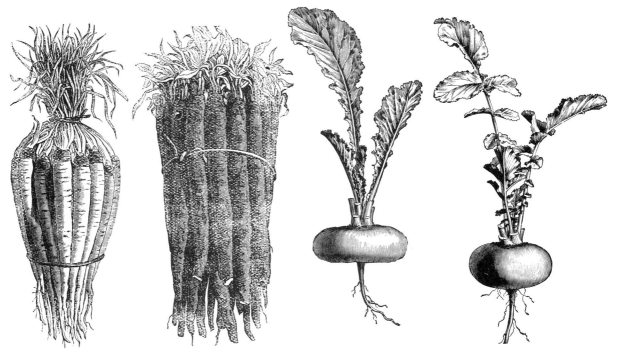

were eaten as spring greens. Turnips, parsnips, carrots, salsify and scorzonera were treated similarly, and even cauliflowers were preserved in trenches, laid head down and covered with earth by 'an intelligent horticulturalist', according to the author of *A New System of Practical Domestic Economy*.

Many vegetables were kept in season for much longer than they are today by the use of a spread of varieties and by successional sowing. Broad beans could be picked continuously from the middle of May to September. The earliest, the Mazagan, was a small form, not more than two feet high, which was sown in November and often began to bear in the second week of May. It was followed by the Dwarf Fan, also sown in the late autumn, and by the Long-pods and Windsors, sown in stages from January to the end of June. As breeders improved the larger strains, the Mazagan dropped out of use, and in 1884 *The Gardeners' Chronicle* maintained: 'it is very probable that if the Mazagan were sown in November, and the Seville Longpod in the middle of February, on the same piece of ground, and under similar conditions, the last-named would prove the earliest.' The Aquadulce strain, 'a very fine Longpod Bean of Continental origin', was also favoured. 'It is not nearly so much grown by gardeners and exhibitors as it deserves to be.' The yield of broad beans has been considerably improved since the nineteenth century. According to a report on eleven types grown by the Horticultural Society in 1831, which was quoted by James Anderson as still relevant in the 1870s, the long-pods contained four, five or occasionally six seeds per pod, the Mazagan three or four, and the Windsors usually no more than two. Peas, ranging from the early dwarfs to 'Knight's Marrowfat and other gigantic

Above left: Salsify and scorzonera, from *Hooper's Gardening Guide*. *Above right:* Turnips from *The Illustrated Dictionary of Gardening*, 'Yellow Malta' and 'Early Strap-leaved White Stone'.

The Garden bean: Estimate of sorts: The Mazagan is one of the earliest, hardiest, and best flavoured. Mazagan is a Portuguese settlement on the coast of Africa, near the Straits of Gibraltar; and it is said that seeds brought thence afford plants that are more early and more fruitful than those which spring from home-saved seed. The dwarf-fan or cluster-bean is likewise an early variety, but it is planted chiefly for curiosity; it rises only six or eight inches high; the branches spread out like a fan, and the pods are produced in small clusters. The long-pod bean has been long noted for its fruitfulness. Of all the large kinds, the Windsors are preferred for the table. When gathered young, the seeds are sweet and very agreeable; when the plants are allowed room and time they produce very large seeds, and in tolerable plenty, though they are not accounted liberal bearers. The green China is late, but very productive; and the fruit remains green even when ripe and dried.

J. Loudon, *An Encyclopaedia of Gardening*, 1834.

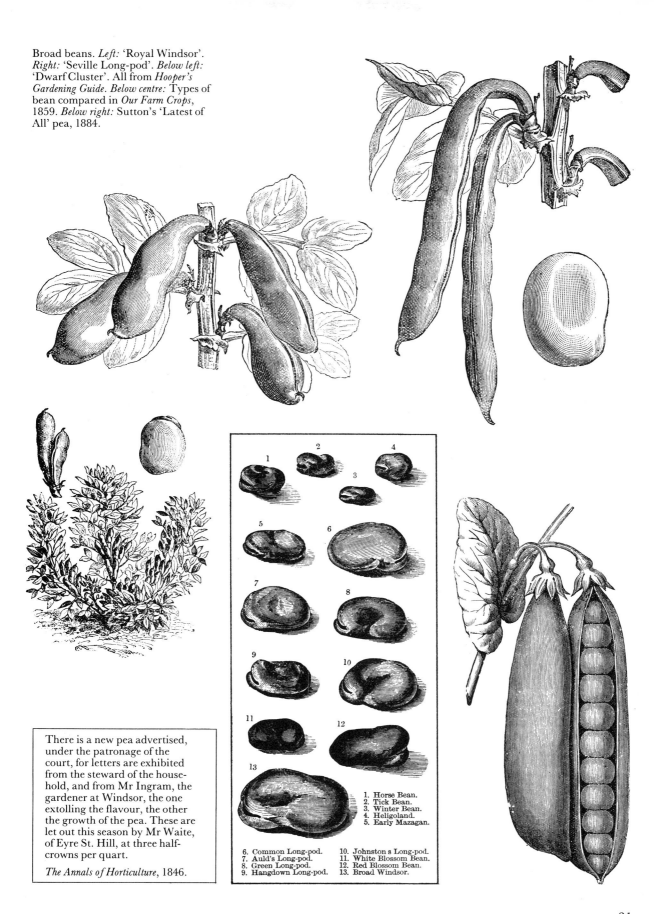

Broad beans. *Left:* 'Royal Windsor'. *Right:* 'Seville Long-pod'. *Below left:* 'Dwarf Cluster'. All from *Hooper's Gardening Guide*. *Below centre:* Types of bean compared in *Our Farm Crops*, 1859. *Below right:* Sutton's 'Latest of All' pea, 1884.

There is a new pea advertised, under the patronage of the court, for letters are exhibited from the steward of the household, and from Mr Ingram, the gardener at Windsor, the one extolling the flavour, the other the growth of the pea. These are let out this season by Mr Waite, of Eyre St. Hill, at three half-crowns per quart.

The Annals of Horticulture, 1846.

1. Horse Bean.
2. Tick Bean.
3. Winter Bean.
4. Heligoland.
5. Early Mazagan.

6. Common Long-pod.
7. Auld's Long-pod.
8. Green Long-pod.
9. Hangdown Long-pod.
10. Johnston s Long-pod.
11. White Blossom Bean.
12. Red Blossom Bean.
13. Broad Windsor.

varieties', were similarly sown in succession from January to the end of May, and dwarf French beans and runners at intervals from May to the first week in August.

Every garden had its potatoes, its leeks and its onions of various types. Garlic, the rather similar rocambole, and shallots were planted either in late autumn or early spring and harvested towards the end of June or in July. Mrs Loudon says of the shallot, 'It is very difficult to grow, as it is apt to be attacked by a kind of maggot; but it has been found to succeed, planted in cup-shaped hollows like the leek.' Welsh onions, or cibouls, were grown for their green stems, and tree onions for the clusters of small bulbs produced on the stalks, which were normally pickled. The potato-onion, also known as the underground onion and the Burns's onion, was regarded as a distinct form (*Allium aggregatum*), and developed clusters of bulbs below the surface of the soil. According to the 1834 edition of Abercrombie's *Every Man His Own Gardener*, 'This kind of onion is now grown very generally in the West of England: the vegetable markets of Bristol, Bath, Exeter, &c. are supplied abundantly with it in the early part of summer.'

Salad plants were extensively raised to provide a supply throughout the year, including not only the many forms of cos and cabbage-headed lettuce (also used for soup), but endive, both curled and Batavian, radishes, and a number of 'small salads'. This category covered seedling lettuce as well as mustard, cress and rape, sown three or four times a month from March onwards, and cut when an inch or so

Onions from *Hooper's Gardening Guide*. *Above:* 'Strasbourg', 'Rocca' and 'Naseby Mammoth'. *Below:* 'Tripoli', 'Blood-red' and 'Globe'.

Right: Frontispiece of *The Annals of Horticulture* for 1846, showing a selection of recently introduced greenhouse climbers.

Below: Tree onion, from *Vegetable Substances used for the Food of Man*, 1832.

J. Andrews Zincog.

Max. & Cᵒ Liᵗ

ANNALS OF HORTICULTURE

Published by Houlston & Stoneman, 65, Paternoster Row, January 1ˢᵗ 1846

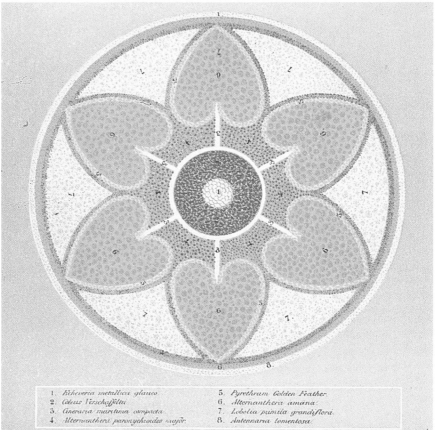

1. Echeveria metallica glauca.
2. Coleus Verschaffeltii.
3. Cineraria maritima compacta.
4. Alternanthera paronychioides major.
5. Pyrethrum Golden Feather.
6. Alternanthera amoena.
7. Lobelia pumila grandiflora.
8. Antennaria tomentosa.

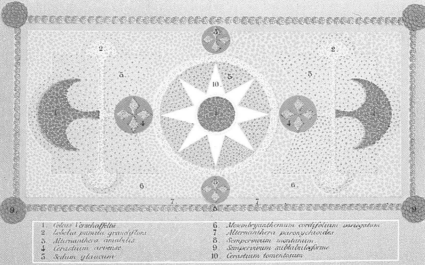

1. Coleus Verschaffeltii.
2. Lobelia pumila grandiflora.
3. Alternanthera amabilis.
4. Cerastium arvense.
5. Sedum glaucum.
6. Mesembryanthemum cordifolium variegatum.
7. Alternanthera paronychioides.
8. Sempervivum montanum.
9. Sempervivum sublalnulaeforme.
10. Cerastium tomentosum.

A Ballad of Salad
I cannot eat the red, red rose,
I cannot eat the white;
In vain the long laburnum glows,
Vain the camellia's waxen snows,
The lily's cream of light.

The lilac's clustered chalices
Proffer their bounty sweet
In vain! Though very good for
   bees,
Man, with unstinted yearning
   sees,
Admires, but cannot eat.

Give me the lettuce that has cool'd
Its heart in the rich earth,
Till every joyous leaf is school'd
To crisply-crinkled mirth.

Give me the mustard and the
   cress,
Whose glistening stalklets stand
As silver-white as nymphs by
   night
Upon the moonlit strand;

The winking radish, round and
   red,
That like a ruby shines;
And the faint blessing, onion-
   shed,
Whene'er LUCULLUS dines.

The wayward endive's curling
   head,
Cool cucumber sliced small,
And let the imperial beet-root
   spread
Her purple over all.

While shrinking poets still prefer
The common floral fashions,
With buds and blossoms hymn
   their Her,
These vegetable loves would stir
A flint-heart's mineral passions!

Punch, 1st June 1889.

high. Celery was used in salads, though more often made into soup or cooked on its own. Corn salad, or lamb's lettuce, and American cress were useful in winter, and the leaves and flowers of the 'nasturtium', or Indian cress (*Tropaeolum majus*), were added in the summer. An occasional winter substitute for radishes was rampion (*Campanula rapunculus*). Brassicas as a group were, of course, a mainstay of the garden. Cabbages provided spring, summer and autumn crops, and some were harvested young, before they formed heads, to be cooked as coleworts. Savoys came into season in November, as did Brussels sprouts (which many gardeners preferred to grow from imported Belgian seed). The many forms of kale, or borecole, could be relied on to survive the worst frosts, 'continuing to yield an abundance of green tender shoots, even in very cold weather, when other vegetables have ceased to grow.' (*The Garden Manual*, c.1860.) Cauliflowers were sown in August for use in the following June and July, with a second sowing in February, but, since the plants were considered too tender to withstand most winters without protection, broccoli was generally grown in addition. By careful management, which included retarding it under cool conditions in the summer, broccoli could be kept in production in all seasons—one demanding employer was said to have insisted that his gardener had it ready for the table in every week of the year. Although the sprouting purple form was grown, most of the broccolis, whether white, purple, brown or green, formed single heads and were used exactly as cauliflower. The distinction between the two, always vague, has disappeared altogether in twentieth-century market usage, the winter cauliflowers of today being broccolis a hundred years ago. Loudon reports that a head of Portsmouth broccoli 'sent by Oldacre [also spelled Oldaker in the *Transactions* of the Society and elsewhere] from the garden of Sir Joseph Banks, to the Horticultural Society, on the 5th of May, 1819, measured more than two feet in circumference, although it was quite close.' Various authors write approvingly of other brassicas

The parsley is scarcely acknowledged to be indigenous; but it has become perfectly naturalized on the walls of our Abbey at Faversham, and has occupied them at least 60 years: the locality being recorded by Mr Jacob.

The leaves are a pleasant stimulating salad. They are diuretic. The plant is occasionally sown in pastures to counteract the liver rot in sheep. Burnet says, that the fruit is a deadly poison to parrots.

M.H. Cowell, *A Floral Guide for East Kent*, 1839.

BROCOLI is generally supposed to be a variety of the cauliflower; but it differs essentially, both in being much hardier, and in being very apt to vary. Thus, while only two kinds of cauliflower are known, the early and the late, and even these can hardly be distinguished from each other, – there are ten or twelve distinct sorts of brocoli, and more are being raised every season. All these kinds, however, appear to have sprung from two, the purple and the green, which are said to have been brought from Italy.

Mrs Loudon, *Gardening for Ladies*, 1840.

Left: Savoy cabbage and cauliflower, from *The Illustrated Dictionary of Gardening. Below:* Sutton's 'Autumn White' Broccoli, 1884.

Right: Degenerate form of *Brassica oleracea* var. *costata*, the Portugal cabbage, with funnel-like appendages to the ribs, described by Augustin de Candolle in the Horticultural Society's *Transactions* in 1824. Engraved by Enoch James. *Left:* Lettuce leaf with a similar deformation, reported in *The Gardeners' Chronicle*, 1854.

Sinapis Pekinensis. This plant is more extensively used by all classees of the Chinese than any other, perhaps than all the others together. It is carried about the public streets for sale, boiled, in which state its smell is extremely offensive to Europeans... It grows best in the cold weather, and doubtless will thrive well in England. Its rapid growth may recommend it to the agriculturist as a cheap food for cattle, but it gives to milk the peculiar taste of its genus.

Transactions of the Horticultural Society, 1824.

among which are kohl-rabi and the couve tronchuda, or Portugal cabbage (*B. oleracea* var. *costata*)—'Sow in March and April, and prick out and cultivate in soil the same as directed for the *Cabbage.* It then becomes fit for use in November, and when it has endured some night frosts it is the most tender and sweetest of all the Cabbageworts.'

The Chinese cabbage, though known, does not seem to have been cultivated. In 1821, John Livingstone dispatched seeds of a number of Chinese vegetables from Macao to London, and described the plants in a paper printed in Volume V of the Horticultural Society's *Transactions.* His *Sinapis pekinensis* corresponds to the *Brassica pekinensis* of modern classification, while the winter brassica of 'procumbent habit' was probably the flat cabbage, *B. chinensis* var. *rosularis.* Robert Fortune, too, sent seeds to the Society in 1846, including some of the Shanghai Oil Plant—'It is grown over the whole country round that city.' This must have been *B. chinensis* var. *utilis*, which provides an oil like that produced from rape seed. (*See* G.A.C. Herklots *Vegetables in South-East Asia*, London 1972.) *The Annals of Horticulture* dismissed it:

'This appears to be of no importance in a horticultural point of view. It may be cultivated by farmers for feeding cattle, or it may be grown for the same purpose as in China.' Fortune also sent back the Chinese spinach, *Amaranthus gangeticus*, which, though not completely hardy, was thought to be more likely to succeed in Britain.

That the diet of many Victorians was unimaginative, as much from inclination as from circumstance, is certainly true. A French observer, Léonce de Lavergne, wrote in 1855 (*The Rural Economy of England, Scotland and Ireland*) that the English 'are not great consumers of fruit and vegetables, and they are right; for both the one and the other of them are very tasteless.' In *The Complete Cottage Cookery*, Mrs Esther Copley, a clergyman's wife dedicated to improving conditions for the poor, proclaims, 'The best and most agreeable diet comprehends a due proportion of the various substances that are adapted for human food.' She holds,

Above left: Somewhat the appearance of a plot of cow cabbage that I saw growing in Jersey', from *The Gardener's Magazine*, 1829. *Above right:* Jersey Cole, from *Our Farm Crops*, 1859. *Below left:* 'Monstrous broccoli' sent to *The Gardeners' Chronicle* in 1856: 'I have been an extensive grower for more than 20 years, and I have never seen anything like it before.' *Below right:* Strasburg cabbage, from *Our Farm Crops* – 'under favourable conditions it may be seen weighing as much as from 50 to 70lbs.'

Esther Copley, who brought to her writings 'the resources of a strong and ardent mind, deeply imbued with sympathy for the oppressed.'

however, that 'Good bread is the most nourishing of all food, and that on which life can be longest sustained. Meat, taking a pound to a pound, and allowing for bone and waste in cooking, contains about half the nourishment of bread; potatos, barely one-fourth part; carrots rather less—about one sixth. Parsnips, broad-beans, red beets and vegetable marrow, and asparagus, are among the most nutritious vegetables. Next come French beans and peas, and then, turnips and greens, which last yield about one-third the nourishment of potatos.' Her last chapter, on preparing and cooking vegetables, covers asparagus, Jerusalem artichokes and globe artichokes, as well as the more usual roots and greens. Mrs Copley includes a section devoted to the interests of 'families of four or five, or even more, to be maintained on wages varying from 9s. to 13s. a-week, with rent 1s. or 1s. 6d. a-week, and fuel dear,' or those 'in circumstances even yet more straitened,' where she comments: 'Those who have no garden should not forget at the proper seasons certain things that may be had for the gathering. Young nettle-tops in spring are delicious boiled as greens: hop-tops gathered young are as good as asparagus: turnip-tops, any decent person who asks civilly and engages to gather them without injuring the roots may generally have leave to do so; they are among the most delicious and wholesome of vegetables. The cardoon or thistle head is as good as an artichoke. When people take a walk they might as well think of such things.' It would have been wise to ask civilly, for the law prescribed a penalty of 10 shillings, or a month's hard labour, for stealing or maliciously destroying turnips, potatoes, cabbages, parsnips, peas or carrots; a person repeatedly spoiling or carrying away any root, shrub or plant in cultivated ground was liable to transportation.

Ladies in more comfortable circumstances were also the target of advice and instruction. Apart from celebrated works, such as *The Lady's Country Companion* and Mrs Beeton's manual, first published in 1861, there were many smaller handbooks. By the time that Mrs Beeton's book appeared, *Household Hints to Young Housewives*, with *the Arrangements and Receipts for Forty Dinners* by 'Martha Careful' was into a twelfth edition and sold for one shilling. 'Martha Careful' addresses herself to the young lady who 'while her mother was arranging domestic affairs...was idling hours away, and the accomplishment of managing a home was not among those she learnt.' She expects a 'small genteel house' to have a cook and a housemaid, and opines that 'the union of a cultivated and domestic mind is quite compatible with the most delicate notions.' She gives directions concerning a fairly wide range of vegetables and salads, but normally recommends little more than to boil them till tender—suggesting an hour's cooking for young carrots and two hours for old, which may explain the lack of flavour remarked on by Lavergne.

The development of new strains of plants for the table, and their improvement, which had been an important task for eighteenth-century nurserymen such as London and Wise, was carried on energetically by later seedsmen and by horticulturalists, among them Thomas Andrew Knight, co-founder of the Horticultural Society with Sir Joseph Banks, in 1804. Knight was the younger brother of the eccentric Richard Payne Knight, whose notorious study of ancient Priapic cult-images, and an unfortunate single-handed crusade to prove that Lord Elgin's marbles were Roman copies of the Greek originals, at the time overshadowed his achievements as an antiquarian and accomplished scholar. The elder Knight was also much against the Capability Brown landscape school and in his didactic poem, 'The Landscape', deplored the constraints that Brown and his followers imposed on Nature—'They shave the Goddess that they came to dress.' Richard Payne Knight built the extravagant Downton Castle in Herefordshire to his own designs, laying out the grounds in a picturesque and romantic style. In 1809, he left the house to the care of his brother, who carried on the horticultural experiments which he had begun twenty years earlier at nearby Elton. Thomas Andrew Knight was a central figure in the horticultural establishment until his death in 1838, and varieties of vegetables and fruits which he had originated continued in cultivation for a long time.

Many plant breeders resorted to wild forms as a source of improvement, a practice that is now recognised as essential for the injection of robust genes into inbred strains. Philip Miller had failed in his efforts with the wild carrot in the eighteenth century, but Professor Buckman achieved better results in 1860, and his work with the wild parsnip produced an addition to the existing hollow-crowned varieties, described in F.W. Burbidge's *Cultivated Plants* (1877) as 'the Student or Hollow-Crowned Parsnip of gardens'.

As the number of varieties increased, many of them came to be known by the names of their growers or suppliers, but in the first half of the nineteenth century some strains were still identified with their habit, their place of origin or their cropping season. In a list of sixteen varieties of the potato, for example, John Loudon includes the Ash-leaved Kidney, the Lancashire pink-eye and the white long keeper, as well as Fox's Seedling and Prince's Beauty. Cobbett, discussing the raising of potatoes from seed rather than tubers, comments: 'Few people take the pains to do this, the sorts being already as numerous as the stones of the pavement of a large city.'

The spread of blight (of which the true cause was not identified until 1860) and crop failures in the 1840s encouraged experiments in raising potatoes from seed. However, potato seed usually fails to breed true, and the outcome was generally unsatisfactory.

The problem is still being tackled in the 1980s, though now with better results. Some gardeners, following theories advanced by Knight, thought that varieties degenerated

List of Potatoes.

EARLY VARIETIES

Early Frame
Fox's Seedling
Fox's Early Globe
Fox's Early Kidney
Ash-leaved Kidney
Early Manly
American Native
Early Shaw
Taylor's Fortyfold
Early Betty
Hopetown Early
Ladies' Fingers or Rufford Kidney
Soden's Early Oxford
Cornwall Kidney
Chapman's Early Kidney

LATE VARIETIES

Champion
Old Flat White
White Bread-fruit
Early Field Kidney
Albany Kidney
Edinburgh Dons
Blue Dons
Devonshire Apple
Irish Apple
Black American Pink-Eye
Dork Red
Perthshire Red
Poor Man's Profit
Red Bread-fruit
Red-nosed Kidney
Bedfordshire Kidney
Irish Lumpers
Irish Cup
Connaught Cup
Oxnoble
Kentish Seedling Goldfinder
Goldfinder
Sheep's Tail Kidney
Regent
Leathercoat
Mangold-Wurtzel Potato
Prince de Rohan

The following potatoes, which are but little known, in this country, (and are perhaps more curious than useful), have been grown in the garden of the Horticultural Society, and are thus described in their *Transactions*:

Golden Potato of Peru
Pied Golden Potato
Asparagus Potato
Mouse Potato
Pine Apple or Cone Potato
Spanish Dwarf Potato

The Annals of Horticulture, 1847.

after a life-span of as little as four or eight years. *The Gardeners' Chronicle* in 1854 confessed itself unable to reconcile this view with experience, doubting any deterioration in some common market potatoes of thirty years earlier, 'the Ash-leaved Kidneys, Champions and Oxnobles'. These names still appear in advertisements of the 1850s (where seed potatoes are listed at between six and ten shillings a bushel, and seed itself, 'saved from the best varieties', at sixpence a packet, but the strains then most commonly grown are given as the Shaw, the York Regent and the Fluke. Further varieties were introduced over the next two decades, many of them claimed as disease-resistant. In 1871, a contributor to *The Journal of Horticulture* reported well of the Red-skinned Flourball. An important introduction, the Magnum Bonum, was on the market from 1876 and is mentioned by Flora Thompson in *Lark Rise* as one of the varieties grown on Oxfordshire allotments in the 1880s. Writing in *Gardening Illustrated* in 1879, 'J.S.W.' prefers Magnum Bonum to the Flourball, finding it and York Regent the best croppers. The name, which was also given to strains of other vegetables and fruit, is a curious, though presumably coincidental, echo of the racehorse, Magnum Bonum, whose sire, Pot8os (always spelled in this way after a stable lad's initial mistake), was an influential stallion at the end of the eighteenth century—another of his sons, Waxy, won the 1793 Derby.

The potato was a common topic for horticultural writers, and there are many essays on its history, culture and nutritional merits. Article 2 in the first volume of the *Transactions* of the Horticultural Society was 'An Attempt to ascertain the Time of the Introduction of the Potato' by Banks. There was controversy not only about its arrival in Europe—traditionally after Sir Walter Raleigh's attempt to colonise Virginia, more probably via the Spanish trade routes—but also about its nutritive value. Although some communities were wholly dependent on potatoes, as in Ireland, others were less ready to accept them as human food. The Scots had shown reluctance partly because of their 'ignorance of

'Everyone should plant Disease-resisting Potatoes', from a Sutton's advertisement of the 1880s.

the proper mode of cooking them' and partly because they were not mentioned in the Bible. Bishop Heber reported some success in overcoming the prejudice against them that he encountered in India. In France, Parmentier had to persuade Louis XVI to wear a nosegay of potato flowers before the 'unwholesome plant' was thought better than 'fit to be eaten by cattle and the most wretched of human beings'. The Russian peasants were suspicious of potatoes as coming 'recommended by their Lords, who were not unnaturally perhaps suspected of some selfish or sinister motive.'

The other notable introduction of the sixteenth century, the tomato, was accepted much more slowly into kitchen gardens. In 1904, Owen Thomas wrote that it had been regarded as of little value in England until twenty or thirty years earlier and, even then, suggested that it should be classed as a dessert fruit. Tomatoes do not seem to have been used in salads until the very end of the nineteenth century. For most of the period they were looked on as possibly dangerous exotics, still known by the name of Love-apple. When used at all, they were pickled, preserved in syrup, or put into soups. In the 1813 edition of Abercrombie, they are placed among other half-hardy annuals used for purely decorative effect in the flower border. Abercrombie may here be referring to the cherry tomato (*Lycopersicum esculentum* var. *cerasiforme*), a small-fruited primitive form which was still noted in *The Illustrated Dictionary of Gardening* (Nicholson) in 1887 with the even smaller currant tomato (*L. pimpinelli-folium*), as 'chiefly grown for ornament'. Tomatoes occasionally appear in the Covent Garden Market reports in early numbers of *The Gardener's Magazine*, and are listed under 'Stalks and Fruits for Tarts, Pickling, &c' at ten to twelve shillings per sieve in 1829. They do not feature in *The Gardeners' Chronicle* market reports in the 1850s, but were on sale again by 1871 at an average of two shillings a dozen.

The development of improved strains of tomato began seriously in about 1860. The early Victorians made do with types listed by Loudon as 'the large, small, cherry, and pear-shaped red' and 'the large, and small, or cherry-shaped yellow'. Noting its widespread cultivation in Italy, where 'scarcely a dinner is served up in which it does not in some way or other form a part,' he suggests that in one respect it appealed to the British palate then as it does today: 'Its use for sauce in this country is greatly on the increase, and it is

Tomato varieties from *The New Practical Gardener*, 1880: 'The Dwarf Orangefield (centre) is one of the most useful and one of the best for this country. Key's Early Prolific (right) is a quick grower and comes to maturity quickly, which suits our climate; and the Trophy (left) is said to be one that will eclipse all, if we may accept the testimony of our American cousins.'

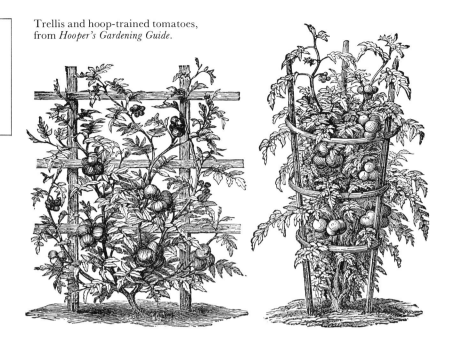

Trellis and hoop-trained tomatoes,
from *Hooper's Gardening Guide*.

cultivated to considerable extent near London.' Both Cobbett and Abercrombie mention a white form as well as the red and the yellow. This does not seem to have lasted beyond about 1840, although it appears in the 1845 edition of *Hortus Cantabrigiensis*, the Cambridge catalogue of Indigenous and Exotic Plants. According to *The Annals of Horticulture* in 1847, 'A variety with white fruit appears to be entirely lost, although that it once existed admits of little doubt, as it is distinctly mentioned in various old botanical works. Such being the case, a similar variety may, perhaps, again be detected by some curious observer.' A similar type was to be found in early twentieth-century America, and *The Standard Cyclopedia* by E.H. Bailey includes the White Apple tomato, described as 'the best variety for eating out of the hand.'

By the mid 1880s, there were 'somewhat numerous sorts of Tomatoes in cultivation', and seedsmen offered a considerable range of varieties, in contrast to the simple 'Tomato' entry in a typical list of thirty years earlier. Nicholson's *Dictionary* contains a selection of twelve recommended varieties, some ribbed, some smooth, and ranging in colour from the purplish-crimson Acme to the citron-yellow Greengage. Breeders produced intermediate forms, for example the Grape Tomato, a cross between the cherry-fruited variety and 'Hepper's Goliath' exhibited in 1875, and curiosities, such as a hybrid between the tomato and the sweet pepper, *Capsicum annuum*, reported by Dr Kanitz in Germany in 1867. F.W. Burbidge refers in *Cultivated Plants* to an American experiment carried out in 1847, when a tomato was grafted on to the stem of a potato, 'both Tomatoes and Potatoes having resulted from the union.' He continues: 'Mr A. Dean, of Bedfont, exhibited a bushy plant of a Potato in 1876 which had been grafted on a Tomato stock; and the Potato haulm being thus elevated above the earth, it produced tubers abundantly in the axils of its leaves.'

While the tomato was becoming more popular, some long-established vegetables lost favour. Alexanders, or Alisander (*Smyrnium olusatrum*), a plant native to Britain and fairly extensively grown until the middle of the eighteenth century, was entirely superseded by celery. Its blanched stems had been used in a similar way, and the leaves were an occasional pot-herb. The skirret (*Sium sisarum*), too, which had once been called 'the sweetest, whitest and most pleasant of roots', was in decline and is scarcely referred to after 1850. The *Annals* of 1847 had observed that skirrets 'are boiled or stewed in various ways, and vary the supply at table in winter, although they are not so much in demand now as formerly, when the number of vegetables procurable at that season was not so great as at present.'

The increased availability of vegetables resulted in part from the breeding and sale of more productive strains with a longer cropping season. However, the transport revolution which followed the spread of the railways in the 1830s and 1840s was more important, at least for the population in towns and cities. Steam locomotives made possible the cheap and reliable distribution of perishable goods over distances far beyond the range of horse-drawn wagons, while steamships brought foreign produce into British markets. Despite the Duke of Wellington's view that the train would not force itself into extensive use, 1800 miles of track were in use by 1843. The triumph of the railway was reflected in the gruesome gesture of the ostler at the White Lion posting inn at Hartford Bridge, near Camberley, who cut his throat on the day when the London and South-Western Railway opened. The Great Northern Company carried nearly 46,000 tons of potatoes and 1,940 tons of other vegetables into London, in 1853, and in another year the Brighton line brought 300 tons of produce from Jersey and Dieppe. The South-Eastern Railway carried in a single night 100 tons of peas, 25 tons of plums, 16 tons of black currants, 50 tons of other fruit and 10 tons of Kentish filberts. Steamers were loaded with up to 500 tons of walnuts from Antwerp.

Even before the steam age there was substantial traffic of vegetables and fruit into the London markets of the Borough, Farringdon, Portman and Spitalfields, as well as the main centre, Covent Garden. Market gardens had been established since the Middle Ages, mostly in villages close to the city, although the first was reputedly at Sandwich in Kent. At the end of the eighteenth century, about 5,000 acres were devoted to commercial vegetable-growing within twelve miles of London, 1,700 acres to potatoes and 800 acres to fruit. The business went on all round the city, but mainly in the parishes of Deptford, Chiswick, Barnes, Battersea and Mortlake, where the river carried the barges full of horse manure 'procured in great abundance from the London stables.' Seventy acres in Mortlake were set

The flowers and roots of the Skirret, from *Vegetable Substances used for the Food of Man*, 1832.

Skirrets – Wash them thoroughly clean, and when you have boiled them until they are tender, skin the roots, and cut them into slices. Have ready a little cream, a piece of butter rolled in flour, the yolk of an egg beaten fine, a little grated nutmeg, two or three spoonfuls of white wine, with a very little salt, and stir all together. Put your roots into the dish, and pour the sauce over them.

J.C. Schnebbelie, *The Housekeeper's Instructor*, 1808.

Pearls of Price
Mr Ruskin has in a recent letter described Railroads as "the loathsomest form of devilry now extant; animated and deliberate earthquakes, destructive of all wise social habit or possible natural beauty, carriages of damned souls on the ridges of their own graves"...

Punch, 1887.

The hunt aroused the bitter hostility of the market gardeners and farmers of Harrow... Lord Alvanley, a well-known figure in Leicestershire, was once asked in White's how his day with Grantley Berkeley had gone. 'Devilish good run,' he replied, 'but the asparagus beds went awfully heavy; and the glass all through was up to one's hocks.' Grantley Berkeley gave up in 1829.

Raymond Carr, *English Fox Hunting*, 1976.

aside for raising asparagus, and Carew Hazlitt noted that a fair quantity was still grown there in the 1800s. Rhubarb was produced in New Cross. The market gardener Joseph Myatt had nearly twenty acres of it under cultivation in the 1840s, sending three wagon-loads, of a ton or more each, to Covent Garden at a time. Twenty-five years earlier, he had sent his sons to Borough Market with a mere five bundles, and they sold only three. Myatt had been given his first dozen plants by Mr Oldacre, and the stock, originally from Russia, was 'of a kind' according to E.S. Delamer 'finer and much earlier than the puny variety cultivated by the Brentford growers.' Myatt's perseverance in the face of public apathy and in defiance of suggestions that he had taken leave of his senses when he first proposed planting a whole acre of 'this useful *vegetable fruit-stalk*' was much admired by later commentators. 'Mr Myatt' wrote Delamer, quoting James Cuthill, 'had to contend against many prejudices; but time, that universal leveller, overcame and broke down every barrier, and rhubarb is no longer called *physic*, as it was then.' His assertion that 'in our own day it forms most delicious and wholesome tarts and puddings, as well as an excellent preserve,' could have been the war-cry of a regiment of Victorian nannies.

Covent Garden had been a recognised market 'for buying and selling of all manner of fruits, flowers, roots, and herbs whatsoever' since 1677, when the Earl of Bedford first granted a lease. Arrangements in the eighteenth century were described as miserable, and the market remained an open space surrounded by stalls and sheds until the Bedford estate undertook its improvement in 1827. The grand new buildings designed by Charles Fowler were completed in 1830 at a cost of £42,000, and furnished not only with 'a handsome fountain of Devonshire marble, highly polished', but also with cellars for washing potatoes fed by the central artesian well, a steam engine for pumping water to the higher levels, and conservatories heated by hot water or steam 'at pleasure'.

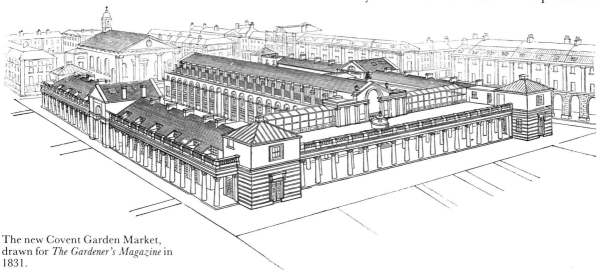

The new Covent Garden Market, drawn for *The Gardener's Magazine* in 1831.

The new Covent Garden Market, from *The Gardener's Magazine. Left:* The East front, engraved from a drawing 'obligingly lent by Mr Fowler'.

The market is a filthy scene, soiled by putrid refuse, leaves of cabbages, shells of peas, and roots, the air of which is impregnated with a stench that is wafted in every direction by the wind; and yet the centre walk has many attractions for the botanist and epicure, who may there feast their eyes and their appetites with rare and beautiful flowers and rich fruits – but not at the cheapest rates.

James P. Malcolm, *Anecdotes of the manners and customs of London*, 1808.

Produce for the market: the 'Covent Garden Mammoth' cauliflower, from *Hooper's Gardening Guide*.

Covent Garden as it was in 1745, engraved from a painting by Joseph Vanaken for *The Journal of Horticulture*, 1872.

Apart from warehouses, shops, and stands for fruit and vegetables, there were two seed and herb shops, two rooms where fruit and ices were served, and three public houses.

The range of produce available in the market was fairly wide throughout the nineteenth century, and reports of prices were a regular feature in the horticultural press. They note a number of delicacies that would be hard to find on present-day stalls. *The Gardener's Magazine* of the early 1830s mentions truffles and morels, both English gathered, as well as ordinary mushrooms. The trade in garden snails (sixpence the quart, in season) does not seem to have survived much beyond the rebuilding of the market, and silkworm eggs (one penny the dozen) disappear from the lists at about the same time. Loudon noted with regret in December 1829 that the mulberry plantation near Slough, which supplied leaves to feed the silk moth larvae, had been utterly abandoned: 'The cause assigned is, that the air is too humid for the vigorous health of the insect.'

Covent Garden, however, was a service for the metropolis, providing Londoners with a wide choice of bought produce all through the year, but most households in the country were dependent on their own resources until well into the twentieth century. The kitchen garden was a vital part of the domestic economy, and for cottagers and estate-holders its proper management remained a necessity.

The new Covent Garden Market. *Right:* design for a fountain and for shelf-support brackets in the conservatories.

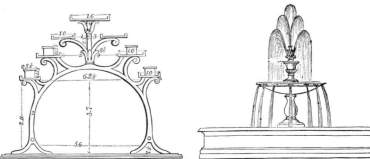

Artifice

Left: 'The Horticulturist', frontispiece of William Robinson's 1871 revision of John Loudon's work, *The Culture and Management of the Kitchen, Fruit and Forcing Garden.*

'An intellectual man who has to think, to contrive, to plan his work, and shape his course, according to the seasons' —so one employer defined the ideal gardener in 1842. 'Argus', advocating higher wages in *The Gardener and Practical Florist*, recounted his horror at the discovery that his own men earned only twelve shillings a week. His solution was to order the sacking of one man in five and a rise of three shillings for the rest—a neat form of philanthropy. 'I seize this opportunity of giving my sentiments upon this import-ant subject, because I really do feel that there is something exceedingly cruel to the employed, and beyond measure degrading to the employer, in the very fact of establishing a rate of wages which dooms the men to be only half fed, or only half honest.' The sentiments of a fifth of the gar-deners are not recorded.

Gardeners' pay had, in fact, risen since the post-war depression of the 1820s, when the average weekly figure was ten shillings. The head gardener in a large household then expected only about forty pounds a year, compared with the butler's fifty. Self-employed men and jobbers were even worse off, since they did not have the advantage of free board and lodging. In a letter to *The Gardener's Magazine* (1826), Archibald McNaughton catalogues the trials of a fifty year career in the profession: 'I left Edinburgh in the year 1777, and, after working some time in Mr Christopher Gray's nursery at Fulham, I got a very good place with a Mr Rolls, a great stockbroker, whose affairs went wrong after I had been six years with him, and I was obliged to quit. After going down to Scotland to see my friends, I came up again and got a place from Mr Hare, then a seedsman in St James's Street, to go to Mrs Wilson at Putney, where I remained till her daughter married, when her husband having an aversion to Scotch servants, I was obliged to leave.' He then set up a nursery at Epsom, which failed, and turned to jobbing work. 'When I first began, the highest wages I could get were 3s. a day, and obliged to find my own tools. I had a good deal of employment at first, partly from the circumstance of being a Scotchman...' But more disasters followed, and the unfortunate McNaughton had 'no other prospect than the workhouse.' His story ends with the hope that 'it will be a warning to gardeners when they are in good situations to keep in them, and not let discontent or ambition prey on their minds... And, especially, let them never give up any place whatever for the condition of a jobbing gardener, for that is greater slavery than being a common labourer.'

Low wages remained an issue throughout the century, and the complaint that gardeners were paid less than common labourers was often repeated. Many men sold surplus produce on the side, but that could be risky. One of them complained to *The Journal of Horticulture* in 1871 that an elderly lady employer, had apparently condoned his sale of plants 'for a trifle' and later sacked him for it without a reference. He was better off than Christopher Young, gardener to Mr Bowden of Clapham Common, who was sent to prison for two months in 1857, having encountered constables on his way into Covent Garden with boxes full of his master's camellias. A market 'haggler', giving evidence, claimed that 'It was a common practice to purchase flowers of gentlemen's gardeners. If it were not for the gentlemen's green-houses they would not be able to supply Covent Garden Market with flowers in the winter.'

Most professional gardeners were reasonably well placed, however. Theirs was acknowledged to be a respectable calling which entitled them to be addressed as 'Mr'. Often, they had a measure of independence denied to indoor servants—a good gardener, said Mrs Loudon, could not bear to be interfered with—and some even aspired to a measure of friendly conversation with the ladies, gentlemen and children of the house. Many gardeners did not like to be too closely associated with the rest of the servants. Another correspondent to *The Gardener's Magazine* writes 'On the Evil Effects of a Head Gardener being lodged anywhere else than in his Garden' and wonders, 'the gardener of England, placed, as he is, in the housekeeper's room,—I say, whether he can there improve himself? I answer, all that he can do there, admitting it to be an improvement, is,—he may read a little, play at cards, dance, and flirt with ladies' maids.' Even worse, if he were an inmate of the servants' hall, he might turn to drinking, swearing and low language. 'But it requires no more than common sense to see the absurdity of any other arrangement than that of a proper house for a head gardener in the garden.'

To be worth his place, the nineteenth-century professional had to be adept in techniques that have since been made redundant by easy importation and improvements in the preservation of fruit and vegetables. For many people, the ordinary seasonal succession of crops was not enough, and there was a constant demand for out-of-season produce. At Sandringham in the 1870s, where the

Sir,—I wish to bring the following to the notice of your readers:Every man who enters upon the profession of a gardener, does so with the ultimate view of acquiring a sufficient knowledge of his business to qualify him for a master gardener's place. It must, however, be observed, that, as the number of situations bears no proportion to the number of men qualified to fill them, it necessarily follows that a great number of deserving men must remain in a state of probation, perhaps to the end of their lives; and it is appalling to think of the miseries endured by these men, from the time of their apprenticeship until they arrive at such a state of perfection as would warrant them in taking master places. And, after having arrived at such perfection, they see no prospect of an alleviation of their miseries: twelve shillings a-week, and the hope of a better place, is all that they have to subsist on... Places that give more than fifteen shillings, are considered of no importance in the horticultural world; for, strange as it may appear, exactly as the establishment rises in grandeur, and its proprietor in wealth, so does the remuneration of the men (who by their skill and industry add to its beauties) gravitate towards the starvation point.

Letter from 'One in the Chiswick Gardens' in *The Gardener and Practical Florist*, 1843.

Below: The gardener's lodge at Ingestrie Hall, Staffordshire, from *The Journal of Horticulture*, 1872.

'Summer costume of a journeyman gardener in the neighbourhood of London; the hat of straw, and the jacket and trowsers of cotton' from *The Gardener's Magazine*, 1826. The illustration shows a plant of *Yucca gloriosa* flowering in Viner's nursery at Windsor.

Right: The gardener's cottage at Belrath Bury, County Meath, Ireland, from *The Gardeners' Chronicle*, 1884.

head man, Mr Carmichael, had turned a turnip field into a garden in the course of six years, strawberries were provided from February onwards, and green peas were available in December. While few other establishments operated on so lavish a scale, with ten thousand pots of strawberries under glass, most serious growers, professional and amateur, liked to pit their skill against the climate. In the 1847 edition of *The Young Gardener's Assistant* (adapted for American readers) Thomas Bridgeman, an expatriate Englishman, wrote: 'I shall endeavour to show the utility of an artificial climate suited to the various species of useful plants. In England, a regular succession of vegetables can be obtained from the natural ground every month of the year, and the fruits of that country, from the summer heat being moderate, are of longer continuance than with us, and yet the English make gardening a science, and employ the elements, as well as the ingenuity of man, in the production of fruits and vegetables out of the ordinary season.'

For their ingenuity to be effective, gardeners had to be attuned to the elements, and weather observation was always an important talent. Many people kept their own records in the hope of achieving systematic predictions. Exceptional conditions, such as the particularly cold and stormy winter of 1859-60 (when the Meteorological Office introduced gale warnings), were lengthily documented and discussed in the horticultural press. In 1854, *The Gardeners' Chronicle* reported gloomily on the catastrophic April frost: 'It is to be feared that all around London the hopes of the gardener have been destroyed by a sudden and most

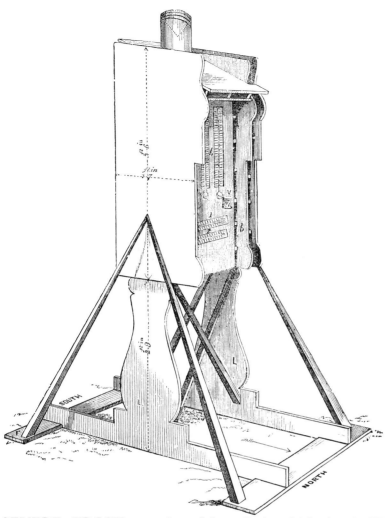

SEVERE FROST on the night of the 24th inst.' The temperature had fallen to 18° Fahrenheit after a maximum of 77° on the 19th, and many plants suffered—including a number of tender species in Kew Gardens. 'Another barren fruit year has to be added to our long list of failures,' Thomas Rivers subsequently wrote to the *Chronicle*, noting that late frosts had caused damage every spring since 1846. A correspondent from Cork described the ruin of the early potato crop and the loss of many trees and shrubs.

Recording the state of the weather was easy enough, but predicting it was not. Among the solutions put forward were systems dependent on the changing phase of the moon. Thomas Bridgeman dismisses 'moon-planting' as 'the practice and prejudices of many persons in choosing the first quarter of the moon for planting such vegetables as yield their produce above the surface, as Cabbage, &c., and the last quarter or wane of the moon for such as grow and yield their produce chiefly in the earth, and below the surface, as Potatoes, &c.,' but goes on to quote the 'justly celebrated' Dr Adam Clarke: 'About twenty years ago, a table purporting to be the work of the late Dr Herschel, was

Left: The Lawson Meteorological Thermometer Stand: a portable 'weather station' incorporating maximum and minimum thermometers, a hygrometer and a rain-gauge. From *The Journal of Horticulture*, 1872.

If it be New or Full Moon, or she enter into her first or last quart. at twelve at noon, or between		SUMMER.	WINTER.
12 & 2	aftern.	Very rainy	Snow and Rain.
2	4 aftern.	Changeable	Fair and Mild.
4	6 even.	Fair..............	Fair.
6	8	{ Fair if Wind N. W	{ Fair & Frosty if wind at N. or N. E.
8	10	{ Rainy, if Wind at { S. or S.W....	{ Rain or Snow, if S. or S. W.
10	12 night.	Fair..............	Fair and Frosty.
12	2 morn.	Fair..............	{ Hard Frost unless wind S. or S.W.
2	4	{ Cold, with frequent { showers	{ Snow and Stormy.
4	6	Rain	Snow and Stormy.
6	8	Wind and Rain	Stormy Weather.
8	10	Changeable .....:	{ Cold Rain, if wind be { W., Snow if E.
10	12 noon..	Frequent Showers..	Cold with High Wind.

The above Table, constructed upon philosophical considerations of the relative positions of the Sun and Moon in respect to the Earth, and confirmed by experience of many years actual observation, furnishes the observer, without further trouble, with a knowledge of what kind of weather there is the greatest probability of succeeding, and that so near the truth, that in very few instances will it be found to err.

Right: 'A table purporting to be the work of the late Dr. Herschel, professing to perform prognostics of the weather, by the times of change, full, and quarters of the moon,' contributed by Dr Adam Clarke to Thomas Bridgeman's *The Young Gardener's Assistant*, 1847. *Above:* A similar table from a pocket diary for 1852.

MOON.	TIME OF CHANGE.	IN SUMMER.	IN WINTER.
If the New Moon—the first Quarter —the Full Moon—or the last Quarter, happens	Between midnight and 2 in the morning,	Fair.	Hard frost unless the wind be south or west.
	Between 2 and 4 morning,	Cold with frequent showers.	Snow and stormy.
	" 4 and 6 "	Rain.	Rain.
	" 6 and 8 "	Wind and rain.	Stormy.
	" 8 and 10 "	Changeable.	Cold rain if wind be west.
	" 10 and 12 "	Frequent showers.	Snow, if east.
	At 12 o'clock at noon, and 2 P.M.	Very rainy.	Snow or rain.
	Between 2 and 4 P.M.	Changeable.	Fair and mild.
	" 4 and 6 P.M.	Fair.	Fair.
	" 6 and 8 P.M.	{ Fair if wind NW., { Rainy if S. or SW.	Fair and frosty if wind N. or NE. Rain or snow, if S. or SE.
	" 8 and 10 P.M.	Ditto.	Ditto.
	" 10 and midnight,	Fair.	Fair and frosty.

OBSERVATIONS. 1. The nearer the times of the Moon's change, first quarter, full and last quarter, are to midnight, the fairer will the weather be during the seven days following.
2. The space of this calculation occupies from ten at night till two next morning.
3. The nearer to midday or noon the phases of the moon happen, the more foul or wet weather may be expected during the next seven days.
4. The space of this calculation occupies from ten in the forenoon to two in the afternoon. These observations refer principally to the summer, though they affect spring and autumn, nearly in the same ratio.
5. The moon's changes—first quarter—full, and last quarter, happening during six of the afternoon hours, i. e., from four to ten, may be followed by fair weather; but this is mostly dependent upon the wind, as is noted in table.
6. Though the weather, from a variety of irregular causes, is more uncertain in the latter part of autumn, the whole of winter, and the beginning of spring, yet, in the main, the above observations will apply to those periods also.

> Many a time, even in tender youth, I have watched the heavens with anxiety, examined the different appearances of the morning and evening sun, the phases of the moon, the scintillation of the stars, the course and colour of the clouds, the flight of the crow and swallow, the gambols of the colt, the fluttering of the ducks, and the loud screams of the seamew, not forgetting the hue and croaking of the frogs. From the little knowledge I have derived from close observation, I often ventured to direct our agricultural operations in reference to the coming days, and was seldom much mistaken in my reckoning.
>
> Dr Adam Clarke, quoted in Thomas Bridgeman's *The Young Gardener's Assistant*, 1847.

Straw protector illustrated in *The Gardener's Magazine*, 1831.

variously published, professing to perform prognostics of the weather, by the times of change, full, and quarters of the moon. I have carefully consulted this table for years, and was amazed at his general accuracy.'

Whatever the value of such methods might be, gardeners of the time were remarkably successful in overcoming difficulties imposed by the British climate. Forcing was an important part of horticultural practice, and even the simplest means, skilfully applied, brought good results. Although developed to a high degree of sophistication during the nineteenth century, it was, to begin with, only an extension of common-sense ways of protecting plants from extremes of weather. A plain wall or fence round the garden was enough in itself to shelter tender growth in winter, and could be supplemented by reed matting, canvas, or paper screens. Mats woven from lime-bark and sedge fibre were important articles of trade with Russia, and are described in Mortimer's *Commercial Dictionary* (1827) as 'justly entitled to rank as commercial commodities...of which we annually import vast quantities from Petersburgh and Archangel.' Market gardeners used a covering of loose straw to keep the frost from early salads, but Loudon recommends as a 'more economical and neat mode of practice' that the straw be tied into rolls and strung

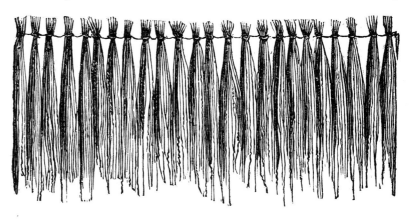

together. In this form it could also be draped over fruit-trees to protect the blossom.

Dressings of straw, peat or leaf mould were laid over parts of the kitchen garden as a winter mulch, and the technique of forcing crops in the open ground was a step on from this. The difference lay in the use of decomposing matter, in this case almost always dung, to warm the soil. Before the development of hot-water systems and, in the twentieth century, electrical methods, the so-called fermentation of stable manure and other organic materials was the only available source of heating the soil. Dung was valued as much as a heat-source as for its fertilising properties, and enormous amounts of labour went into its collection, stacking and turning. If used too fresh it would scorch; if too old it would be useless.

Asparagus was forced outdoors in England from the early 1800s, although it had been raised under glass in winter since the seventeenth century. In accordance with continental practice—Loudon notes that the Danish royal gardener had to have some ready for the king's birthday on 8th January—trenches about two feet wide and three deep were dug between the beds and filled with hot dung. The beds themselves were covered with litter. When rhubarb had become popular it, too, was brought on early by piling manure on the surface around plants which were enclosed in chimney pots or wooden framework.

Plants raised in this way were inevitably blanched, and this was not to every taste. Shirley Hibberd objected: 'Though the books are against me in their indiscriminate counsels to blanch, blanch, blanch, I say blanched rhubarb is only fit for the London market, where any delicate-looking tasteless stuff is sure to sell if offered early in the season; and asparagus without colour can only be tolerated by those who are utterly ignorant of its proper shape, and substance, and flavour. You can get very white drumstick asparagus and very tasteless rhubarb at the guinea table of the London Tavern and the Albion, when the dinner season is in full swing; but no gardener who has tasted the genuine produce of his own growing, would venture on the forlorn hope of attempting to eat it.' A curious, and potentially dangerous, eating habit appears in *The Annals of Horticulture* (1847): 'Mr A. Forsyth, the Earl of Shrewsbury's gardener, at Alton Towers, in Staffordshire, suggests the use of the flower-stalks of Rhubarb, as an excellent addition to our list of culinary vegetables. He says:- "We have been in the habit of eating the leaves of the Rhubarb plant for many years; and, seeing that the fruit stalks were counted as waste, I thought it very likely that they were the better part of the plant, and I now find that the pouches of unopened flowers bear the same relation to the leaves of Rhubarb, that Cauliflowers do to Cabbage leaves, and may be obtained in great abundance, and that at a time (April) when all kinds of vegetables are valuable. The pouches of flower-buds are of a beautiful colour, when dressed in the

These mats, which are in constant use in every garden for protecting trees from the frost, are made principally in Russia, where there are large forests of the lime tree. In spring, when the sap begins to move, and the bark will part readily from the tree, it is stripped off in pieces six or eight inches long. These are steeped in water till the inner bark will separate freely from its outer casing into what are called ribands, or strands. The strands are then hung up in the shade to dry, and in the course of the summer they are ready to be manufactured into mats.

Peter Parley's Tales of Plants, 1839.

It is customary with some persons in the southern parts of England, to keep this plant [rhubarb] growing in their kitchens, so that they may have it for use at any time. They have strong neat boxes, made for the purpose, about three feet deep and two wide, and in length according to the demand, from four to eight feet; these being kept clean, have the appearance of flour-bins, and they are sometimes so contrived as to have shelves over them in imitation of a kitchen dresser. The plants being taken up out of the garden towards winter, are placed as close at the bottom of the box as they can be, with their crowns level: and some sand being thrown over, sufficient to fill up the interstices, and to cover the crowns about half an inch, finishes the operation. No farther trouble is necessary, except to give a little water, just to keep the roots moist, as they need no light at all.

Thomas Bridgeman, *The Young Gardener's Assistant*, 1847.

same manner that Rhubarb is dressed, and resemble the
inside of a fig; the flavour is milder than that of Rhubarb
stalks, but I do not look upon it so much in the light of an
article for making tarts of, as I do for its use as a boiled
vegetable, to be used like Brocoli".'

The one ground-blanched vegetable which was universally approved was sea-kale, *Crambe maritima*. Young shoots,
naturally blanched by growing through banks of sand or
shingle, had been gathered wild from the sea-shore for
centuries and appreciated as a supplement to the sparse
diet of the early spring. Sea-kale was brought into cultivation during the eighteenth century, but was still uncommon
at the start of the nineteenth. It appears in the 1810 edition
of *A New System of Domestic Cookery*, but was obviously still considered a rarity by the author of *A New System of Practical
Domestic Economy* in 1825: 'There is a wild plant which might,
with great propriety and advantage, be introduced more
frequently into our smaller kitchen gardens. We allude to
the *Sea Kale*.' William Curtis had written in 1799 of his attempt to introduce it to London markets: 'Though it was
not attended with all the success I could have wished, I
flatter myself it has been the means of making the plant so
generally known, that in future the markets of the first city

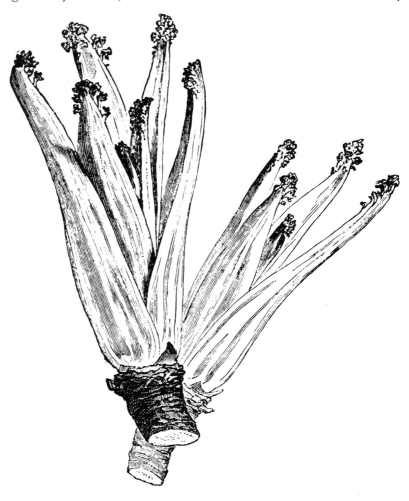

Sea-kale ready for the kitchen, from
Hooper's Gardening Guide, 1883.

53

in the world will be duly supplied with this most desirable article.' By Loudon's time, it was indeed reckoned a common vegetable in the markets, and remained so throughout the rest of the century. In 1872-73, for example, it was on sale in Covent Garden from late November to mid May and dropped from three shillings a basket to about one-and-sixpence.

Charles McIntosh considered that 'Few vegetables are improved more by cultivation than the sea-kale, and few are more improved by forcing. In its cultivated state, it is found to be in April and May, far superior to what it is in its natural habitats; but, when forced at mid-winter, it is superior to any other vegetable with which we are acquainted.' (*The Practical Gardener*, 1830.) It was grown rather like rhubarb. Two-year-old plants raised from seed or from 'thongs' (cuttings from the whip-like roots) were covered in winter with a layer of sand or coal ashes; pots were set over them, and the rows ridged up with mounds of dung. The temperature was kept between 50° and 60° Fahrenheit by careful ventilation, and, according to McIntosh, 'in about three weeks after covering up, the crop will be fit for use.' The covers could be large, up-turned garden pots with the drainage holes blocked to exclude light, or specially-made sea-kale pots with close-fitting lids which could be lifted for easy inspection of the crop. Gardeners timed the process to provide a succession of shoots, which were normally cut at a length of about six to eight inches. For very early cropping, the crowns were lifted in autumn, planted in pots or boxes, and brought into a shed or cellar. E.S. Delamer, who looked on the forcing of 'this valuable esculent' as 'an improvident extravagance' for readers of *The Kitchen Garden*, recommended that it be brought in at its natural time. It still had to be blanched, and there were various opinions of the best method. The *Gardener and Practical Florist* of 1843 prescribes fallen leaves, gathered on a dry day in November and spread in a layer two-and-a-half to three feet deep all over the rows: 'The bed will require no further care until the Kale is fit to cut. The proper time for cutting will be seen by each plant, as it gets ready, pushing up the leaves over-head, like large mole-hills.' Delamer, however, believes in earth rather than leaves: 'This plan has not a single advantage over the earthing system, except indulging the laziness of the cultivator; for any decrepit old woman could sprinkle a few apronfuls of leaves over her garden; but the other mode requires an able-bodied man to execute it properly... autumnal leaves are damp; there is some green rubbish amongst them; and consequently, a slight fermentation takes place, slight putrefaction follows, and the produce grown beneath, which delights the eye like a beautiful branch carved in ivory, disgusts the palate by a flavour as nauseous as it is undoubtedly unwholesome.'

The expense of pots, manure and labour became increasingly a factor against sea-kale forcing, and *Gardening Illustrated*

The best and cheapest method of growing sea-kale

The sea-kale bed is to be planted, in March, in straight rows five feet asunder; the plants in each row to be eighteen inches apart. Some time in December, not too soon, when the foot-stalks of the leaves have fairly separated themselves from the crown of the plants, heap over each about a quarter of a peck of sea-sand or wood-ashes, if these are not to be had, any light soil will do. Then earth up the plants from a trench dug along the space between the rows, exactly as if you were earthing up celery, only that no leaves appear above the top of the mound. The earth should be heaped up till it is about two feet above the crowns of the plants, and then flatted down with the back of the spade, and the whole made very smooth and neat. The long trench between the rows of sea-kale will act as a drain during the dead time of winter. In the spring, when the shoots begin to push, large cracks will be seen in the bank of mould, and a trial may be made with a trowel, as soon as they are supposed to be sufficiently advanced for cutting.

Shirley Hibberd, *Profitable Gardening*, c.1860.

Pascall's Patent Sea-Kale Pot: a convenient means of indoor forcing. From Shirley Hibberd's *Profitable Gardening*.

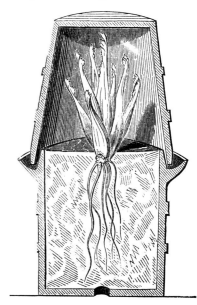

54

The cultivation of this plant is but little attended to, and apparently not very well understood on the Continent. In the 'Manuel du Jardinier', for 1807, a French horticulturalist described the *chou marin d'Angleterre*; but he was not aware of its proper application as an esculent, since he used the broad green leaves instead of the blanched shoots. This of course proved no very tempting preparation, and caused the plant to be condemned as only fit for the coarser tastes of the inhabitants of colder climates.

Vegetable Substances used for the Food of Man, 1832.

The adulteration of chicory may be detected as follows:
1. Powdered chicory thrown on water turns it reddish brown, and rapidly sinks, leaving light impurities either floating or diffused through the liquid.
2. The cold decoction tested with tincture or solution of iodine gives a brown colour; if it turns purple, blue, or black it indicates the presence of roasted beans, rye, or some other like substance containing starch.
3. The dry powder, when incinerated, should not leave more than 4 1/2 or 5 degrees of ash, which should be of a grayish or fawn colour; the contrary indicates the presence of reddle, red clay, ochre, or the like. The adulteration of coffee with chicory is visited with heavy penalties, unless such mixture is properly labelled and sold according to the excise regulation.

The Dictionary of Daily Wants, 1858.

Gardens of Ships. – To sow in the temperate zone and reap between the tropics, is singular, yet constantly done. Our great East India ships have little salad gardens in flat wooden boxes on their poops, where the seed, acted upon by a heat increasing daily, shoots up in a surprisingly rapid manner. In these gardens the number of crops in the year are more numerous than in any spot on earth.

A Dictionary of the Arts of Life and Civilization, 1833.

condemned it as extravagant in 1879, while giving instructions elsewhere in the same volume that were identical to those of McIntosh fifty years earlier. Production of sea-kale seems to have declined towards 1900, and it became as uncommon by the middle of the twentieth century as it had been in the middle of the eighteenth.

Unlike sea-kale which, according to Delamer, 'furnishes a truly British dish, being as yet scarcely known on the continent' and was never much in demand outside Britain, chicory (*Cichorium intybus*) has never been as much favoured in Britain as in the rest of Europe, despite frequent recommendation of its excellence and ease of cultivation. Its history is confused with that of its relatives, the Batavian and curly endive (*Cichorium endivia*), by the perverse tendency of the French to call chicory *endive*, and endive *chicorée*. Loudon mentions succory, the wild form, in *The Cottager's Manual* as good food for rabbits, and says that 'the tops, blanched, either by covering with pots, or by planting in sand in a cellar, make an excellent spring salad, much used in Germany; while its roots, and also those of the dandelion, form one of the best substitutes for coffee.' Chicory was grown on a commercial scale in Flanders, where a bitter extract was used to replace hops in the brewing of beer, and the main product was the dried and roasted coffee-substitute. Increasing imports of chicory-root coffee into Britain led to the imposition of a duty of £1 per ton in the 1830s. Its use, at one time liable to a fine of £100, was allowed under licence by an act of George IV. Later, ground chicory itself was frequently adulterated by the addition of carrot, parsnip, mangold-wurzel, beans, roasted grain, biscuit-powder or burnt sugar.

Two forms of chicory can be produced by forcing. The first, is the *barbe de capucin*, a salad plant originally grown in France from a variety known as *chicorée sauvage* (although it was a cultivated form). Further muddle arose from names, since *barbe de capucin* (friar's beard), has also been called *barbe de bouc* (goat's beard), and the young shoots of English goat's beard, or salsify, (*tragopogon*) are sometimes served in salad. In *The Gardener's Assistant* (1860), Thompson gives directions for the treatment of *barbe* : 'The seed is sown thinly in April or May. In November or December, one or several beds of light sandy soil, or well-decomposed dung, about 2 feet in width, and 3 inches thick, are formed in a cellar. On these is placed a row of chicory roots laid on their side, with the crowns outwards; next comes another row of roots, and so on. The mild and equable temperature of the cellar, and the want of light, soon occasion the production of blanched leaves, which are cut as soon as they have attained a sufficient size.' An alternative practice was to lay up the roots in a perforated barrel filled with earth or sand, the crowns projecting through the holes. This was often advised as a way of providing a supply on board ship. The outcome of either method, as described by Delamer, is that 'the roots begin to vegetate, and send forth long, narrow, yellowish-

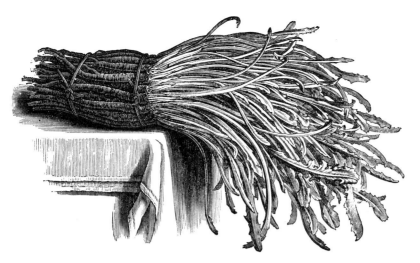

Barbe de capucin chicory, from *The Illustrated Dictionary of Gardening*.

white leaves, which constitute the salad.' He adds that the French deliberately grew the roots in poor soil to produce small, slender shoots. British growers tended to produce less delicate shoots by forcing 'fine roots', raised in rich, well-cultivated ground.

The tight, blanched heads of Witloof chicory, now often referred to as chicons, are said to have been first grown in Brussels in the 1840s, and have been a Belgian speciality ever since. Gibault's *Histoire des Légumes*, cited by Jane Grigson in her meticulous unravelling of the chicory-endive confusion (*Vegetable Book*, 1978) attributes to the head gardener of the Brussels botanical garden the discovery that the roots form compact heads when forced in a covering layer of soil. Even in the 1830s, however, Dr Lippold had acknowledged a distinction between the French and Belgian varieties. 'There is, however, one difference, the thick roots of the Chicorée de Bruges produce broad leaves and luxuriant young shoots, whilst the roots of the Barbe de Capucin, or wild Chicory, have such small leaves, that a bundle of fifty roots scarcely produces a moderate-sized plateful of salad; while from one dozen roots of the other, a good-sized dish of salad can be obtained.' (*The Gardener's Magazine*.)

Although plenty of skill and hard work went into extending the season of crops in the open ground, the heart of any true forcing enthusiast was in pits and frames. Tender plants had for centuries been housed in protective structures, covered first with oiled cloth, later with glass, but in the nineteenth century this branch of horticulture became a high art.

The most general application of forcing in kitchen gardens was in the growing of cucumbers and melons, and the fact that areas in which frames were kept were known as 'melon-grounds' indicates their importance. Both cucumbers and melons had been much prized in Britain since their introduction in the 1570s. John Evelyn described the melon in 1675 as 'the most precious fruit that your kitchen-garden affords'. Dr Johnson's remark about throwing cucumber out of the window has often been quoted, but

In the winter of 1839, or early in 1840, I carried in a basket of this fine salad, tied up in sixpenny bundles, at a price which I thought would pay well. No one had ever seen it, – no one had ever heard of it, – and no one would buy it. An old herbalist (a Mr Steptoe) came along; he was a buyer of pure dandelion leaves, and all sorts of things for foreigners. He bought all the chicory leaves, and paid nine shillings for it. Thinks I, 'my fortune's made.' Next market morning, I carried a still larger quantity in; but when Mr Steptoe came past, he merely shook his head, and passed on. 'Then,' thinks I, 'is my first-born child to fall to the ground like this, and in the first market in the world?' When he returned, 'Here, I have plenty more for you,' said I. ''Tis of no use,' said he; 'I have only sold a few bunches to foreigners.' Then I said, 'Take the lot this time for nothing.' He did so a third time, with no better success; then I gave it up.

Mr Cuthill, in E.S. Delamer, *The Kitchen Garden*.

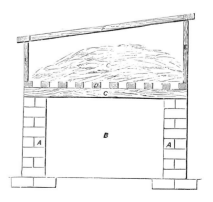

nineteenth-century writers were almost unanimous in their recommendation, which was often derived, no doubt, from Abercrombie's remarks on early cucumbers and melons: 'As it is generally the ambition of most gardeners to excel each other in the production of early cucumbers &c...' (*Every Man His Own Gardener*, 1813 edition). Charles McIntosh wrote, 'The production of these fruits at an early season is an object of emulation amongst gardeners' (1830); John Loudon, 'To produce cucumbers at an early season is an object of emulation with every gardener' (1834); Thomas Bridgeman, 'To produce Cucumbers at an early season, should be an object of emulation with every gardener' (1847). Introducing a moralistic tone, the 1857 edition of Abercrombie states, 'it is the duty of gardeners to excel in the production of early cucumbers.' Anderson, in *The New Practical Gardener*, an updated version of McIntosh's work published c.1872, repeats the words of the original, but a fresh note appears in the cucumber entry of *The Illustrated Dictionary of Gardening* (Nicholson) at the end of the century: 'Its cultivation is a matter of importance in almost every garden, and there are very few of any pretentions where it is not grown.'

The most popular structure for frame-culture was the 'common hot-bed' surmounted by a simple frame. Here again, stable-manure was the usual material so long as it was readily available, but dead leaves and tan could be used, alone or mixed with dung. When the fresh manure had been stacked and repeatedly turned for a fortnight, the construction of the bed could begin. Mrs Loudon's instructions are relatively concise: 'The size of the hot-bed must depend principally on the size of the frame which is to cover it; observing that the bed must be from six inches to a foot wider than the frame every way. The manure must then be spread in layers, each layer being beaten down with the back of the fork, till the bed is about three feet and a half high. The surface of the ground on which the hot-bed is built, is generally raised about six inches above the general surface of the garden; and it is advisable to lay some earth

Left: Cucumber frame supported on brick piers; the space 'B' is for 'Hot Manure'. From *The Illustrated Dictionary of Gardening*. *Right:* Design for a cucumber pit submitted to the Horticultural Society by John Mearns in 1823. Warm air passed from the dung linings through the walls of open brickwork into a cavity below the frame. The soil, contained in a trough of stone, slate or wood, was built up to the level of the dotted line as the plants grew.

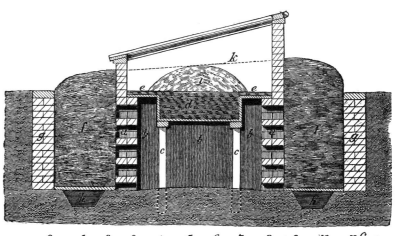

round the bottom of the bed, nearly a foot wide, that it may receive the juices of the manure that will drain from the bed. As soon as the bed is made, the frame is put on and the sashes kept quite close, till a steam appears upon the glass, when the bed is considered in a fit state to be covered three or four inches deep with mould; observing, if the bed has settled unequally, to level the surface of the manure before covering it with earth.' (*Gardening for Ladies*, 1840). She also had a concern for appearance: 'When hotbeds are made of spent tanner's bark or decayed leaves, a kind of box or pit must be formed of bricks or boards, or even layers of turf, or clay, and the tan or leaves filled in so as to make a bed. Where neatness is an object, this kind of bed is preferable to any other; but a common hotbed of stable manure may be made to look neat by thatching the outside with straw, or covering it with bast mats, pegged down to keep them close to the bed.'

The directions given by Mrs Loudon are for a small bed to take a frame four feet by three, and this would have been suitable for raising seeds. Her readers are advised against more ambitious projects. The larger hotbeds for cucumbers and melons were made to suit frames of two or three glazed lights or sashes, each usually six feet long. Larger lights than this were difficult to handle.

With the hotbed settled and the plants established, constant attention was needed to regulate the temperature. Careful ventilation was generally enough to prevent overheating, but in extreme cases sections of the bed might have to be dug out and replaced with cooler material. Keeping the heat up was the more likely concern, especially when cucumbers were required in midwinter. As the sides of the heap decayed and cooled, they were continually reinforced by application of fresh dung round the sides, the 'lining' of the bed. Screens of canvas helped to protect the whole structure from winter winds, and mats were laid over the glass at night, sometimes till as late as June.

Loudon's *Encyclopaedia of Gardening* (1834 edition) lists fourteen principal varieties of cucumber including both cucumbers forced for salads and cooked dishes, and the types grown outdoors for pickling. Many of the fruit are noted as bearing spines, although the Smooth Green Roman, the White Turkey and the Green Turkey were 'destitute of prickles'. There was also a large, coarse 'Patagonian' variety pickled in the manner of the mango, presumably similar to the fruit referred to by 'A Lady' in *A New System of Domestic Cookery* under the heading 'Melon Mangoes'. The cucumber was often grown, in hothouses as well as frames, for exhibition. The sorts preferred were the ones which reached great lengths, such as the Longford, a 'handsome fruit, originated at Longford, near Manchester, the seat

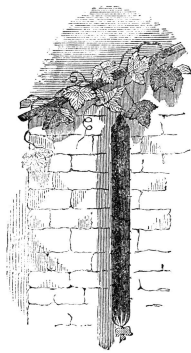

Above left, 'The Perfection of a Cucumber' and, *above right*, one 'not so handsome'. Both from *The Gardener and Practical Florist*, 1843.

Melon Mangoes
There is a particular sort for this purpose which the gardeners know. Cut a small square piece out of one side, and through that take out the seeds, and mix with them mustard seeds and shred garlick; stuff the melon as full as the space will allow, and replace the square piece. Bind it up with a small new pack-thread. Boil a good quantity of vinegar, to allow for wasting, with peppers, salt, ginger, and pour boiling hot over the mangoes four successive days; the last, put flour of mustard, and scraped horse-radish, into the vinegar just as it boils up. Stop close. Observe that there is plenty of vinegar. All pickles are spoiled if they are not well covered. Mangoes should be done soon after they are gathered. Large cucumbers called green turley [turkey?], prepared as mangoes, are excellent, and come sooner into eating.

A New System of Domestic Cookery, 1810.

Cucumbers advertised in the 1880s: Sutton's Purley Park Hero and Hamilton & Son's Sir Garnet Wolseley. *Below left:* Mr Gauen's device for restoring the bloom to cucumbers, from *The Gardener's Magazine*, 1828. Powdered magnesia was puffed into the box by bellows and distributed by the rotating brush. *Below right:* Glassware advertisement from *The Gardeners' Chronicle*, 1857.

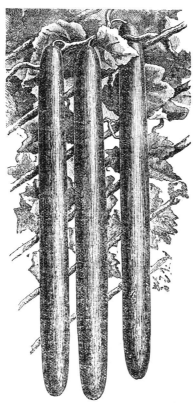

NEW CUCUMBER SIR GARNET WOLSELEY.—Joseph Hamilton & Son, Wellington Place, near Carlisle, are now prepared to supply Seed of the above. Price 2s. 6d. per packet of six seeds. Special quotations to the trade on application.

"The handsomest Cucumber I have ever seen. The brace shown grew from one joint."—THE GARDEN, Sept. 27, 1879.

"The points in which Cucumber Sir Garnet Wolseley surpasses all other long-fruited varieties are the symmetry of its fruit, and the abundance with which they are produced, there being no shank or handle to Sir Garnet." –*Gardeners' Chronicle*, Sept. 27, 1879.

"It is the most handsome Cucumber we have ever seen, is entirely destitute of shank or shoulder, and is of excellent flavour ; it produces three fruits to every joint, which swell rapidly to maturity in succession."—*The Gardener*, August, 1879.

JOSEPH HAMILTON & SON, Wellington Place, near Carlisle.

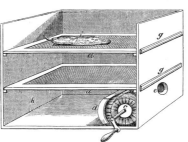

CUCUMBER GLASSES.

24 inches long .. .. 2s. 6d.	16 inches long .. .. 1s. 4d.	
22 ,, ... 1 10	14 ,, ... 1 2	
20 ,, ... 1 8	12 ,, ... 1 0	
18 ,, ... 1 6	Made to any length.	

PROPAGATING GLASSES.

2 in. diameter 0s. 3½d. each	12 in. diameter 1s. 9d. each
3 ,, 0 4½ ,,	13 ,, 2 0 ,,
4 ,, 0 5½ ,,	14 ,, 2 5 ,,
5 ,, 0 6½ ,,	15 ,, 3 0 ,,
6 ,, 0 8 ,,	16 ,, 3 6 ,,
7 ,, 0 10 ,,	17 ,, 4 0 ,,
8 ,, 1 0 ,,	18 ,, 5 0 ,,
9 ,, 1 2 ,,	19 ,, 6 0 ,,
10 ,, 1 4 ,,	20 ,, 7 0 ,,
11 ,, 1 6 ,,	

GLASS PRESERVE JARS.—Per dozen.

	Without lid. With lid.		Without lid. With lid.
3 inches .. 4s. 6d. 6s. 6d.		7 in. £0 12s. 0d. £0 16s. 0d.	
4 ,, .. 6 0 9 0		8 ,, 0 16 0 1 0 0	
5 ,, .. 8 0 11 0		9 ,, 1 9 0 1 6 0	
6 ,, .. 10 0 14 0		10 ,, 1 4 0 1 12 0	

WASP TRAPS, 3s. 6d. per dozen,

JAMES PHILLIPS AND CO.,
116, Bishopsgate Street Without, E.C.

He was extremely successful in producing melons, having invented a method of suspending them in baskets of wire gauze, which, by relieving the stalk of tension, allowed nutrition to proceed more freely, and better enabled the fruit to grow and ripen. Amongst his other erections, he built a joiner's shop, where he kept a workman regularly employed in carrying out his many ingenious contrivances of this sort.

He took much pride also in his growth of cucumbers. He raised them very fine and large, but he could not make them grow straight. Place them as he would, notwithstanding all his propping of them, and humouring them by modifying the application of heat and the admission of light for the purpose of effecting his object, they would still insist on growing crooked in their own way. At last he had a number of glass cylinders made at Newcastle, for the purpose of an experiment; into these the growing cucumbers were inserted, and then he succeeded in growing them perfectly straight. Carrying one of the new products into his house one day, and exhibiting it to a party of visitors, he told them of the expedient he had adopted, and added gleefully, "I think I have bothered them noo!"

Samuel Smiles, *Life of George Stephenson*.

of C.F.S. Walker Esq., and grown there sometimes to the length of 27 inches.' Ipswich was a centre for exhibition growing, and competitors there put great emphasis on the size of their fruit. Perfectionists encased developing specimens in cylinders of glass to make sure that they grew straight and free from blemishes, and unscrupulous exhibitors resorted to trickery to improve the look of individual cucumbers or the matching of a pair or a 'leash' of three. *The Gardener's Magazine* of 1828 disapproved of dusting the fruit to restore the surface 'bloom', and glueing on individual prickles. Many varieties were developed throughout the century, including the Captivation and the Phenomenon in the 1850s. By 1870 the Telegraph had appeared, and has been a favourite ever since. The Marquis of Lorne was endorsed by 'a Market-gardener' in the 1872 *Journal of Horticulture*: 'Mr Jenner, fruiterer, of Tonbridge Wells, told me it gave general satisfaction to his customers, and he is no mean authority'. The same writer praised J. Douglas's Tender and True, which had won a first-class certificate from

59

the Royal Horticultural Society two years previously. At about the same time, *The New Practical Gardener* mentioned 'the extraordinarily growing Sodly Qua, which grows to a length of from five to six feet. In China it is used as an article of food, served up with rice.' The Chinese, kwa, is applied to many cucurbits—this is probably the tropical Snake Gourd, *Trichosanthes cucumerina* var. *anguina*, common in the East and sometimes grown in Britain as a hothouse ornamental.

It is now usual to pinch out the male flowers of cucumbers grown under glass, since fertilised fruit develop a bitter flavour. This would have horrified many gardeners of the early nineteenth century. Abercrombie, quoted by McIntosh, Loudon and Bridgeman, instructs the grower to fertilise the female flowers with the 'farina' or pollen of the male: 'The males are often erroneously called false blossoms; but they are so far from being false bloom, that they are by

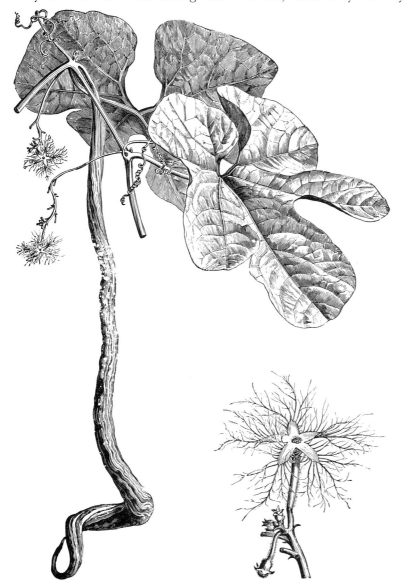

The Snake Gourd, *Trichosanthes anguina*, from *The Illustrated Dictionary of Gardening*.

Plan and sections of a hotbed and frame recommended by John Smith in *A Treatise on the Growth of Cucumbers and Melons*, 1839. The smaller frame on the left, warmed by air passing through the tube 'K', is for mushrooms or asparagus.

PLAN. FIG. 1.

LONGITUDINAL SECTION. FIG. 2.

TRANSVERSE SECTION. FIG. 3.

We have recently seen a curious account of a subterraneous garden, formed at the bottom of the Percy Main Pit, Newcastle, by the furnace keeper, which was communicated at the last quarterly meeting of the Caledonian Horticultural Society. The plants are formed in the bottom of the mine, by the light and radiant heat of an open stove, constantly maintained for the sake of ventilation. The same valuable work throws out a hint worthy the notice of residents in all the coal districts, where it describes an extensive natural hot-bed, near Dudley, Staffordshire, which is heated by means of the slow combustion of coal at some depth below the surface. From this natural hot-bed, a gardener raises annually crops of different kinds of culinary vegetables, which are earlier by some weeks than those in surrounding gardens.

A New System of Practical Domestic Economy, 1825.

nature designed to impregnate the female flowers, to render them fruitful; for the antherae in the centre of the male blossom, being furnished with a fine powder, which being dispersed on the stigma in the centre of the female, the fecundation is effected, and the fruit in a day or two after will begin to swell.' He explains that 'without the assistance of the male blossom, the females, having the embryo fruit at their base, wither and decay, and the infant fruit turns yellow and drops off.' It was, however, the rule to gather cucumbers for the table well before they were fully mature —at four to eight inches long, according to Loudon—so that the bitterness would have been less pronounced than in a ripe fruit. The habit of hand pollination, dismissed by Cobbett as 'arrant nonsense', was later discontinued with cucumbers (perhaps because the improved varieties were not liable to shed the unfertilised embryos), though not for melons. Thompson remarks in *The Gardener's Assistant*: 'Formerly great pains were taken to fertilize the female flowers, but it has been proved that this is not necessary except where fruit is to be grown from seed.'

Keeping the fruits for seed was in any case a risky undertaking, as cross-pollination by other varieties often produced inferior strains. 'When a really first-class Cucumber or Melon is obtained, the only safe plan is to banish all others from the garden, and if possible it should be perpetuated by cuttings rather than by seeds,' is the advice given in *Cultivated Plants* (1877) by F.W. Burbidge, who adds a note that 'The Hon. and Rev. J.T. Boscawen of Lamaran Probus has a remarkably well-flavoured seedless variety of Cucumber in his garden which he has perpetuated by cuttings for thirteen years.' He also quotes the 'rather doubtful' case of a cucumber plant in Mr J. Watson's St Albans nursery which was claimed to have borne 'a globular fruit, exactly like a Melon in form, together with normal Cucumbers.' Seeds of the cucumber and of the melon were very generally kept up to four years before being sown, since they were thought to produce shorter-jointed and more productive plants. 'When old seeds are not to be had, gardeners give them an artificial age by wearing them in their pocket.' (E.S. Delamer, *The Kitchen Garden*, 1860). Shirley Hibberd, though, states that 'the seed should be new and plump.'

One method of raising cucumbers without the need for artificial heat produced disastrous results, as reported in *A New System of Practical Domestic Economy*: 'Attempts have been made to concentrate the Sun's rays upon them by means of copper sheet reflectors. This, however, has been ascertained to render the plants reared by them completely deleterious, even to the loss of life. It is not impossible that the rain water and dew dripping from these reflectors may have aided much in the unhappy consequence; but, in whatever way the morbific action may have taken place it would be the height of imprudence to adopt, or to prolong the practice, the results of which have been fatal in more than one instance.' In the eighteenth century, housewives were encouraged to boil their pickles in brass pots 'to green them', and to repeat the process until the colour was satisfactory. By about 1810, the dangerous effect of using copper and brass as containers for vinegar had been recognised, together with the risk of using earthenware vessels with lead and arsenic in the glaze. *A New System of Domestic Cookery* recommended boiling with vine leaves to improve the colour, 'as it is now known that the very fine green pickles are made so by using brass or bell-metal vessels, which, when vinegar is put into them, become highly poisonous, few people like to eat them.' The public had evidently become wary of the whole process.

Melons were raised on hotbeds in exactly the same way as cucumbers, but, whereas it could be said that 'there is scarcely any person, not even the humblest tradesman, who has not his cucumber-bed in his garden,' the attempt was less generally made with melons. Since the bed had to produce a constant heat of about 75° Fahrenheit, the melon-frames were normally used only in the summer, sometimes

Melon-seeds improve by age, and should not be sown, if it can be avoided, under two years old. They will retain their vegetating properties for twenty years or more. If seeds of the growth of last season be sown, they for the most part produce plants of very gross habits, and will not be so fruitful, but grow more to vines than fruit.

To obviate this disadvantage, when older seeds cannot be procured, the seeds may be worn in the pocket, near the body, for some weeks previously to sowing, which will have the effect of fully maturing them.

C. McIntosh, *The Practical Gardener*, 1830.

Rules to be observed with Pickles. Keep them closely covered, and have a wooden spoon, with holes, tied to each jar, all metal being improper. They should be well kept from the air, the large jars be seldom opened, and small ones, for the different pickles in use, should be kept for common supply, into which what is not eaten may be returned, and the top closely covered.

Acids dissolve the lead that is in the tinning of sauce-pans. When necessary to boil vinegar, do it in a stone jar on the hot hearth. Pickles should never be put into glazed jars, as salt and vinegar penetrate the glaze, which is poisonous.

The Young Woman's Companion or Female Instructor, c.1830.

Covered with vinegar, caper buds will keep many years. It is said that in order to increase the green colour, it is customary to put filings of copper in the first pickle. Bosc states that, in order to effect the same object, they use sieves formed of copper wires, when separating the large buds from the small ones, previously to placing them in fresh vinegar; the consequence is, he says, that capers are always more or less poisonous.

J. Loudon, *Arboretum and Fruticetum Britannicum*, 1838.

Melons from *The Illustrated Dictionary of Gardening. Above:* Cantaloup and 'Persian' melons; *below:* Queen Anne's Pocket Melon, 'Figari' and 'Embroidered Market'.

doubling as protection for other tender subjects in the winter. Mr Cuthill suggested a first sowing on 1st February, and wrote in 1843 that over four years he had cut ripe fruit between 5th and 10th May. But melon culture was always more popular with professionals than amateurs, and E.S. Delamer discouraged it: 'The Melon has no right to make its appearance here, except for the sake of mentioning that a pretty little old-fashioned variety,—Queen Anne's Pocket Melon,—which produces green-fleshed well-flavoured fruit, the size of a large orange, may, in very fine English summers, be grown on a trellis against a south wall.' In the 20th century, though, Edward Bunyard described this as seldom seen, and best left 'for soured bachelors and other solitary folk.'

Loudon's list of melons contains thirty varieties, including Persian melons, of which the Housainee type was popularised by Thomas Knight in the 1830s, and a selection from the separate genus of water melons. These, he observes, 'form both the food and drink of the inhabitants of Egypt for several months in the year.' Cobbett grew water melons from Maltese seed, and had a high opinion of them: 'They are a totally different thing from the other tribe; and being so much better, I have often wondered that, where people have great space under glass, and great heat at command, they do not raise them in England.' Thomas Bridgeman tells his American readers that 'they afford a very refreshing article of luxury in our warm summers.'

In *The Gardener's Assistant*, Thompson recommends four scarlet-fleshed and nine green-fleshed dessert melons, noting that 'the varieties of both are exceedingly numerous...new ones are being continually produced.' However, the process of improvement does not seem to have been altogether successful and in 1884 *The Gardeners' Chronicle* complained: 'it would be of exceeding interest to be enabled now to compare with the best acknowledged Melons

Blenheim Orange melons, from *Garden-Work*, 1887.

of the day the best of twenty or more years since, for gardeners then prided themselves that they produced first-rate fruits... What will our Melon breeders say to a proposal to hark back, as it were, to some new and distinct breeds?—new so far, of course, that they have not been utilised in this country, and through the instrumentality of which it is just possible some genuine and desirable novelties may be produced. We have now all that can be desired in form, size, and beauty, and there is little fault to find on the score of productiveness, our chief want is richer flavour, something more than mawkish sweetness, or mere sugar and water. Who will strike out a new path in Melon productiveness?'

The simple hotbed, when properly prepared and tended, was a remarkably efficient producer, not only of melons and cucumbers, but of strawberries, out-of-season salads, herbs and tender annuals. The disadvantages of hotbeds were the constant care needed to manage them, and the large amounts of manure which had to be supplied—an average of one cartload for each light of the frame, with more still for the linings. For 'humble gardeners and small establishments', Sir Joseph Paxton suggested a more economical arrangement: a 'homely pit' built of sods of turf, covered over with oiled calico or paper as a substitute for glass. Two or three barrowloads of dung could be thrown into the pit to give some degree of heating (*Cottager's Calen-*

64

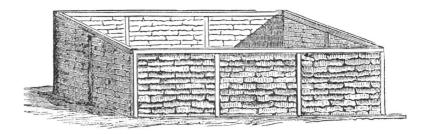

Unheated turf pit, from Shirley Hibberd's *The Amateur's Kitchen Garden*, 1877.

dar). Here and elsewhere in the literature, the word 'pit' does not necessarily mean a hole in the ground; usually it just signifies an enclosed structure, part of which might be sunk in the earth.

Many designs for pits and patent frames appeared from the end of the eighteenth century onwards, one of the first being that of James McPhail, author of *A Treatise on the Culture of the Cucumber*. The essential feature of McPhail's pit was a wall built of bricks, with gaps between each, which supported the frame. 'Round these perforated walls, linings of hot dung, or dung and leaves are placed, the heat of which enters the flues, and heats the mould in which the plants grow. The chief advantages of this pit, are, that the dung requires no preparation before using, and consequently none of the heat is lost... Where neatness and order are looked to, pits of any sort are preferable to dung beds, and this one, if partially sunk under the ground-surface, or surrounded with a neat wall as high as the perforations in the side walls, will have a neat and respectable appearance.' (Charles McIntosh, *The Practical Gardener*, 1830.)

The Edmondstone pit, a similar construction, was popular in Scotland: dung was retained by a wall and covered with a wooden lid, 'which prevents the dung of the linings from being chilled by rain or cold, and completely hides all

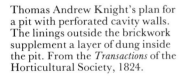

Thomas Andrew Knight's plan for a pit with perforated cavity walls. The linings outside the brickwork supplement a layer of dung inside the pit. From the *Transactions* of the Horticultural Society, 1824.

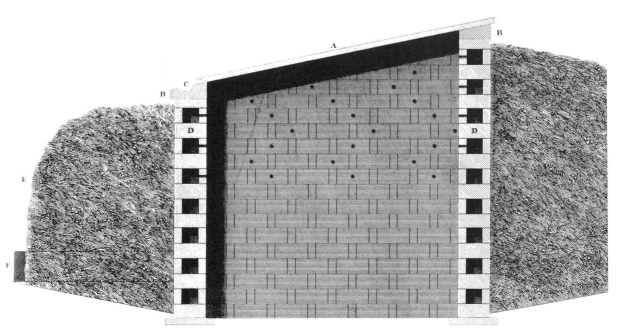

that is so offensive to the eye in ordinary hot-beds and pits where the lining is exposed.' As well as the many more or less elaborate variants of this type, there were pits with mechanisms for raising and lowering the frames, pits heated by flues from coal fires, and eventually, pits with their own steam or hot-water circulating systems. At their most sophisticated, the forcing-pits of a prosperous garden were not so much refined hotbeds as miniature hothouses.

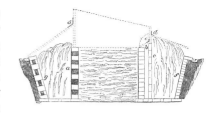

Sections of pits from *The Gardener's Magazine.*
Above: Atkinson's Melon Pit (1827): 'These have been found far superior to any other yet constructed.'
Left: Alfred Kendall's double cucumber or melon pit (1828).

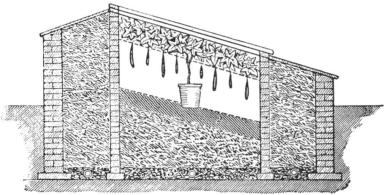

Cucumber pit with sloping bed from David Thomson's *Handy Book of Fruit Culture under Glass*, 1881. The plants were raised in eleven-inch pots with the bottoms knocked out so that the roots could extend into the layer of soil.

Summer cucumbers in Stoke Newington, from Shirley Hibberd's *The Amateur's Greenhouse and Conservatory*, 1873.

Glass

'Madam, I do not see your glawss,' remarks a boorish English visitor to Mrs Knox in a story by Somerville and Ross (*In Mr Knox's Country*). The old lady retorts that all the glass on her estate is on top of the walls keeping out intruders, but for more conventional property-owners some 'glass' in the form of greenhouse, hot-house or conservatory had become a must. In the first half of the nineteenth century, such structures had still been rarities and were often impractical. 'In former times,' according to *Beeton's Book of Garden Management* in the 1870s, 'greenhouses were not only costly to fit up, but inefficient when erected. The proper principle of their construction was not very well understood: heavy rafters, complicated sashes, at once costly and inefficient, encumbered many a fine garden.' This follows the observation that 'Glass structures of even the smallest kind would, a very few years ago, have been considered a piece of great extravagance for any but the affluent.'

One spur to the development of early forms of horticultural building had been the fashion for decorative citrus trees in the gardens of great houses, which started with the growing of oranges in England at the end of the sixteenth century and lasted until the increasing importation of other exotics some hundred and fifty years later. The trees were usually arranged outside in pots and tubs during the summer. The orangeries built for their winter quarters, many of which still survive, were not so much horticultural structures as adaptations of domestic architecture—in Loudon's phrase, 'mere chambers distinguished by more glass windows in front than were usual in dwelling houses.' Some were built and equipped in a style well beyond that of the ordinary dwelling house, and their designs often followed the decorative fashions of the period.

An alternative approach was to plant the trees in a permanent position, as in the gardens of Heidelberg Castle laid out by Solomon de Caus. There, in 1619, the orangery covered an area of just under 9,000 square feet, with 30

Charles McIntosh's design for an orange-tub, made of slate or wood and easily taken apart for root-inspection and re-potting. Illustrated in Volume I of *The Gardener's Magazine*, then in McIntosh's *The Practical Gardener* (1828), the same engraving was still being used in 1873 in Shirley Hibberd's *The Amateur's Greenhouse and Conservatory*.

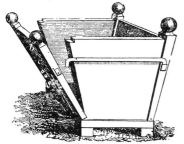

'large' trees, about 25 feet high, and roughly 400 others. A wooden building was erected on the site from autumn until Easter, and four furnaces were kept burning through the winter. The same practice was followed in England, although on a smaller scale, and the portable covers were sometimes dispensed with in southern counties. At Combe Royal in Devon, lemons, limes, shaddocks and several varieties of orange grew in recesses in a south-facing wall, unprotected except for reed mats in severe weather. A Bergamot Lemon was lost in 1859-60, but an orange still flourishing in 1871 was said to have survived for more than 250 years.

The use of walls to protect and train trees was, of course, commonplace, and the walls of kitchen gardens were lined with apples, pears, peaches, apricots and other fruit. As well as straight brick walls, there were others built on a zig-zag, angular, or serpentine plan (rather preciously titled 'crinkle-crankle' walls). Their main value seems to have been in greater stability and decorative effect, and Loudon says that their supposed advantage of providing more effective shelter was 'generally denied by practical men'. However, a further development, flued walls, contained hollow sections to conduct heat from fires, and eventually walls were made with glass. Robert Thompson describes

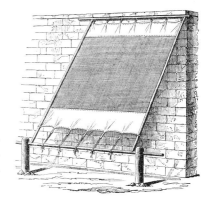

Above: Calico and netting screen for wall-fruit from *The Gardeners' Chronicle* for 1854.

Below: The orangery at Combe Royal, from *The Journal of Horticulture,* 1871.

Solid-roofed camellia and orange house in chinoiserie style, from *The Gardener and Practical Florist*, 1843: 'The only subject, connected with a garden, in which the Chinese have exercised any thing like taste, is their Conservatories.'

Colonel Challoner's wall-frame, a glazed framework erected against a wall and equipped with ventilation flaps and counter-weighted sashes. *The Gardener's Assistant* also contains a paragraph on Ewing's Glass Wall—a fully-glazed design. Glass walls, Thompson remarks, 'have been erected in different parts of the country, but their adoption has been but partial, the expense being great in proportion to the area enclosed. On the other hand, the vegetation within them has the advantage of being near the glass; but the greatest drawback is the little protection they afford compared with a lean-to structure, which might be put up for the same, or perhaps less expense... They might also be introduced in particular situations where something is required to hide a bad view, but where a solid wall or a house would be unsightly.'

Orangeries and conservatories with extensive windows, but with conventional roofing, were built all over Europe throughout the eighteenth century. They ranged from the 'greenhouse' in the Chelsea Physic Garden to the opulent winter garden in Prince Potemkin's estates at St Petersburg, which was reported as 'too gloomy for the growth of plants ...those grown in the glass sheds of the kitchen-garden are carried there and sunk in the ground.' The true glasshouses and plant-stoves of the nineteenth century owed

The winter garden of the Potemkin estate, from J. Loudon's *An Encyclopaedia of Gardening*, 1834.

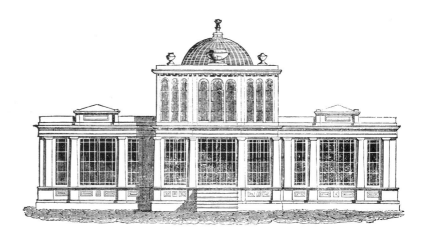

their origins to the development of glazing for roofs as well as walls.

Theorists of the early 1800s were anxious to discover the best form of glass roof and discussed at length the most suitable angle of slope for ripening fruit at different times of the year. According to Loudon, the investigation culminated in a 'fortunate discovery' by Sir G. MacKenzie in 1815 that 'the form of glass roof best calculated for the admission of the sun's rays is a hemispherical figure'—not, perhaps a very surprising conclusion. Designs for glazed roofs in the first quarter of the nineteenth century were often extremely complex: an 'acuminated semi-globe', a 'parallelogram with curved roof and ends' and a 'polyprosopic house' are described by Loudon.

The construction of elaborate glazed buildings was possible only in an industrial age. Without improved standards of glassmaking, theoretical calculations of the transmission of light would have been pointless, and the often huge areas of curvilinear roofing could not have been supported without the use of cast iron. Many gardeners prophesied that metal would never supplant wood for ribs and rafters, since its expansion would break the glass. In the hot weather of 1827 hundreds of panes in the roof of the Regent's Park Colosseum were shattered, but in normal British summers this was rarely a problem. Curved roofs called also for complicated ventilation systems, with carefully contrived linkages of pulleys, rods and chains controlling a series of lights.

One of the reasons why many gardeners achieved poor results under glass was the low quality of much of the material. 'Glazing', says Loudon, 'was formerly performed with the very worst description of glass, called green glass; and, accordingly, Adanson, in 1710, recommends the adoption of Bohemian glass, then the best in Europe, but now equalled by our best *crown* or *patent crown* tables.' Loudon adds that green glass reflected as much as three-quarters of the light falling on it, so that plants took on a 'sickly, pale, etiolated appearance'. Crown glass came only in small sizes, since each pane was cut from circular sheets spun by hand. The largest panes were about three feet by two, and many

were much smaller. This problem was partly overcome by rolling sheets from large blown cylinders, then by the development of good quality plate glass, cast on iron tables up to seventeen feet long. As late as the end of the nineteenth century, green glass (apparently tinted intentionally to prevent the scorching of plants) was used at Kew, though the plants grew better when it was finally removed. The name 'greenhouse' is sometimes said to refer to such coloured glass, but is in fact derived, as in John Evelyn's seventeenth-century usage, from the evergreen plants kept inside.

The high cost of glass restricted its horticultural use to botanical showplaces and great estates for years. The great 'domical botanic hot-house' at Bretton Hall, Yorkshire, cost £14,000 to put up in 1829, although it was sold a couple of years later for only £560. Between 1792 and 1845, the glass industry was virtually stagnant. A tax first imposed under Pitt's austerity budget became so heavy that, as Sir Robert Peel stated in a House of Commons debate, the duties exacted on glass finally amounted to two or three times its actual value. Manufacturers paid a license fee of £20 per year for each works, imported materials were taxed on entry, and the glass itself was assessed at threepence per pound in the melting-pot or sixpence after it had been taken out. In 1833, there were only 126 glassworks in the whole of the United Kingdom, and George Dodd's *British Manufactures* reported no more than four or five makers of plate glass in England in 1845.

In that year, the duties on glass were removed, and the occasion was celebrated in *Chambers's Edinburgh Journal*: 'Now the whole of these restrictions are to be taken off, and it is impossible to foresee to what useful purposes glass will be put, and how cheaply it will be possible to obtain it. It is not merely a release from the sums paid for excise duties, but relief from the vexatious regulations imposed on its manufacture, which will bring down the price. An elasticity will be given to the trade, and new enterprisers will embark in it... It is impossible to foresee the advantages of cheap glass which will be reaped by horticulturalists. Conservatory frames and other glazed implements of their art are so serious an item of expense that recent insurance companies have thought it worth their while to afford insurances

The following are the principal regulations relative to the glass trade:

Glass-makers must take out a licence at the excise office, and are not to begin to charge any pot without giving *twelve hours'* notice, in writing, of the time of beginning, the weight of metal, and species of glass.

Manufacturers of flint-glass are allowed three hours for beginning to charge their pots, after the time specified in their notices.

Cast plate is to be charged by weight if squared, and measured in the presence of the officer; and makers are to give six hours' notice in London, and twelve hours in the country, before drawing plates out of the annealing arch, on penalty of £50.

Manufacturers are to permit officers to take samples, and are entitled, on demand, to copies of the officers' return.

Entries to be made in writing, upon oath, and duties to be paid monthly in London, and every six weeks in the country.

Duty on materials lost or spoiled to be allowed, due proof being made of such fact.

Officers at all times, by day or night, are to have access to workhouses, to gauge the materials, and mark the pots as they shall think fit.

Mortimer's *Commercial Dictionary*, 1827.

against hail—a severe storm of which has been known to ruin many a struggling gardener. Private individuals also will be able to have conservatories; and we hope to see the majority of town residences adorned with cases for containing plants.'

Nevertheless, glazed buildings that had been erected regardless of expense were significant in marking the start of a tradition in horticultural architecture distinct from the domestic pattern: 'The grand cause of the improvements which have been made in hot-houses may be traced to their being no longer, as formerly, under the control of mansion architects. To civil architecture, as far as respects mechanical and chemical principles, or the laws of the strength and durability of materials, they are certainly subject, in common with every description of edifice; but in respect to the principles of design or beauty, the foundation of which we consider, in works of utility at least, to be "fitness for the end in view", they are no more subject to the rules of civil architcture than is a ship or a fortress.' (Loudon, *An Encyclopaedia of Gardening*). Much of the credit for 'breaking through the old system' was later given to Sir Joseph Paxton, and his part in broadening the appeal of gardening under glass was certainly crucial.

Paxton was described by Samuel Smiles as 'a man who cultivated opportunities—a laborious, pains-taking man, whose life had been a life of labour, of diligent self-improvement, of assiduous cultivation of knowledge'. He started out as an assistant to his brother (then gardener at Battlesden Park in Bedfordshire), achieved fame with his design for the Crystal Palace and ended his career as Liberal Member of Parliament for Coventry. He was 'first employed in a responsible capacity' at Wimbledon by the Duke of Somerset. By the time he was 23, he was foreman of the Arboretum at the Horticultural Society's Chiswick gardens. He encountered the Duke of Devonshire, from whom the

Society leased the land at Chiswick, and rapidly became not only superintendent of his Chatsworth estate, but his confidant and travelling companion as well. After overseeing the construction of a range of buildings, including a glass wall, at Chatsworth in the late 1830s, he started work on the Great Conservatory, which was completed in 1840. Two years later, the Queen described it as 'stupendous', and the King of Saxony called it 'a tropical scene with a glass sky.'

Among growers of exotics, Paxton became known as the first person in Europe to coax into flower the gigantic water-lily *Victoria regia* (properly *V. amazonica*), which had been discovered early in the century by European travellers in South America, among them the Spaniard Haenk and

Above: Interior of the Great Conservatory at Chatsworth, from *The Annals of Horticulture*, 1847.

Left: The Horticultural Society's Garden at Chiswick, where 'a lofty conservatory has been erected, and planted with many curious specimen plants' (*The Annals of Horticulture*, 1847). Ten years later Donald Beaton described it in *The Cottage Gardener* as 'perhaps the ugliest and the worst-arranged house of this kind in England.' It was converted into a vinery (*see page 97*).
Above right: The water-lily *Victoria regia* in flower at Weeks's nursery, from *The Illustrated London News*, 1851.
Right: The tank at Syon House, constructed from slate slabs for *Victoria regia*. Heated pipes kept the temperature at about 85° Fahrenheit, and a flow of fresh water passed over the wheel at one end to agitate the surface. The plant, like Paxton's, came from seed distributed by Kew Gardens in 1849 and was grown as a perennial: at Chatsworth new plants were raised each year. From *The Journal of Horticulture*, 1861.

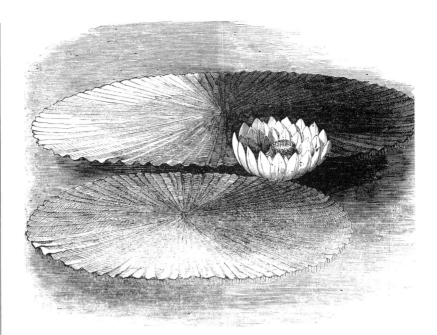

The train of circumstances by which this very plant was mainly contributary to the success of the Great Exhibition is so interesting as to merit recapitulation. We give it in Mr Paxton's own words: "Having in contemplation the erection of the great conservatory (at Chatsworth) in its present form, it was determined, in 1836, to erect a new curvilinear hothouse, 60 feet in length and 26 feet in width, with the elliptical roof on the ridge and furrow principle, to be constructed entirely of wood, for the purpose of exhibiting how roofs of this kind could be supported. The plan adopted was this – the curved rafters were composed of several boards securely nailed together on templets of wood cut to the exact curve; by this means a strength and firmness was obtained sufficient to support an enormous weight. This house was subsequently fitted up for the *Victoria Regia*; and it was here I invented a waterwheel to give motion to the water in which the plant grew; and here this singularly beautiful acquatic flowered for the first time in this country on November 9, 1849. You will observe that *nature was the engineer in this case*. If you examine this, and compare it with the drawings and models, you will perceive that nature has provided it with longitudinal and transverse girders and supporters, on the same principle that I, borrowing from it, have adopted in this Building."

The Illustrated London News, 31st May 1851.

the French botanist D'Orbigny, who sent dried specimens to Paris in 1828. Details were published by Dr Pöppig in 1832, but the plant seems not to have come to British notice until 1837, when it became 'an object of unceasing interest' according to *The Illustrated London News* from the moment of its discovery by Sir Robert Schomburgk, in 1837, in one of the rivers of British Guiana. The magazine reported Paxton's presentation of a leaf and flower to the Queen and Prince Albert at Windsor. His achievement in cultivation was capped in 1851 by Messrs Weeks of the King's Road in Chelsea, who, on the 16th of May, produced a flower in an open-air tank.

Paxton claimed that his design of the Great Exhibition building, christened the Crystal Palace by *Punch*, was derived in part from the leaf-structure of *Victoria regia*. It also recalled the conservatory at Chatsworth. Over two hundred designs submitted for the building in Hyde Park had been rejected in favour of a plan drawn up by members of the Exhibition Committee, which did not impress the public.

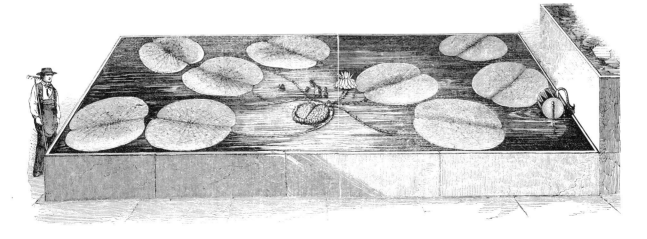

Mr Paxton, 'apprehensive that an irreparable blunder would be committed', put in his own scheme. *The Illustrated London News* described the process:

> On the morning of the 18th of June, whilst presiding at a railway committee, he sketched upon a sheet of blotting paper his idea for the great Industrial Building. He sat up all that night, until he had worked out the design to his satisfaction; and the elevations, sections, working details and specifications were completed in ten days. Next morning, Mr Paxton started from Derby by railway for the metropolis; and in the same train and carriage was Mr Robert Stephenson, the engineer—a member, moreover, of the Royal Commission, and who, at Mr Paxton's request, examined the plans.
> 'Wonderful! (exclaimed the engineer)—worthy of the magnificence of Chatsworth!—a thousand times better than anything that has been brought before us! What a pity they were not prepared earlier!'
> 'Will you lay them before the Royal Commission?'
> 'I will,' was the reply.

This was probably not a chance meeeting. Paxton was an old friend of Stephenson's father, George, who had been a keen gardener since his days as a workman in a mining village. He had outdone his neighbours in growing vegetables, and had also invented a mechanical 'fley-craw' or

We have still to refer to the chief glory of Chatsworth in a horticultural point of view – the great conservatory... The house was the precursor of the Crystal Palace. The whole is built of iron and glass, and the roof framed on the ridge-and-furrow principle, or what was called the Paxton roof, as having been first designed by him; but, unfortunately for this supposition, we saw the exact principle at Shaines Castle in Antrim, the seat of Lord O'Neill, in the roof of an old conservatory that had been erected some eighty years ago – another proof that there is but little that is new under the sun.

The Gardener, September 1867.

Joseph Paxton: an engraving in *The Illustrated London News* of 1851, based on a photograph by Kilburn.

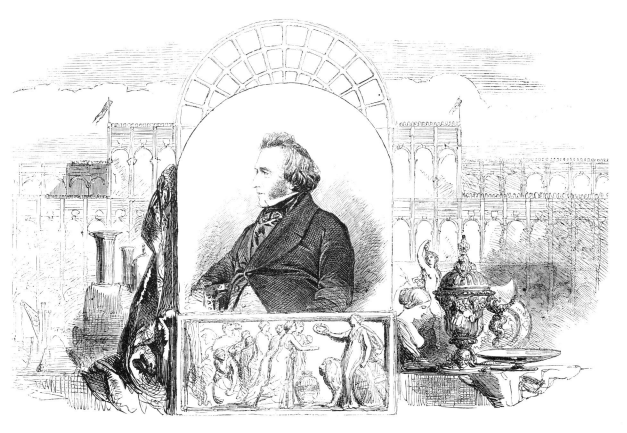

'Raising the Trusses of the Central Aisle' – this view of the Exhibition Building in *The Illustrated London News* shows part of the 'ridge and furrow' roof in place.

Like a fairy palace, there sprang up in Hyde Park the transparent walls and roof of the great building in whose grand transept the lofty trees of the park stood untouched. It would trespass too much on our space to begin telling of the triumphs of art and skill that adorned the First International Exhibition. Before the opening, the Queen paid a private visit. On her return she wrote: "We remained two hours and a half, and I came back quite beaten, and my head quite bewildered from the myriads of beautiful and wonderful things which now quite dazzle one's eyes. Such efforts have been made, and our people have shown such taste in their manufactures. All owing to this Great Exhibition, and to Albert – all to him!"

T.F. Ball, *Queen Victoria*, 1886.

bird-scarer. In retirement at Tapton, near Chesterfield, he took up horticulture again, and in 1845, 'began to build new melon-houses, pineries and vineries, of great extent; and he now seemed as eager to excel all other growers of exotic plants in his neighbourhood, as he had been to surpass the villagers of Killingworth in the production of gigantic cabbages and cauliflowers some thirty years before.' (Smiles, *Lives of the Engineers*.)

Paxton's plans were put to the Committee, though not, in fact, by Stephenson, and turned down, in spite of a personal approach by Paxton to Prince Albert. They were finally accepted only after some careful manoeuvring and a well-organised campaign in the press. Paxton designed a system of prefabrication, and the Palace was assembled and built in only six months.

The Exhibition Building was opened by Queen Victoria on May Day 1851, amid scenes of general rejoicing. Among prudent measures taken to ensure the building's safety were several experiments to test the strength of the gallery floors. Three hundred workmen assembled on a small section, stood still, walked to and fro—in and out of step—and

all jumped up and down. A party of sappers repeated the performance and 'were, finally, made to mark time in the most trying manner.' The building was pronounced sound. It was said that not a single accident occurred during the extent of the Exhibition, although 6,200,000 people visited it. After the opening, the Queen wrote: 'Albert's name is immortalised, and the wicked reports of dangers of every kind, which a set of people, viz., the *soi-disant* fashionables, the most violent Protectionists, spread, are silenced.' The whole undertaking was a triumphant success, vindicating the faith of the organisers in the face of gloomy forecasts from its opponents. These included the colourful Colonel Sibthorp, M.P. for Lincoln, an arch-Tory whose grandfather and uncle had both held the Sherardian chair of botany at Oxford, and whose deep and immovable dislike of foreigners had led him, in 1840, to introduce a successful parliamentary amendment cutting the Prince Consort's salary by twenty thousand pounds.

Prince Albert closed the Exhibition on 15th October: 'How sad and strange to think this great and bright time has passed away like a dream.' Paxton was knighted, together with Cubitt, the engineer, and Fox, the contractor. Controversy over the future of the Palace had started almost as soon as it was erected and went on after the closure of the Exhibition. A condition of the project from its inception had been that any buildings would be taken down after the event, but the popularity of what the Queen called the 'gigantic edifice' led to many appeals for its preservation. 'Will the House of Commons, in July, 1851,' asked *The Illustrated London News*, 'with Mr Paxton's beautiful Palace in existence, an object of admiration to all Europe, affirm its decision of 1850, and insist that the fairy structure shall be removed?' Paxton wanted it to stay in Hyde Park, and for a while it looked as though it would be moved to Battersea. At last, in 1853, the whole structure was transferred to Sydenham and enlarged as part of an enormous 'leisure centure'. It was a prodigious business. *The Gardeners' Chronicle* commented:

MR MECHI, in proposing the health of Sir Joseph Paxton, believed, that not only in the present time, but in days to come, the name of Paxton would be honoured. He would say, in the words of his friend Lord Braybrooke, that "there was nothing in the laws of this country to prevent the humblest individual from becoming what he (Lord Braybrooke) was – a peer of the realm" – and Sir Joseph Paxton was one of those who fully exemplified this. Let any one go to Sydenham, and see the vast structure he had erected there, a work worthy of the greatest genius, and they could not fail to admire his taste and judgment. Architects, he said, were fond of building structures of bricks and mortar, with loop-holes for windows; but this was one which was all window, and no bricks and mortar. "In fact," said Mr Mechi, "Sir Joseph has let daylight in upon us." Long may he be spared to carry out the great work he has begun.

Sir Joseph, in returning thanks, said, "I happened to come in the flood-time, and by the energies that God had given me, and by the able assistance of many eminent men, I have been enabled to carry out these great works, and to attain the position I now occupy."

Report of the 13th Anniversary Dinner of the Gardener's Royal Benevolent Institution in *The Cottage Gardener,* 1856.

80

'What it must become will be most readily understood by those who have gazed upon such pictures as Martin's Destruction of Babylon; the principal difference consisting in the architect having realised more than the painter ventured to imagine.'

Paxton's most lasting contributions to the arts and sciences of the ordinary gardener were on a more modest scale than his 'beautiful Palace'. *The Gardeners' Chronicle*, a weekly paper edited by John Lindley, which Paxton helped to establish, was probably the most influential of the horticultural journals meant for mass circulation. It claimed for itself the role of 'The *Times* of Horticulture', deliberately aiming at a wider range of interests than more conservative periodicals. The stuffy *Gardener and Practical Florist* resented being compared to a 'Garden Newspaper', saying that it was 'like comparing the *Quarterly Review* with *The Times*. The one is a repository of subjects permanently interesting, the other is a record of passing events.' The *Chronicle* appealed to an increasingly affluent middle class, supplementing the horticultural material with general articles and book reviews, and carrying advertisements for patent medicines, household appliances and the works of Dickens, as well as every requirement of the garden. Sir Joseph Paxton's talent for invention, combined with his good business sense, led him also to introduce modular construction in small-scale glasshouse building. 'He has invented and patented a system of hothouses at once economical and, above all, portable.' (*Beeton's*

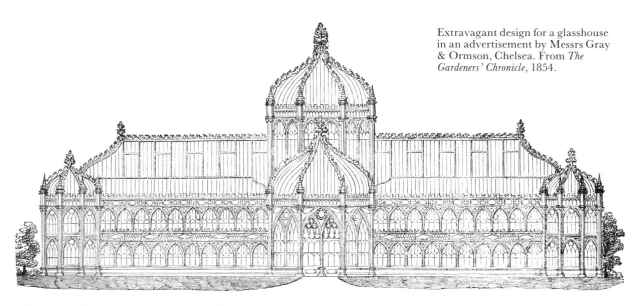

Book of Garden Management.) The system was a simple one, consisting of timber-framed sashes containing a number of glazed lights made up in standard lengths. Various combinations of sashes provided a range of houses either lean-to or span-roofed and easily constructed, with hinged ventilation panels between each pair of sashes. The cost of a span-roofed house in 1871 ranged from £24 for a building 20 feet long with 8-foot sashes, to £253 for one 105 feet long with sashes of 16 feet.

The huge success of the Crystal Palace certainly helped to stimulate greenhouse building on a domestic scale. After the Exhibition many firms were set up to design and erect glass-houses of all sizes, and a whole range of glass was on offer at prices within reach of many pockets. Public interest had been aroused, not only by the Chatsworth conservatory, but by the even larger Palm House at Kew, which was built between 1844 and 1848 from designs by Decimus Burton and Richard Turner. Burton was influenced by the house at Chatsworth, and there is a possibility that he had assisted Paxton in the earlier plan.

Improved building and glazing techniques were accompanied by developments in heating. In Loudon's day, fires and smoke-flues were still widely used and described, but fifty years later they had largely disappeared. 'We have not thought it necessary to mention any other system of heating than the ordinary one with hot-water boiler and pipes, because no one builds smoke flues now,' was the view of Benjamin Williams in *Stove and Greenhouse Flowering Plants* (1883). The flues, of bricks, tiles or earthenware sections, carried the smoke and gases from a coal furnace around the walls of the house. One drawback of this relatively inefficient method was the possible danger to both gardener and plants from leaking fumes. An improvement was the use of steam, sometimes through a series of supply pipes and condensing tubes, sometimes as a means of heating beds by passing the vapour through layers of stones and gravel. But it was the

THE VISITORS OF KEW GARDENS

In a report by Sir William Hooker on the Royal Botanic Gardens at Kew, dated December 1844, the following passage occurs: 'With the fact before me that the vast stores of the British Museum are freely opened to the public, and visited by thousands of persons in a day with impunity, or comparative impunity to the collections, I did not hesitate, on my arrival here, to have it announced that the grounds should be thrown open from one to six o'clock, with free admission to the hothouses and greenhouses, without the ceremony of conductors; and the public have taken ample advantage of this privilege, and prize it highly; the number of visitors is annually increasing, till so many as 15,000 persons have frequented the garden during the past twelvemonth. The experiment was considered by many a dangerous one; but it has been pursued now for nearly four years, and, thanks to the diligence and attention of those employed in the garden, *with little or no damage to the plants*, nothing worth recording; and this being the case it becomes easy to show the benefit accruing to the establishment itself, and to the public, by such an act of liberality.

Chambers' Edinburgh Journal, 16th August, 1845.

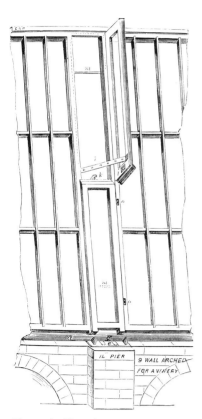

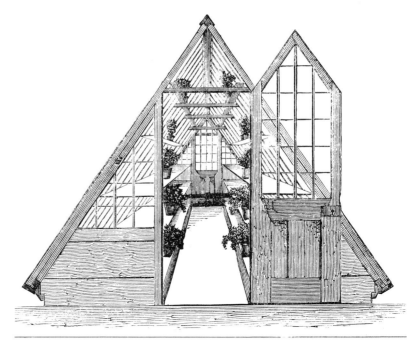

Above right: Plant-house built on the 'Paxtonian' system, from Shirley Hibberd's *The Amateur's Greenhouse and Conservatory*, 1873.

Above: Part of the roof of a Paxton house, showing the ventilation section between the sashes. From the 1881 edition of Robert Thompson's *The Gardener's Assistant.*

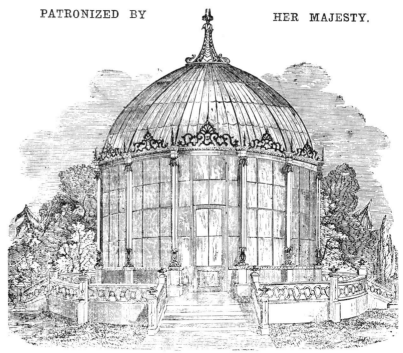

Advertisement from *The Gardeners' Chronicle,* 1856.

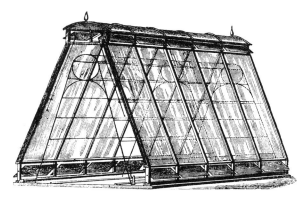

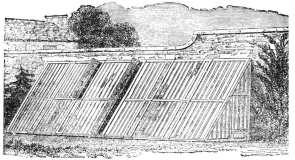

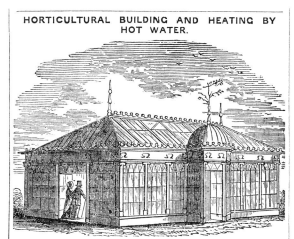

hot-water method which first provided controlled heat in a reasonably reliable manner. 'Fire-flues and steam have hitherto been employed in common with all other kinds of similar erections, but since the introduction of the hot-water system, there are but few who will not avail themselves of it.' (McIntosh, *The Practical Gardener*, 1830.)

Loudon believed that heating by water-pipes was first applied in Britain to a hot-house at Sundridge Park, Kent, by Count Chabannes in 1816, though he conceded that William Atkinson and others were working along similar lines at about the same time. Water-pipes for domestic heating had then been in use for several years and were notably installed by Boulton & Watt. Within a few years, engineers and manufacturers produced equipment capable of heating a whole range of glasshouses and conservatories, devising ingenious ways of circulating the hot water above and below the level of the boiler. A.M. Perkins introduced a sealed system which was installed in Mr and Mrs Loudon's own small greenhouses in Bayswater and received favourable comment in *An Encyclopaedia of Gardening*: 'The advantage in point of neatness, is very great, from the smallness of the pipes; and there is also little or no smell from the inattention or misconception of attendants, as nothing is required to be done but supplying fuel.'

John Loudon himself had suggested, in *The Gardener's Magazine*, a visionary scheme for extracting heat from the earth's crust by tapping sources of subterranean hot water: 'It seems not unreasonable to suppose that, if a bore or artesian well is carried so deep as to penetrate into a stratum of water at a sufficient temperature to expand itself into

Above left: A moveable greenhouse invented by Mr Spencer, gardener to the Marquess of Lansdowne, at Bowood. *The Cottage Gardener* (1856) commented: 'Such a structure is often desirable for a tenant who has an unreasonable landlord.'
Left: Lean-to Paxtonian fruit-house, from *Beeton's Book of Garden management.*
Above: Advertisement from *The Gardeners' Chronicle*, 1853.

Below: Sketch from *The Gardener's Magazine*, 1828, illustrating a scheme to store warm water in underground cisterns. The water was to be heated by the sun's rays, acting on the hollow ball.

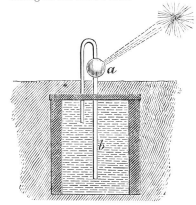

Mr Gauen's invention for ripening fruit. The rays of the sun, focused by the lenses (a) 'which may be self-adjusted by watch-machinery', heat the air in the cast-iron ball (b). The hot air was then supposed to be piped over the tree as required. *The Gardener's Magazine,* 1828.

steam, there will be no difficulty in the water ascending to the surface. If ever so complete a command of water should be obtained by man, in every part of the world, except, of course, the frozen zone, the climate and culture of the whole would be altered: and who can tell what may be the ultimate result of the operation of man, in one way or another, chemically, electrically, and mechanically, upon the globe?' His predictions went further: 'The next step would be to call down fire from the clouds, in the form of electricity, so as to facilitate the operation of cooking, and the driving of machinery.' Predictably, *The Gardener and Practical Florist* treated these futuristic ideas with ponderous irony: 'The consternation which this last discovery of Loudon's has created can scarcely be imagined. The tea-kettle makers, seeing that their "occupation's gone", meditate some violence towards our ingenious friend, and the police on the Bayswater station has been doubled for the good old gentleman's protection... Scarcely any living being but Loudon would have thought of penetrating into the earth deep enough to find boiling water, and none but he would have conceived the idea of bringing it up to the surface of the ground in its boiling state... Mr Loudon's name has always stood high, and it is to be deplored the influence of an author should be applied to the promulgation of absurdities which shake people's confidence in his better writings.' (February 1843.) Futurology seems to have been a family characteristic—in her book *The Mummy*, 'a tale of the twenty-second century', published in 1827 before her marriage, Jane Loudon wrote of such modern improvements as electrical rain-making machines, world-wide communications by telegraph, universal air travel (by balloon) and inflatable beds. Loudon and *The Gardener and Practical Florist* were not on good terms. A few months before Loudon's death in December 1843, a proposal in the second volume to raise a testimonial fund to purchase some mark of respect for Mr Loudon's 'long and useful services' was followed by a report of his absolute refusal to have anything to do with it.

For houses where a humid atmosphere was wanted, a modified heating system incorporating open tanks of water was introduced. A writer in *The Journal of Horticulture* (1871) noted that 'it was suggested some time ago—I believe first by Mr Rendle—that bottom heat from a tank of heated water was the nearest approach to the genial warmth of fermenting leaves or dung; for whilst it afforded the necessary warmth it was accompanied by vapour, as in the case of fermenting materials, which is essential to plant-growth.' In 1843, *The Gardener and Practical Florist* had reported on 'A paper read from Mr W.E. Rendle, of the Union Road Nursery, Plymouth' setting out the plan. The tank was covered by slate slabs as a secure base for beds of soil. The scheme was never wholly a success, particularly in early forms where the water in the tanks formed part of the circulating flow from the boiler. It was difficult, too, to build tanks that stayed watertight. Most of all, the humidity was excessive, as a nurseryman wrote in *Gardening Illustrated*: 'The objectionable feature of this system is that in spite of the covering the moisture escapes into the house so freely as to be detrimental to nearly all plants grown... The result of our experience is that the system is useless for amateurs and small houses where a little heat is required to keep out the frost and dry the atmosphere of the house.' (30th August 1879.)

The various glazed buildings of the nineteenth century were classified according to their purpose, although the same techniques of construction and management could be applied to all of them. Greenhouses, conservatories and hot-houses were designed to be decorative; the more functional forcing houses, mainly for fruit, were the natural extensions of pits and frames. 'The green-house and conservatory,' says McIntosh, 'may be defined to be garden structures, dedicated to the exclusive cultivation of ornamental plants, and are considered as the highest grade of horticultural erections. The former is distinguished from the latter by having all the plants portable, and generally placed on stages; whereas, in the latter, the major part are planted out permanently in beds or borders prepared for them.'

The greenhouse proper was an adjunct to the flower garden, and was sometimes a central feature of the pleasure ground. In the winter it was only slightly warmed—a temperature between 40° and 55° Fahrenheit is recommended in *The Gardener's Assistant*. It might accommodate a variety of subjects, according to the taste of the owner: 'It is very generally the case, that the green-house is made to contain a perfectly miscellaneous assemblage of plants. All plants, whatever their nature may be, which require a temperate climate, are congregated together in a structure known by this name.' (*The Annals of Horticulture*, 1847.) Serious gardeners preferred to have specialised houses for several groups of flowers and shrubs, typically a Camellia House, which would also have space for citrus trees, magnolias and rhododendrons; a cool Heath House, principally for the winter-flowering ericas (several hundred species had been introduced from southern Africa at the end of the eighteenth century); an Australian House, with plants native to 'New Holland', such

We have very recently seen an extraordinary fact stated, which deserves peculiar notice here. It is averred that in Russia, particularly in the vicinity of St Petersburg, it is now common to see green-houses heated on an entirely new plan which promises to become general. It consists simply in substituting the breath of cattle for the old method of heating by fuel or steam; and its superiority was evident from the fact, that in a climate where they have often twenty-four degrees of frost, vegetables were raised far superior to any thing produced in this country. So far as the plan can be described, without a plate, the byre, containing the cattle, is built in the form of a double house, with a partition wall, through which are a number of square holes, opposite the different cribs, leading to the green-house, and which open and shut at pleasure. These holes are placed a few inches above the cribs, and when the animals lift their heads for the purpose of breathing, the warm air immediately finds its way under the glass frames on the opposite side. The byre is, of course, kept very close, and for this purpose is provided with double doors... Independently of the saving in fuel and men's time, the breath of the cattle serves for both heat and moisture, and completely supersedes the necessity of watering.

A New System of Practical Domestic Economy, 1825.

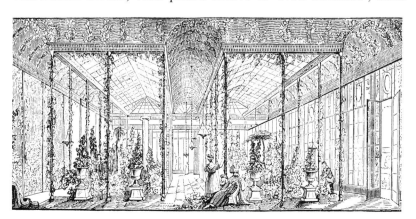

Interior of the conservatory built for Alexander Baring at The Grange, Hampshire, in 1824. The house itself, 'one of the best works of Inigo Jones', had been remodelled in the form of a Doric temple; the conservatory, a 'spacious area of perpetual spring', was a cast-iron-framed structure put up by Messrs. Jones and Clark to designs by C.R. Cockerell. From *The Gardener's Magazine*, 1827.

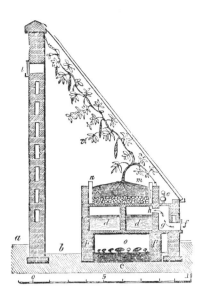

Above: Lean-to cucumber house with tank heating, from Shirley Hibberd's *Profitable Gardening*, c.1860. The water in the slate tanks (d) circulates by way of the flow and return pipes (e), which also warm the air above. Fresh air enters through the ventilator (f).
Below: Iron-framed conservatory built by Handyside & Co. for Henry Bessemer Esq. From Shirley Hibberd's *The Amateur's Greenhouse and Conservatory*, 1873.

as the banksias and callistemons, together with the protea-ceae from the Cape; a Geranium House to raise, according to the *Annals*, pelargoniums, calceolarias, cinerarias, fuchsias and tropaeolums, and a Miscellaneous House, with green-house bulbs, climbers and succulents.

The conservatory, though occasionally free-standing, was most often attached to the owner's living quarters: 'Among the various appendages which it is desirable that a house should possess, few are more important than the conservatory, which, when appropriately placed, may be regarded as an extension of the drawing-room.' (*The Diction-ary of Daily Wants*, 1857.) As part of the house, the structure was often more elaborate than an ordinary greenhouse, sometimes extravagantly so. The interior was carefully arranged so that 'disagreeable elements' such as heating pipes were concealed beneath iron or brass gratings in the floor. The plants themselves were mainly chosen for a showy effect—climbers were especially popular. Mrs Lou-don describes a scheme from the 1840s in *The Lady's Country Companion*: 'There is usually a walk all round the conserv-atory, next to the glass, and one down the middle, on each side of which are the beds containing the plants, and under which are placed the hot-water pipes that warm the house. The consequence of this arrangement is, that the beds on each side of the middle walk are so planted with tall camellias, acacias, metrosideros [callistemons], eucalyptus, &c.; while near the walk are placed oleanders, myrtles, fuchsias of different kinds, together with chorozemas, and many of

the other most ornamental New Holland plants; and up the pillars that support the roof are trained kennedyas, bignonias, ipomoeas, and passion-flowers in great variety. Clianthus puniceus and polygala oppositifolia ought to find a place in every conservatory; and a plant of Wistaria sinensis may be trained under the rafters so as to afford shade to the camellias; as, under shelter, the wistaria will flower twice in the year, and its flowers will yield a delightful, though very delicate, fragrance.'

Eventually the conservatory became a Victorian cliché—a necessary attachment to any house of even modest pretensions and, often, no more than a place where pot plants could be brought in 'so that the Conservatory may be as gay as possible during the dull months, at which time this part of the garden is the most enjoyable to the ladies of the family.' (Williams, *Stove and Greenhouse Flowering Plants.*) After the mid-nineteenth century, the excitement of building in glass and iron wore off, and some designers began to look for ways to conceal, rather than to flaunt, the form of the building. 'There are many modes,' says an authority quoted in *Beeton's Book of Garden Management*, 'by which the conservatory might be rendered both picturesque and interesting, apart from the actual brilliancy of the flowers. The principal feature being to relieve the spectator, as far as possible, of the idea that he is walking under glass, I propose to do this by making the frame-work for receiving the glass of some irregular form, resembling the branches of trees or ribs of large leaves, such as the palm. This would greatly tend to encourage the illusion that the openings between

Exterior and interior (*below*) of a rustic conservatory put up by Shirley Hibberd's neighbour in Stoke Newington: 'A structure combining plant-house and smoking-room, the whole of which is encased in a rockery.' From Shirley Hibberd's *The Amateur's Greenhouse and Conservatory.*

the branches are not glazed.' The plan includes a naturalistic layout of low-growing plants in the centre of the house, with 'some of the finest Ipomoeas and Passiflora trailing round the slight pillars, and forming a matted roof overhead, at once to give shade and conceal the artificial nature of the edifice.'

If greenhouses and conservatories displayed the greatest achievements of architects and builders, the art of the plantsman and the gardener reached its height in the hothouse, which was still throughout the century known as the stove, from its original meaning of a closed, heated room, rather than the later usage, which limited it to the heating apparatus. According to McIntosh in 1830, stoves 'are much less numerous in the British gardens than other plant structures, and consequently the management of them is

Hothouse interior from James Anderson's *The New Practical Gardener*, 1880.

The Horticulturist, when he steps into this department, aspires to the top and mastership of his art. A full acquaintance with what his predecessors knew, as principle – a vigilant attention to what his contemporaries offer as improvements, with a capacity to estimate new practices – a considerable personal share of intelligence, experience, and invention – will not more than qualify him for his profession.

Without an imitation of warmer climates, travellers alone could survey the beautiful and interesting plants with which Nature has arrayed her local gardens. When Discovery exhibits an extraordinary plant by the pencil of Descriptive Elegance, how inadequate is the picture? In the Hot-house, information is complete, and curiosity gratified.

Abercrombie's Practical Gardener, 1834.

89

A plant of the Abyssinian Banana,
Muse ensete, in the Glasgow Botanic
Garden. From *The Gardeners'*
Chronicle, 1884.

90

generally much less understood. The expense attending them is the most probable cause of their limited number, and certainly not any want of interest or splendour in the plants or their flowers.'

The 1834 edition of Abercrombie's *Every Man His Own Gardener* defines a general hot-house as 'an artificial garden for the cultivation of exotics requiring constantly a warm climate, of which the minimum heat is 60° of Fahrenheit.' All authorities agreed on this figure as the lowest that could be allowed. Most stoves were kept at between 60° and 70° Fahrenheit in the winter, when the low level of daylight in British latitudes made it unwise to encourage tropical plants into growth, while the summer temperature was raised to about 80°. Thompson recommends a maximum of 86° Fahrenheit, basing this on his calculation of 80.38° as the average in Singapore. The maintenance of constant heat was a major problem when flues and dung or tan beds were the only source, but became easier with the spread of more reliable systems. Even in houses fitted with boiler-heating, plants were still plunged in tan to give additional warmth and humidity—the 'bark-stove' was the home of most exotics, while a separate 'dry-stove' was provided for cacti and tropical succulents.

As well as such general hot-houses, enthusiasts built specialist stoves to suit their own interests. 'Aquarium Stoves' were designed to display tropical water-plants, of which Paxton's house for *V. regia* was the most celebrated example. Charles McIntosh quotes Loudon's plan to equip an aquarium with a rotating, underwater platform, driven by clockwork, to simulate the motion of running water: 'Those plants, which grow naturally in rapid streams, might be planted or placed on the circumference of the bottom, and those requiring less agitation towards its centre. If reverse motion were required to imitate tides, where marine aquatics were cultivated, nothing could be easier than by the sort of wheel used in the patent mangle to produce it to any extent.'

Orchids were another class of plants needing special arrangements, and only experienced gardeners attempted them. 'The use of two separate houses is indispensable,' says the *Annals*, one for growing and flowering specimens, the other, cooler and dryer, for dormant plants. In the second half of the century the fashion for them spread more widely, and an article by George Gordon in Shirley Hibberd's *The Floral World* of 1874 notes that 'the cultivation of orchidaceous plants is extending in the gardens of amateurs at a very rapid rate', but recommends three houses, or at least a single building divided into three compartments at different temperatures.

In addition to the expense of housing them, the cost of the plants themselves was a deterrent. Prices were said to have fallen from the point where 'only the favoured few could indulge in their cultivation,' but a report in *The Journal of Horticulture* of a collection sold at Steven's saleroom in

August 1871, lists an *Aerides veitchii* at £22 1s and a *Cattleya labiata*, admittedly 'the finest specimen in the country', at £36 15s. Nothing went for less than £5. Even though orchids were beyond the scope of most gardeners, however, they appealed strongly to a curious public, and nurserymen vied to produce the showiest and most exotic specimens. In 1884, *The Gardeners' Chronicle* described the successful importation by Messrs Sander & Co. of a 'Monster Cattleya Skinnerii', weighing about 12 hundredweight: 'The specimen was originally planted by a native many years ago in the crown of a tree belonging to the species Euphorbia, in his garden near the city of Cartago, Costa Rica.' Though he had refused all offers, the firm at last 'made him a fancy bid, which proved too much for his desire to gratify his love for his pet monster by keeping it.' The tree was cut down, and the orchid conveyed 'with infinite labour and great cost' to St Albans.

The hot-house was not only a place for gardeners to practice sophisticated skills, it was widely seen as a means of instruction and enlightenment. Attitudes to the contents varied from astonishment at the wonders of nature to plain Imperial pride. The 20th edition of Abercrombie (1813) encourages readers to 'cultivate collections of the most curious and singular exotic plants from the various different and most distant hot parts of the known world, all collected together within the small compass of the above repository:- seen immediately, as it were in one point of view, [they] must afford an entertaining variety in their different nature, habit and dimensions of the growth, and in their foliage, flowers and fruit.' In *The Practical Gardener* (1830), McIntosh mentions the 'splendid flowering, eccentric, and curious plants, and indeed those which supply us with some of our most valuable species, vegetable medicines, oils, gums, and dyes, together with food plants which are 'beneficial, not only as a lucrative reward to the spectator, but also as diffusing comfort and sustenance to a large portion of the community.' He lists 'Coffee, sugar, cocoa, sago, and chocolate...and Jesuit's-bark, cinnamon, ipecacuanha, balsam of capivi, cassia and gum-arabic'—rather an optimistic catalogue for the owner of a modest hothouse, especially as he goes on to describe the gigantic and foul-smelling parasite *Rafflesia arnoldii*, discovered in 1818 'in a jungle in Sumatra'.

The range of plants available in nineteenth-century Britain was constantly increasing as more and more specimens were sent home from abroad, and as colonial territories were opened up. Williams's *Stove and Greenhouse Flowering Plants* includes a tribute to the plant-hunters: 'To collect and send home the riches of these tropical regions is a work of much cost, and is attended with great difficulties and danger, in the prosecution of which many highly intelligent and talented travellers have fallen victims either to the pestilential climate, the wild beasts of the country, or the treachery of, in many instances, the equally wild aborigines.

'The Monster Cattleya Skinnerii' – the owner poses before cutting it down for transportation to St Albans. From *The Gardeners' Chronicle*, 1884.

To these men, who, by their arduous and self-sacrificing labours, have so largely increased our knowledge of the vegetable kingdom, all honour is due, and we cannot pass them in this place without recording our best thanks and highest praise for their services, and at the same time expressing our deep regret for their loss.'

One lamented collector was David Douglas, who travelled in North America for over a decade, and was killed by a wild bull in an animal trap in the Sandwich Islands in 1834. His loss was an embarrassment to the Horticultural Society of London. The 'awful visitation', which befell him while he was 'treading almost unknown lands in search of botanical novelties, caused for a time a lapse in the supply of new subjects, and the council were, in some measure, bound to supply the subscribers of four guineas per annum with something.' Nurserymen complained that the Society was distributing common plants and spoiling their trade, but *The Annals of Horticulture* noted in 1847 that this practice had abated.

The gardening Establishment was quick to take advantage of colonial activities. In 1843, the Horticultural Society observed that 'the occupation of Hong Kong and Chusan,

The body of David Douglas, removed from the bull-trap by two Sandwich Islanders and an Englishman, Ned, with his faithful dog guarding his bundle. He was taken to the British consul's house at Wahoo, and there buried. From *Peter Parley's Tales about Plants*, 1839.

Left: Plant-hunting territory – 'a view copied from nature in South America', from *The Journal of Horticulture*, 1872.

When he [Douglas] went back to the same country where he had been before, the Indians were quite glad to see him. "Oh!" said they, "Here is the Man of Grass come back again," – for they called him the Man of Grass because he was always searching among the tall grass for new plants.

One day the Indians saw him mixing powders to make a kind of soda water, and when they saw it bubbling up, they thought it was boiling, and called to him to stop when they saw him going to drink it; and at another time, they saw him use a burning glass to light his pipe, when they cried "Oh! oh! our Grass Man should be called the Man of Fire now; for he drinks boiling water, and brings down the sun to light his tobacco."

Peter Parley's Tales about Plants, 1839.

and the opening of new ports in the Chinese empire, appeared to present so favourable an opportunity of acquiring valuable plants, that the Council deemed it advisable to send a collector to that country, which has for so many years been the richest of all fields in a horticultural point of view.' The job went to Robert Fortune, superintendent of the Society's hot-houses, and he spent the next three years on the Chinese mainland and islands, sending back several shipments during his travels, and arriving home in 1846 with 69 cases of plants and a number of seeds. This mission was particularly successful, since, as Fortune reported: 'At the present day whatever relates to China and the Chinese has a degree of interest peculiar to itself: and this is quite as much the case with relation to gardening and horticultural matters as with matters of more general importance.' Many new plants were introduced, including twelve or fourteen varieties of tree pæony and the kumquat (Fortunella). The love of exotics was shared by many British expatriates. Fortune mentions Dr Maxwell, of the Madras army, who was stationed at Tinghae in North China: 'This gentleman, who was an ardent lover of botanical pursuits, had been most indefatigable in his researches, and was consequently able to give me a great deal of valuable information' (*The Annals of Horticulture*, 1847). His namesake, Captain Murray Maxwell, had played a part in the opening of the Chinese ports with his voyage to the Far East in the frigate *Alceste*, and in 1816 had made a horticultural gesture in the opposite direction by presenting the inhabitants of Lewchew (now Okinawa) with corn and potatoes.

The garden of the temple at Lewchew, drawn by Lieutenant Dwarris during the visit of the frigate Alceste and the brig Lyra in 1816. From the *Voyage of H.M.S. Alceste*, 1818.

Fortune returned to the East and continued his travels in China and Japan until 1861. John Scarth's *Twelve Years in China*, published in 1860, describes an encounter with the 'celebrated traveller' in Che-Kiang province. Scarth had left a cache of drink under the case of a one-eyed priest at T'heen-Tung with instructions for him to give it to the next passing westerner. Sadly, the priest lost or forgot his orders: when Fortune came across the miraculous sight of a row of beer bottles he was forbidden access and 'in the midst of plenty could not get a drop of the "Allsopp's Pale". Only Scarth's providential arrival persuaded the old man to relent: '...he handed over every bottle. This for a priest, one of a class that is the most degraded in China, was more than I expected.'

Glass-houses for fruit were a feature of many nineteenth-century gardens, and peach, fig and cherry trees, in particular, were grown under protection for earlier and more certain crops. But the two areas in this department which received the most attention were the vinery and the pinery. The grapevine had long been cultivated in Britain, with varying success, and the pineapple was introduced in the seventeenth century.

Almost all British grapes were grown for dessert use, but nineteenth-century recipes for grape wine can be found. Home winemakers used fruit of all kinds, and gooseberries were especially popular. Horticultural shows generally included classes for wines, and a report from the Caledonian Horticultural Society in the first volume of the *The Gardener's Magazine* claims that it 'has always paid particular attention to the subject of home-made wines. Thirty-seven varieties were now (1825) presented to them for examination. The qualities of the wines seem to have improved materially from year to year, not only in the Champagne, both still and mousseux, from the unripe gooseberry becoming more palatable; but various attempts at imitating the drier continental wines have succeeded beyond expectation.' Commercial wine-making was based very largely on imported raisins. The industry had been encouraged in the eighteenth century, partly as an attempt to wean the drinking classes away from gin and partly because the residue of raisins after fermentation was in great demand as a filtering medium for vinegar. Raisin wine and similar fruit products were known to the Excise as 'Sweets', and duty was levied on them. By 1851 the official attitude toward the wine industry was turning to disapproval and, apart from a few bottles of rhubarb champagne and a bottle of potato spirit, alcoholic drinks were excluded from the Exhibition. The reporter from *The Illustrated London News* was clearly on the vintners' side: 'Regardless of their value in the arts, or as an article of food or medicine, they were not allowed to exhibit, because they are sometimes turned to bad purpose...but the majority of the most eminent medical professors consider that the moderate employment of alcoholic stimuli tends rather, at any rate in large cities, to the preservation of

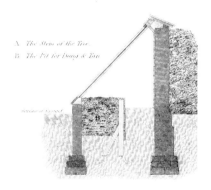

Section of a peach forcing house from the 1824 *Transactions* of the Horticultural Society. The back wall has a lining of leaves, and the interior is warmed by a pit of dung or tan.

The ripening of wall fruit may be greatly facilitated by having the wall covered, previous to the trees being trained against it, with a thick coat of black paint. Mr H. Dawes of Slough, near Windsor, tried the experiment with respect to a vine, and found that the weight of grapes gathered on the blackened part of the wall was 20 pounds 10 ounces; whilst the other part yielded only 7 pounds 1 ounce.

A New System of Practical Domestic Economy, 1825.

Pressing soaked raisins in the production of wine. From Dodd's *British Manufactures*, 1845.

The Vinery at Chiswick, illustrated in *The Journal of Horticulture*, 1871: 'Is there any gardener in the British Isles who has not heard something of Chiswick and its celebrated vinery?' Originally the Horticultural Society's conservatory (*see* page 74), it was converted to a vine house in 1857. Eventually it contained 83 vines of 26 varieties, which were tended from 'an elegant light wrought-iron ladder on wheels'.

How to eat Grapes. – Dr. Underhill has reduced eating grapes to a science. Here are his directions: When in health, swallow only the pulp. When the bowels are costive and you wish to relax them, swallow the seeds with the pulp, ejecting the skin. When you wish to check a too relaxing state of the bowels, swallow the pulp with the skin, ejecting the seeds. Thus may the grape be used as a medicine, while at the same time it serves as a luxury unsurpassed by any other cultivated fruit. An adult may eat from three to four pounds a day with benefit. It is well to take them with or immediately after meals.

The Gardener's Weekly Magazine, 1860.

Below: 'Bottled grapes' – the system used for keeping bunches through the winter. In the 1870s, the fruit-room at Heaton Grange, Bolton, was equipped with about 300 bottles in racks, filled with rainwater and charcoal. Some of the grapes lasted until the middle of May, when the first of the new season were cut.

life...we are informed by assurance office examiners, that the majority of those who confine their drink to water alone are pale, flabby, and do not exhibit the full standard of strength and health.'

The use of artificial heat in vine houses began in 1718, according to Loudon, and a century later he wrote, 'The art of forcing has made such rapid progress that no kitchen-garden worth notice is now without a vinery: the fruit is produced in some vineries during every month of the year; and in the London market is to be had in the highest degree of perfection from March to January.' He did not consider the actual form of the building of great importance: 'The vinery offers the greatest latitude of construction; for the fruit tree the most easily cultivated of all that are grown under glass is the vine.' Sometimes the house had to be en-larged as the contents grew—as with the Hampton Court vine and another Royal specimen at Cumberland Lodge, two of the 'Celebrated Vines' quoted in William Thomson's *Cultivation of the Grape Vine* of 1862. Many famous examples were, like these, Black Hamburghs, but numerous varieties

were cultivated, some of them suitable for planting outdoors as well as under glass. Loudon's list has fifty names,
while Thomson describes the varieties as endless.

Disputes over cultivation mostly concerned pruning systems. Some growers preferred the 'extension' method of
allowing a single stem to produce as many fruiting branches
as possible, others supported 'restriction', with many individual vines, each close-pruned. On this question Thomson
concludes, as he began, 'by saying that there is much truth
on both sides of this question.' There were differences, too,
over ways of supplying nourishment to the roots. A reader
wrote to *The Gardeners' Chronicle* in 1856 to ask: 'Noticing in
your last week's Number that you are averse to using blood
in Vine borders, will you do me the favour to inform me
what you consider the best suited to the purpose? The border at present consists of pasture loam and dung, with a

'A Wonderful Vine', a Black
Hamburgh at Manresa House,
Roehampton, illustrated in *Garden-
Work*, August 1888. Mr. Davis,
shown by the stem, had raised it
from a cutting taken in 1862. The
seven branching stems extended
over a total length of 1,400 feet. In
1886, 807 bunches were cut, and
were sold in the market for £107.

Right: Cats in the
greenhouse – Shirley Hibberd's
view of the drawbacks in *The
Amateur's Greenhouse and Conservatory*,
1873.

98

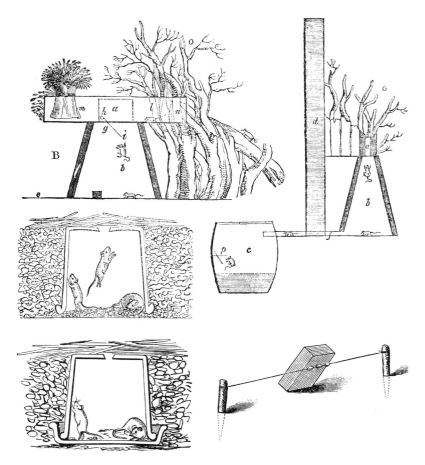

Right and far right: Rat-trap 'invented by the late Mr Robert Paul', shown from two angles in *The Gardener's Magazine*, 1830. The rat, passing along the trough to get at the wheatsheaf, falls through the trapdoor into 'Forlorn Hope' (b); from there it escapes through a pipe into the 'Slough of Despond' (c), a sunken barrel half full of water, where it drowns.
Below right: Suggestions for mouse-traps from the horticultural papers – the Hidden Flowerpot and the Suspended Brick. In the second type the mouse eats through the string, which is baited with peas, and 'down falls the brick and crushes the intruder.'

VINE BORDERS V. CARRION. – Carrion is very seriously recommended by one writer on the cultivation of the Vine, while others, with reason I apprehend, think differently. I have seen a dead dog buried in a Vine border, and I have seen upon examination after the carrion was decomposed that all the roots near it were dead – could any other result have been expected?

Letter in *The Gardeners' Chronicle*, 8th November 1856.

small quantity of bones, but having been recommended to use flesh as an addition, your advice will much assist me.'

Vineries, like all heated houses, suffered from pests. Usually mites and insects were the problem, but 'J.C.J.B.' complains in *The Journal of Horticulture* of 1872: 'My vinery has suffered from rats; they have made their way into the border, and at night they carry off and eat the Grapes; they have also been doing damage to plants.' Two weeks later W. Graves, of Tonbridge, sent the magazine a design for a rat-trap using a spring-loaded pointed stick: 'When the rat is caught he pulls the stick out of the hook and is immediately suspended in the air and out of the way of the next comer, which passes on to the next trap, and is very soon suspended likewise.' Another solution proposed by 'C.P.' of Goldthorn Hill was that 'A cat may be secured to a wire, so that she can go the whole length of the house, whilst her kittens may be left free.'

The pineapple was a curiosity when first introduced into Britain and remained a status symbol for much of the nineteenth century. Until imported pineapples began to arrive in quantity, mainly from the Azores, a ripe fruit on the dinner table represented just about the highest achievement of the gardener's skill. In a series of articles on pine culture in *The Journal of Horticulture* in 1872 a contributor regretted that it was receiving less attention than it had thirty years earlier:

Plate XVII.

Pineapple plant or 'ananas' from Richard Bradley's *A General Treatise of Agriculture*, 1757.

'The Pine Apple, however, holds the same position now as then in the scale of importance, being still regarded as the king of fruits. One reason, doubtless, why its cultivation should have made less progress is the fact that large quantities of fruit from tropical countries arrive here at a time when home-grown fruit of other kinds is also plentiful: hence both the market and the appetite are glutted, and the once-aristocratic Pine Apple figures on the costermonger's barrow, and is retailed at the lowest figure imaginable... Although a noble Pine is an ornament to any table, it becomes rather commonplace when it is seen too often, and I have heard of one going the round of a series of west-end dinner parties for some weeks.'

Successful pine-growing called for constant care, particularly in keeping up a high temperature. To begin with, pits were heated by beds of tan, but already when Bradley wrote of the 'ananas' in his *Treatise of Agriculture* (1726), hothouses were being put up for the purpose: 'We have instances of their being brought to extraordinary perfection. There are several stoves now built by curious gentlemen on this account.' They were then fitted with flues, but as soon as the hot-water method became available it was enthusi-

SENTRY CATS. – Robert Brook, Esq., of Melton Lodge, near Woodbridge, has four or five cats, each with a collar, and light chain and swivel, about a yard long, with a large iron ring at the end. As soon as the gooseberries, currants, and raspberries, begin to ripen, a small stake is driven into the ground or bed, near the trees to be protected, leaving about a yard and a half of the stake above ground; the ring is slipped over the head of the stake, and the cat, thus tethered in sight of the trees, no birds will approach them. Cherry trees and wall-fruit trees are protected in the same manner as they successively ripen. Each cat, by way of a shed, has one of the largest sized flower-pots laid on its side, within the reach of its chain, with a little hay or straw in bad weather, and her food and water placed near her. In confirmation of the above statement it may be added, that a wall of vines, between two hundred and three hundred yards long, in the nursery of Mr Kirke, of Brompton, the fruit of which in all previous seasons, has been very much injured by birds, was, in 1831, completely protected in consequence of a cat having voluntarily placed himself sentry upon it.

The Gardener and Practical Florist, 1843.

CATS. – If you are plagued with these animals they will destroy your garden, or you must destroy them; give them fish rubbed over, or peppered, as it were, with arsenic.

The Gardener and Practical Florist, 1843.

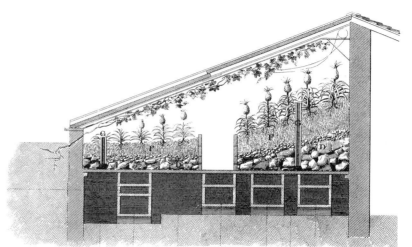

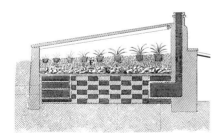

Flued pine-pit and (*right*) combined pine-house and vinery, from Abraham Rees's *Cyclopaedia* of 1820. The vines are rooted outside: this later became the usual practice. The Chiswick vinery went over from inside to outside borders in 1869.

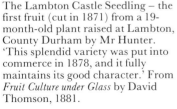

The Lambton Castle Seedling – the first fruit (cut in 1871) from a 19-month-old plant raised at Lambton, County Durham by Mr Hunter. 'This splendid variety was put into commerce in 1878, and it fully maintains its good character.' From *Fruit Culture under Glass* by David Thomson, 1881.

astically applied. McIntosh reproduces a plan of a pine-house designed by Atkinson, one of the pioneers of the method, which was 'found to give the greatest satisfaction, and may be considered the perfection of the principle; the temperature here has been sufficient, under every circumstance, to prove, that the hot-water system, as recommended by that gentleman, is amply sufficient to bring to perfection "the king of fruits".'

Beds of tan or leaves were nearly always included as well as water pipes, and the plants were buried there in twelve-inch pots for bottom-warmth and humidity. Thomas Knight favoured the dry-stove for pines, with the pots on staging, but few people agreed with him. The actual structures used varied from small pits to full-sized hothouses. Affluent growers kept several houses to accommodate different varieties, or plants at different stages of growth. The three houses at Sandringham were each 100 feet long. The disadvantage of a pit was that nothing could be done to the contents without opening it to the weather, while a house could be fitted with double doors. In both, there was a danger that water would condense on the glass and drip on the plants. (For an account of the only pine-stove still in operation after World War I, *see* Horace Parsons 'Growing Tropical Fruits' in *The Garden*, Journal of the Royal Horticultural Society, August 1981.)

Robert Thompson comments that, of the more than sixty varieties of pineapple, 'many are worthless, and others present such slight shades of difference as scarcely to warrant their being considered as distinct sorts.' He lists nineteen useful types, while in *The Illustrated Dictionary of Gardening* (Nicholson), at the end of the century, the number has been pared down to eight. The Queen and its sub-varieties, such as Ripley's Queen, were probably grown more widely than others—the 'tankard-shaped' fruit was reckoned to be 'juicy and sweet', and the plants were relatively easy to manage. According to 'The Amateur's Pine-Pit' in *The Floral World* of 1874: 'Of the comparatively large number of pine-apples in cultivation, there are only two that are of real service to the

101

amateur, and these are *The Queen* and *Smooth Cayenne*.' Fruits for the table rarely weighed more than five or six pounds, but varieties grown for exhibition, like the White Providence, produced pineapples of ten, twelve or even fifteen pounds. George Stephenson announced that he was going to grow pineapples as big as pumpkins, and took first prize with his Queen fruits at a show in which he beat the Duke of Devonshire's entry grown by Paxton.

The fairly common practice of using pine-houses and vineries for other purposes, or indeed of combining them was discouraged, as it tended to spread the insect pests to which pineapples were susceptible, but some exceptions were allowed. French beans, in particular, did well in the warm conditions of a pinery in winter, and produced a valuable forced crop, At Bicton, in Devon, the pits and stoves supplied a rarer speciality in the 1870s: Mr Begbie, the gardener, who was responsible for fruiting bananas as well as sixteen varieties of pineapple, mentioned in *The Journal of Horticulture* that 'The desserts have to be supplied with home-grown Ginger during the year. Begbie harvested 28 pounds for preserving from plants in ten-inch pots, plunged in beds of oak leaves. The only extra care needed was an occasional dose of liquid manure—'that from deer dung is proper.'

GINGER, PRESERVED. – For two weeks put the ginger every night and morning into fresh boiling water. Take off the outside skin with a sharp knife; boil the ginger in water till it is quite tender; slice it thin, prepare a syrup of one pound of sugar to half a pint of water; clarify it, and then put the ginger into it. Boil it until it is clear; leave it to cool, and set by in jars.

The Dictionary of Daily Wants, 1858.

Right: The Kibble Conservatory in the Glasgow Botanic Garden, engraved for *The Gardeners' Chronicle* in 1884, soon after it was taken over by Glasgow Corporation as a winter garden.
Below: Interior of the Kibble Conservatory.

A WINTER GARDEN

Fat children, and food-stuffs, and holly,
The tributes of Art to his sway,
And the struggle all round to be jolly,
Have vanished with Christmas away.

But, true to the season, the weather
Has banded again with the Parks,
To start on the war-path together
For a glacial epoch of larks.

When pale snows on ice-levels glinter,
What cheer for the sun-loving souls
Who seek to escape from the winter
Unaided by skating or coals?

Though frost the broad gravel-path hardens,
The glasses are beaded with dew;
Though it's desolate out in the gardens,
There's life in the greenhouse at Kew.

Good-bye to the reign of December,
To boughs that are leafless and wet;
From the fires of the summer an ember
Keeps warm the chrysanthemums yet.

Narcissus and tulip and lily
The siege of the season abide,
While the fog-demons chubby and chilly
Throng thriftless and baffled outside.

They stand the dull atmosphere scorning,
Like beautiful captives arow,
As white as the mists of the morning,
Or flushing like sunset on snow—

The dress of a fairy of fashion,
Whose skirt a wet rainbow has swept;
The cheek of a pearl in a passion
Whom a moonbeam has kissed while she slept.

Fast-frozen the grey grass beseeches
A token of hope for the lawn
From the high-tow'ring poplars and beeches,
The wind-whisper'd watchtow'rs of dawn.

But we turn from the climate of Sweden
To breathe the perennial balm,
Where aisles like the alleys of Eden
Are arched by the fronds of the palm.

And silvered, unvex'd by the raw gust,
Benignant, and happy and hot,
Is lull'd by that music of August,
The clank of the watering-pot.

Where gardeners, passive and pensive,
Their leisurely labours pursue,
And tropical trunks, comprehensive,
In charity hide them from view.

Though man, more and more, with his crass works
Profanes this sweet Goshen of trees,
Though Brentford, with whistles and gasworks,
Claims more than its share of the breeze,

So much of the fugitive Summer
Is caught in the crystalline cage,
That the thought of sweet Spring, the newcomer,
Makes mirth of Jack Frost and his rage.

The River, again, in the twilight
Gleams silvery grey like a dove,
And birds twitter clear in the shy light
That dawns upon April and love.

'Ode to Kew' in *Punch*, 19th January 1887.

John Lindley, from an article in *The Cottage Gardener* for
29th January 1856. The son of a nurseryman, he was
associated with the Horticultural Society from an early
age, becoming Assistant Secretary in 1826. He kept his
position through a period of mismanagement of the
Society's affairs which attracted angry criticism from
John Loudon and others and led to the resignation of
the Secretary in 1830. Lindley earned respect as a
botanist, but was not universally liked as an
administrator: despite his fairly humble origins, he was
an autocratic figure with a brusque, patrician manner.
The Cottage Gardener, while wishing him many years of
botanical success, hoped 'as fervently that he may not
continue in the Secretariat of the Horticultural Society.'
The magazine felt that he was out of touch with garden-
owners and gardeners: 'No Society in England is
evergreen that is not planted and cultivated by the
middle classes, and Dr. Lindley neither in temperament
nor in habits is calculated to win them to a Society's
subscription list. Much less is he so gifted as to win
golden opinions from the men of the spade.' He stayed
with the Society until 1862, and died in 1865 after
suffering from 'gradual softening of the brain'.

Science in the Garden

'I do believe if botany could be divested of its humbug, many would be glad to study it,' commented a contributor to *The Gardener and Practical Florist* who shared the fairly exasperated attitude of many ordinary growers towards botanical controversies. Most gardeners, breeders and nurserymen preferred to ignore the uncertainties of theory, and rely on traditional empirical methods.

Sales of *The Theory of Horticulture* were disappointingly low when it first appeared in 1840, but the author, John Lindley, a 'most indefatigable' man, brought out a new edition under the title *The Theory and Practice of Horticulture* and turned it into a success. Lindley, who became Professor of Botany at London University in 1829, was the 'eminent botanist' credited on the title-page of *An Encyclopaedia of Plants* by Loudon, and assisted Joseph Paxton both in compiling his *Botanical Dictionary* and in founding *The Gardeners' Chronicle*. According to the bibliographer, William Carew Hazlitt, 'there was no section of botany and horticulture which he did not treat with ability and public advantage.' However, his attempts to overcome readers' aversion to theory were not altogether successful, as a long discussion in the very conservative *Gardener and Practical Florist* in 1843 makes clear.

Lindley's views reflected ideas expressed by many of his British contemporaries, including Thomas Knight, and several botanical theorists in Europe, but he was attacked by reviewers in terms very much like the later criticism of Charles Darwin. The suggestion that flowers, and therefore fruit, were formed by modified leaf-processes was described as 'a stretch of presumptuous folly which we hope and trust is not usual in other sciences.'

Descriptions of plant development soon afterwards accepted as self-evident were regarded not only as 'unmitigated nonsense', 'intolerable twaddle' and 'brainless gabble', but also as 'mountebank doctrines' and 'systems established in opposition to the Scriptures themselves.' 'We are heartily ashamed that such trash should be read by decent people' wrote the author of an article, 'Botanical Fallacies'. 'For the present we assert, without fear of contradiction, that if Botany and Horticulture cannot be taught without founding the theory upon the dangerous notions, that the Creator made flowers and fruit less perfect than other parts of His great work, and that he made parts of the flowers useless, the less they are taught the better.'

Arguments among botanists about the structure of plants were of little importance to the average gardener. As *The Gardener and Practical Florist* observed: 'It has to be premised that the practice of gardening was not founded on theory; it has grown up, as it were, of itself; nature had been the teacher, and each race of gardeners learned something from their own experiments in addition to what they were taught by their predecessors, until thousands who were ignorant of the causes nevertheless produced the best effects, nay, there were gardeners—masters of the profession, who could do all that appertained to their business, in any branch, yet could not read.' One of the founding aims of *The Gardeners' Chronicle* in 1841 was to improve gardeners' education, and Lindley abhorred the gulf between the art of horticulture, 'whatever concerns the mere manner of executing the operations' and the science, which 'explains the reasons upon which practice is founded.' He saw that explanation and instruction had a practical value: 'In the majority of works upon horticultural subjects, the numerous directions given in any particular ramification into which the art is susceptible of being divided, are held together by no bond of union... Horticulture is by these means rendered a very complicated subject, so that none but practised gardeners can hope to pursue it successfully; and, like all empirical things, it is degraded into a code of peremptory precepts.'

At the beginning of the nineteenth century the mechanisms of plant nutrition, if thought about at all, were almost entirely misunderstood. Lindley confessed in 1840 that 'the application of soil and manures to plants must remain at present exclusively within the dominion of art,' but by 1900 the chemistry and biology of soils, plants, fungi and bacteria, and the relationships between them, were thoroughly established.

Experiments in plant chemistry began soon after the discovery of oxygen in 1774 by Priestley (who called it 'dephlogisticated air') and independently two years later by Scheele ('empyreal air'). Scheele, described by Samuel Smiles in *Self-Help* (1859) as working obscurely in a remote Swedish village with a few apothecaries' phials and pigs' bladders, proved that oxygen was necessary for the germination of seeds. Priestley found that plants absorb carbon dioxide from the atmosphere and release oxygen, and his work was developed by de Saussure, as well as by Sir Humphry Davy in his work at the Royal Institution and his lectures to the Board of Agriculture from 1802 to 1813. Another of the early chemists, Dr Ingenhousz, started a long-running hare

Ingenhousz, who published a series of experiments on this subject in 1779, observed, that the *flowers* of plants universally render the air highly noxious, equally by night as by day. A few flowers of the honeysuckle exposed even to the light of the sun in the middle of the day, rendered a body of air equal to two pints very noxious in three hours. "These flowers," he says, "like all others, after having thus rendered fatal a body of air equal to two pints, have lost nothing of their fragrance. The air itself, which they have poisoned, is impregnated with the same fragrant smell as the flowers themselves; so that a person shut up in a small and close room, containing a large quantity of the most fragrant flowers, might lose his life by this most treacherous of all poisons." He also observes, "that many sudden deaths may probably be occasioned by this hitherto unsuspected cause." The same author remarks that the roots of plants detached from the ground, possess the same property, a few excepted, that fruits in general, even the most delicious, have this injurious quality (but principally in the dark) to such a degree, as to endanger the life of a person who should happen to be shut up in a close room where a great quantity of them were stored.

The Gardener and Practical Florist, 1843.

when he put forward the idea of poisonous exhalations from flowers.

Ideas of plant physiology were vague, but some workers were becoming aware of the processes by which plants adapt the substances in their environment. The years leading up to 1840 were later described as 'a very dark interval in plant physiology, chiefly owing to the influence of the assumption of a special "vital force", an assumption which was not allowed merely to serve as a hypothesis put forward to stimulate research and suggest better ideas, but which gained a hold over men's powers of reasoning to an extent which now appears monstrous and phenomenal.' (H. Marshall Ward, *Disease in Plants*, 1901.) 'Many errors crept in during this reign of terror,' Marshall Ward continued, 'One of the most fatal of which was De Candolle's revival of the idea of 'spongioles'; and another, equally disastrous in many of its effects, was the conception of a sort of vegetable food-extract, humus, existing in the soil in a form peculiarly suitable for direct use by plants.'

The belief in the 'vital force'—the mystical spark of life which was supposed to energise every part of the plant as well as the animal world, and which was not susceptible to scientific enquiry—was typical of the period. It was essential both to the thinking of the Romantic Movement and the contemporary view of Nature. Coleridge echoed ideas expressed in poetry by his friend Wordsworth when he wrote of Sir Humphry Davy, 'Every subject in Davy's mind has the principle of vitality. Living thoughts spring up like turf under his feet.'

The work of 'the immortal Liebig' was an important example in the application of rigorous scientific principle to agriculture and horticulture. Dr Justus Liebig, Professor of Chemistry at the German university of Giessen, was the author of *Organic Chemistry in its Application to Agriculture and Physiology*, a title later shortened to *Chemistry of Agriculture*. His book appeared in Britain as a report to the British Association in 1840, and was immediately seen as marking the beginning of a new era. *Chambers' Edinburgh Journal* judged it 'one of the greatest works of modern times,' and even fifty years later Dr A.B. Griffiths, in his textbook on manures, acclaimed it as 'undoubtedly the most important work on agriculture ever given to the world as the results of one man's researches and ideas.' While Liebig was later applauded for his contributions to the destruction of what Marshall Ward called 'the bugbear vitalism', he did in fact use the term, defining it in *Animal Chemistry*, the sequel to his agricultural work, as 'a certain remarkable force, the source of growth... Vitality is a consequence of the action of certain transformations; we can discover the laws which govern the transformation, but we can never learn what life—the ultimate result—actually is.' Liebig's determination to codify these laws introduced a new rationality of approach, based on his methods of analysing the chemical constituents of soils and plants.

Liebig's experiments centred on a comparison of the chemical make-up of ash from plant tissues with the composition of the atmosphere and the soil. Although many of his conclusions were affected by inaccurate techniques and a misunderstanding of the part played by nitrogen in plant nutrition, his work was crucial in replacing vague metaphysical speculation with hard scientific research. Most importantly, he taught that plants do not simply absorb food and excrete waste matter through their roots—the 'spongiole' theory—but convert inorganic substances into organic structures: 'The increase of mass in a living plant implies that certain component parts of its nourishment become component parts of the plant.'

Many of Liebig's admirers conceded that his followers in research concentrated too hard on examining the residues of dead plants and not enough on studying the living plant as a working mechanism. On the other hand, there were scientists like Boussingault, who carried out experiments on crops on his land in Alsace, weighing and analysing the materials put into the soil and the produce taken from it. He established in 1838 that carbon was taken in from the air, although it was not until 1860 that Sachs discovered the mechanism of photosynthesis by which the action of sunlight on chlorophyll powers the process. For the practical farmer and gardener, the most influential event was John Bennet Lawes's establishment, in 1843, of systematic research on his estate at Rothamsted, Hertfordshire. Helped initially by Joseph Henry Gilbert, who had worked briefly with Liebig, Lawes set up the institution which later became Rothamsted Experimental Station. Careful investigations at Rothamsted cleared up many of the confusions over soil fertility and the growth of plants. They quickly showed the essential requirement of phosphate and potash, and, above all, that plants obtain nitrogen in the form of compounds through the roots and cannot take in gas from the atmosphere. The Rothamsted experiments thus explained how crops, apparently surrounded by nitrogen in the air, could starve in exhausted land. German scientists in the 1870s demonstrated that the restoration of available nitrogen during a fallow period is effected by bacteria, whose nitrate products build up when the soil is left to rest. The specific organisms were identified in 1890. The remaining problem, of why leguminous crops, including clover, lucerne and beans, seem to be able to use free nitrogen, was eventually solved by Hellriegel and Wilfarth in 1886, when they isolated the strains of bacteria which live on the roots and convert atmospheric nitrogen into an assimilable form.

One result of these advances was a fuller understanding of soil fertility. The land had been enriched with dung from domestic animals and dressed with lime, chalk and marl for centuries, and the practical value of such treatment was well appreciated long before its effectiveness was explained. The average yield of wheat per acre was thirty bushels in the nineteenth century compared with the nine or ten bushels

Liebig was distinguished at school as 'booby', the only talent then cultivated in German schools being verbal memory. On one occasion, being sneeringly asked by the master what he proposed to become, since he was so bad a scholar, and answering that he would be a chemist, the whole school burst into a laugh of derision.

Dr Gregory on the Head and Character of Liebig, in the Phrenological Journal (from *Chambers' Edinburgh Journal* 1845)

Palingenesy, or the resurrection of plants, was known to Digby, Kircher, Schot, Gafferel, Vallemont and others. These philosophers performed the experiment of Palingenesy after the following manner: They took a plant, bruised it, burnt it, collected its ashes, and in the process of calcination extracted from it a salt. This salt they then put into a glass phial, and mixed with it some peculiar substance, which these chemists have not disclosed. When the compound was formed it was pulverulent, and possessed a bluish colour. The powder was next submitted to a gentle heat, when its particles being instantly put into motion, there then gradually arose, as from the midst of the ashes, a stem, leaves, and flowers, or, in other words, an apparition of the plants which had been submitted to combustion... The rationale of this famous experiment made on the ashes of the rose was attempted by Kircher. He supposed that even the substantial form of every known substance resided in its salt. This salt was concealed in the ashes of the rose. Heat put it in motion, the particles of salt were quickly sublimed, and being moved about in the phial like a vortex, at length arranged themselves in the same general form they had possessed from nature.

Hibbert's Philosophy of Apparitions, quoted in *The Gardener and Practical Florist,* 1843.

produced in the middle ages. Apart from horse, cow and pig manure, many other types of organic waste, such as blood, wool, hair, malt-dust and fish, were used from time to time. Yet there were plenty of authorities who denied the need for additives of any kind, believing that a fallow period would let the land re-absorb from the air all the nutrients it needed. In the eighteenth century, Jethro Tull was persuaded by his success with revolutionary hoeing methods that the simple movement up of the soil produced fertility. William Cobbett was a keen advocate of frequent digging and stirring, and ends his chapter on propagation and cultivation, 'with observing, on what I deem a vulgar error, and an error too which sometimes produces inconveniences. It is believed, and stated, that the ground grows *tired*, of the *same sort of plant*; and that, if it be, year after year, cropped with the same sort of plant, the produce will be small, and the quality inferior to what it was at first. Mr TULL has most satisfactorily *proved*, both by fact and argument, that this is not true.'

Cobbett particularly recommends 'moving the earth' between growing plants: '*Deep-hoeing* is enough in some cases; but, in others, *digging* is necessary to produce a fine crop. If anyone will have a piece of cabbages, and will dig between the rows of one half of them twice during their growth, and let the other half of the piece have nothing but a flat-hoeing, that person will find that the half which has been digged between will, when the crop is ripe, weigh nearly, if not quite, twice as much as the other half.' He suggests that the roots, 'thus cut asunder, shoot again from the plant's side, find new food, and send, instantly, fresh vigour to the plant.' He felt that stirring up the soil, especially in hot weather, caused 'fermentation and dews', and believed strongly in transplanting seedlings in hot dry conditions—an unorthodox practice but one which evidently worked for him.

In about 1850, The Revd S. Smith set out in the pamphlet *A Word in Season* the results of growing corn without manure on a plot of four acres in Northamptonshire. The 'Lois-Weedon' system, named after the village (later Weedon-Lois) where he was vicar, was based on alternate cultivation and fallowing of three-foot wide strips of land, and attracted a considerable following. 'The land is manured by the very act of digging, which enables it *to absorb from the atmosphere* the principles which maintain its fertility,' wrote Shirley Hibberd in *Profitable Gardening*. However, the real reason for the method's success was the stimulus given by cultivation to soil bacteria, whose nitrate products were then allowed to accumulate in the fallow period.

Nevertheless, throughout the century, animal manure remained the gardener's main resource. In a still unmechanised age, most country households kept animals, usually horses, for transport, and the number gradually increased in the towns until the amount of stable-dung they produced became an embarrassment. Dung-barges traded from London to the Essex marshes, and the wholesale dumping of stable refuse by unscrupulous grooms sometimes blocked the city's sewers.

Manure was applied to condition as well as to feed the soil, 'hot' horse-dung to stiff, cold land and the 'cooler' droppings of cows and pigs to sandy ground. The traditional technique was to pile dung into a heap to 'mature', but after the development of a more scientific approach in the 1840s there was an increasing emphasis on proper management. In 1852, for instance, Mr Blundell, of Bursledon near Southampton, was given a prize by the South-West Hants Agricultural Club for an experiment in which he replaced the floor of his stables with a pit of absorbent earth 'by which the greatest amount of manure could be taken up and retained'. He suggested in *The Agricultural Gazette*: 'In the case of stalls bottomed with earth, not a drop of the manure is lost, but it is so completely absorbed and deodorised that the air is quite pure, the animals are clean, and the labour of cleansing the stall is so much diminished, that I do not hesitate to offer the plan to your notice with the greatest confidence, believing that it will be found the cheapest and most effectual mode of retaining the manure, and of affording health and comfort to the horses.' Various methods were introduced for making 'box-manure' in covered containers, and it was claimed that the greater proportion of nitrates and ammonia led to massive increases in crop yield.

There was interest, too, in foreign methods, particularly those of Flemish growers, and of the Chinese, who according to Loudon 'have more practical knowledge of the use and application of manures than any other people existing.' The *Outline of Flemish Husbandry*, published in 1840, describes the careful collection and distribution of animal and human waste: 'As urine and the emptying of privies are sold wholesale and retail, there are many large tanks near the rivers and canals, where the dealers have sometimes great quantities in store... These tanks are gradually filled by boatloads brought from the large towns; and when the season comes for sowing, in spring and autumn, the farmers come with their carts and tubs, and purchase as much as they may want.' Manure was a by-product of the gin trade: 'Attached to the distilleries, where many beasts are constantly kept to consume the refuse wash, there are very large urine tanks of an oblong shape, divided by partitions into different chambers, so that the liquor may be of the proper age when it is used, which some farmers think ought to be six months.' A moderate distillery, with fifty or sixty head of cattle, supplied several hundred acres every year. However, sadly, 'There were a great many distilleries in Flanders, but the duty on spirits and interference of the government has much reduced their numbers; so that the farmers complain of the loss of this manure, and the consequent deficiency of their crops.'

The Chinese, according to French missionaries cited in an article in *The Gardener's Magazine* (which seems to have been the basis of practically every piece of writing on the

It is a wasteful system, and a dirty, slovenly practice, to throw dung out of the cow-house and stable door, and leave it there to be dried up in summer, all the fertilizing gas to evaporate, and contaminate the air you breathe; or in winter the enriching qualities to be wasted away, and destroyed by the rain, or deadened by a superabundance of cold water. It is a dirty, barbarous, beastly practice, making dung in the farm-yard, near your house; the air becomes unwholesome; the house cannot be kept clean.

The Gardener and Practical Florist, 1843.

The numerous towns and villages in Flanders afford great help in the way of manure. The thrifty housewife and her active substitute the maid, know the value of what in our households is thrown away or wasted and lost. A small tank, or a tub sunk in the ground in some corner contains all the liquid which can in any way be useful; soap-suds, washings of dishes, &c., are carefully kept in this reservoir, until, once a week, the farmer or contractor calls with his tub on a cart; and this, mixed with the contents of privies, which are frequently emptied, he keeps in large cisterns for use or sale. In Ghent we were informed that the sum paid to the servants for the liquids collected, and which is their perquisite, often amounts to as much as they receive for wages; and as consequently the wages are proportionally lower, it is in fact the master and mistresses who benefit from it.

Outline of Flemish Husbandry, 1840.

The Metropolitan Sanitary Association Dinner at Gore House, Kensington, in May 1851: 'The banquet was one in every way characteristic of the high artistic and culinary character of M. Soyer – the wines were unexceptionable, the champagne *bien frappé*, and all the accessories in excellent taste.' Toasts were proposed by, among others, Charles Dickens and George Cruikshank.

subject for the next fifty years), 'mix their night-soil with one third of its weight of fat marl, make it into cakes, and dry it by exposure to the sun... These cakes have no disagreeable smell, and form a common article of commerce of the empire.' Human excrement was also sold in France in the form of a powder (*poudrette*), and in London as cakes of 'desiccated nightsoil'. In a communication to *The Gardeners' Chronicle* in 1853 the correspondent R., 'a gentleman long resident in China', makes no mention of dried blocks, but writes that 'manure in its solid state is seldom used by the Chinese.' He describes another system of tanks and reservoirs of liquid, in which labourers distribute the fluid at sunset from buckets at the end of a pole.

Although R. rather coyly refers to 'the produce of the towns and villages...such as in Europe is considered inadmissible for agricultural purposes,' the need to dispose of sewage in London and other British cities stimulated a general movement towards sanitary reform. In some places, the material had been applied raw to pasture land since the beginning of the century, but by 1854, when Chadwick, as commissioner for the government, inspected such a system in Edinburgh, the City Council was aware that the practice was objectionable, 'occasioning the ague and typhus in men, and the rot in sheep.' Near Manchester, Mr Worsley of Platt Hall had his own works constructed with a steam engine pumping sewage on 70 acres of meadow, so diverting the stream of effluent from Chorlton which had previously flowed through his park and past his mansion.

The discovery that dung alone could not supply all a plant's needs was followed by greater use of other fertilisers. At the end of the eighteenth century, Colonel St Leger

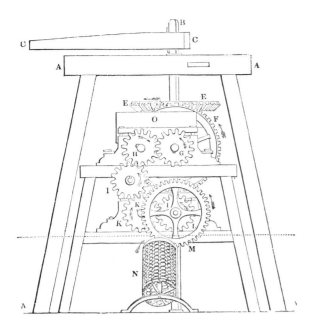
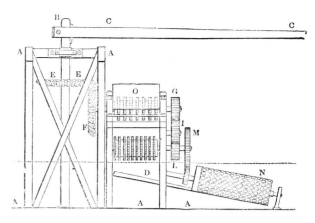

Diagrams of a bone-crushing machine in W.L. Rham's *The Dictionary of the Farm* (1850). 'When the immense quantity of bones from the cattle daily slaughtered is considered, and the readiness with which any commodity for which there is a demand is procured in commerce, there can be no great fear of a deficient supply.'

had made extensive use of ground bones on his Doncaster grassland, and in the early 1800s the grinding and pulverising of bones was a well-established process. As the value of this source of phosphate was realised, more and more bones were needed. Britain imported up to thirty thousand tons a year from Europe—much of it allegedly collected from battlefields. When the French and Belgian governments banned the export of bone, or prevented it by heavy rates of duty, vast quantities were imported from the cattle-raising countries of South America. Sometimes bones and other slaughterhouse offal, together with fish refuse, were combined with treated sewage in proprietorial mixtures, for example the 'Manchester Corporation Manure'.

In 1842, John Lawes took out a patent for the production of superphosphate by treating bones and other 'phosphoritic substances' with sulphuric acid, although he later conceded that Liebig had suggested using bone products in this way in his 1840 report. Lawes began superphosphate manufacture in 1843, using various mineral phosphates as raw material. Two years later, he started to exploit the deposits of coprolites (nodules of fossilised animal droppings from the Tertiary period) that had been found in East Anglia. By the early 1850s several hundred men were employed in the coprolite diggings, and in 1878 Cambridgeshire, Bedfordshire and Suffolk supplied 54,000 tons, valued at £150,000. Lawes found it difficult at first to sell the coprolite-derived fertiliser because of its pale colour—his customers expected something dark and rich.

British growers have always been reluctant to accept innovation—the Tamworth Farmers' Club refused to use iron ploughs presented by Sir Robert Peel because all the members agreed that they made the weeds grow—and they were slow to accept the other important mineral fertiliser

In a purely pastoral or agricultural community, it might be unnecessary to have recourse to any other fertilising substances than those which the manure of animals affords; but in a highly advanced condition of society, in consequence of the large amount of produce consumed by the inhabitants of the great towns, it becomes necessary to seek for new materials to supply the loss which the soil of the country sustains. Thus, bone-dust is procured from South America in such quantities, that it is computed, from calculation, that each head of cattle supplies bony matter equal to 84 lbs in weight; that not less than one million two hundred thousand oxen are slaughtered annually in that country for the supply of bone manure to England alone.

The Athenaeum quoted in *Chambers' Edinburgh Journal*, 4th June 1842.

Announcement in *The Agricultural Gazette*, 1854, of a testimonial fund for John Bennet Lawes. Contributions ranged from £1 to £100; Professor Lindley gave two guineas. The fund reached a total of about £1160, which Lawes used to build a new laboratory.

TESTIMONIAL
TO
J. B. LAWES, ESQ., OF ROTHAMSTED.

A number of Herts Tenant Farmers, influenced as well by their knowledge of Mr. LAWES' private worth as of his public services, met by previous arrangement, at the Town Hall, St. Albans, on December 24, 1853, for the purpose of considering the best manner of promoting and presenting him with a TESTIMONIAL in acknowledgment of those services; and since the benefits which he has conferred upon Agriculture could not be considered as merely local, it was desired, if it were found that the movement was responded to in other districts, that it should be in some degree a national one, though, from the great interest which it is known is taken by many foreign visitors in the researches at Rothamsted, Mr. LAWES' services cannot be considered as even limited to this country.

It was considered—that Mr. LAWES has for many years been engaged in a series of scientific and disinterested investigations, for the improvement of agriculture generally; which, having been carried out to an extent—with an attention to accuracy and detail—and at a cost never before undertaken by any individual, or even by any public institution. That, besides the Laboratory and other labours, from 40 to 50 acres of land are devoted exclusively to these investigations, the results of which, he, from time to time, gives freely, faithfully, and without exaggeration to the public, in the various agricultural periodicals. It was also considered, that he had, after a persevering course of practical experiments, introduced into the Turnip culture of this country, means more successful than any other known, for insuring the crop; whereby, the value of certain lands, and the produce of corn, meat, and wool, particularly in certain districts, has been much increased.

It was unanimously agreed by the Meeting, that a GENERAL ACTING COMMITTEE, from the County of Herts, should be at once formed, for the purpose of promoting such a Testimonial to Mr. LAWES as would be worthy the acceptance of a man who may thus be considered as a benefactor to his country.

It was also agreed, that prior to issuing a General Circular, and thus giving a more national character to the movement, the Herts Committee should, through their Secretary, communicate with owners and occupiers of land in various parts of the kingdom, for the purpose of ascertaining their feeling in regard to it; and also, with a view to the formation of an HONORARY COMMITTEE.

In many of the letters that have thus been received, the most gratifying testimony has been given, as to the respect in which Mr. LAWES' services are held by various classes of the agricultural interest; and, the following is a list of those Noblemen and Gentlemen interested in the improvement of agriculture, who have up to the present time given in their names as members of the Honorary Committee.

HONORARY COMMITTEE.

Ashburton, the Rt. Hon. Lord	Dering, Sir E. C., Bart., M.P.	Lake, James, Esq.	Rivers, The Right Hon. Lord
Ames, Colonel	Dering, Robert, Esq.	Langston, J. H., Esq., M.P.	Rice, E. R., Esq., M.P.
Alexander, Caledon, Esq.	Dorant, Richard, Esq.	Leicester, The Rt.Hon.the Earl of	Scott, S., Esq.
Baker, Sir E. B., Bart.	Dyke, J. Dixon, Esq.	Leigh, J. Shaw, Esq.	Sebright, Sir T. G. S., Bart.
Baldwin, W. T., Esq.	Ducie, The Rt. Hon. the Earl of	Lindley, Professor, Ph. D.,	Simpson, H. Bridgeman, Esq.
Betts, A., Esq.	Essex, The Rt. Hon. the Earl of	F.R.S. and L.S.	Sheridan, R. B., Esq., M.P.
Breadalbane, the Most Hon. the	Eley, George, Esq.	Marshall, W., Esq., M.P.	Sturt, H. C., Esq.
Marquess of	Greaves, E., Esq., M.P.	Mechi, J. J., Esq.	Smith, W. Masters, Esq., M.P.
Bosanquet, G. J., Esq.	Greville, Colonel, M.P.	Meux, Sir H., M.P.	Simpson, —, Esq.
Butt, G. M., Esq., M.P.	Hamond, Anthony, Esq.	Morton, John C., Esq.	Talbot, The Hon. W. P.
Bland, W., Esq.	Halsey, T. P., Esq., M.P.	Munn, Augustus, Esq.	Thompson, H. S., Esq.
Beckford, W., Esq.	Halsey, Rev. J. F. Moore	Newman, Sir Robert, Bart.	Tylden, Sir J. M.
Burlington, the Right Hon. the	Hanbury, R., Esq.	Newman, Thomas, Esq.	Twopenny, Edward, Esq.
Earl of	Harvey, G. H., Esq.	Oakley, Richard, Esq.	Verulam, The Right Hon. the
Cavendish, Hon. C. C., M.P.	Hilton, Captain	Payne, J. Manwaring, Esq.	Earl of
Cavendish, W. H. F., Esq.	Huxtable, Rev. A.	Pusey, Ph., Esq.	Walsingham, the Rt. Hon. Lord
Caird, James, Esq.	Hilton, Rev. H.	Puller, C. W., Esq.	Wilson, Henry, Esq.
Clutterbuck, Thomas, Esq.	Hodges, T. Law, Esq.	Patterson, Captain	Woodward, F., Esq.
Crawley, John, Esq.	Johnson, Cuthbert W., Esq.,	Prime, C., Esq.	Wilshire, William, Esq.
Chichester, the Right Hon. the	F.R.S.	Plomley, F., Esq., M.D.	Whatman, James, Esq., M.P.
Earl of	Jonas, Samuel, Esq.	Rushout, Colonel, M.P.	Walter, William, Esq.
Dacre, the Right Hon. Lord	Kelly, Sir Fitzroy, M.P.	Ryder, Hon. G. D.	Windsor, the Hon. and Very
Dickinson, John, Esq.	Knight, T., Esq.	Romney, The Rt.Hon.the Earl of	Rev. Dean of

Chairman of the General Acting Committee—Mr. F. GOUGH.　　　*Treasurer*—T. W. OVERMAN, Esq.

Honorary Secretary—Mr. WILLIAM KERL, Harpenden, St. Albans.　　　*Bankers*—London and County Bank, and its Branches.

Contributions may be paid by draft or Post-office order, on the St. Alban's Office, payable to T. W. Overman, Esq., Flamstad Bury, St. Alban's; or at any of the Branches of the London and County Bank, to the credit of the Treasurer of the Lawes' Testimonial Fund.

of the late nineteenth century, basic slag. This waste product of steel manufacture, also called Thomas Phosphate after one of the chemists who refined the Bessemer steel-making process in 1879, was initially much more popular in Germany, which imported much of the slag from the British steel mills until World War I. The Germans reciprocated by exporting to the British market large amounts of potash fertilisers, 'kainit', 'sylvinit' and 'carnallite', after mining near Stassfurt in the Harz mountains had begun in 1861.

The one 'artificial' manure which horticulturalists in Britain took to their hearts was guano. It had the glamour of distant lands and was credited with almost mystical potency. Alexander von Humboldt reported the age-old accumulations of bird-droppings on the western coast and islands of South America in 1804, although the Spanish had known about them long before. Garcilaso de la Vega wrote in 1723 of the strict controls imposed by the Incas to protect the 'astonishing great quantities of excrement', prescribing death for anyone disturbing the sea-birds which produced it. The best guano was found on analysis to have a high nitrogen content—which was attributed to the absence of rainfall to wash out the soluble salts—and a single ton was reckoned to be as effective as 33 tons of farmyard manure. British agriculturalists were familiar with similar material shipped by South African colonists from the nearby island of Ichaboe, and in an article later quoted by George Glenny, an Edinburgh agriculturalist claimed that he himself 'had mentioned the subject of guano to persons of influence; among whom were Sir Joseph Banks and the late Lord Sheffield, in 1810.' Guano attracted attention as a fertiliser after the arrival of the first bulk cargo from South America. Though it was said by some later sources to have been landed in 1839, information from George Peacock, 'formerly Marine Superintendant of the Pacific Steam Navigation Company' and commander of the *Peru*, the first steamship in those waters, suggests that the shipment was carried via Bolivia to Liverpool by the vessel *Charles Eyes* in 1841 (*The Agricultural Gazette*, 18th February 1854). In that year, 1,733 tons were brought in, nearly all from the three Chincha Islands off Peru, and reached the retail market at £25 per ton. Because of the high price, importers found themselves with much of the stock unsold and had to cut the rate, while the Peruvian government, suspecting that they were being cheated, cancelled their original contract and improved on the terms. As soon as these initial difficulties were resolved, the trade expanded at an enormous rate, with Britain importing 283,300 tons in 1845.

The Peruvians began to fear that their capital resource would run out, and under pressure from their own farmers sent to the islands their surveyor, Jose Villa, who reported that the guano there would last for nine hundred years. Peacock examined them in 1844 and more cautiously decided that 'it is practically inexhaustible to the present generation'. But after further apprehension, chiefly among investors in Peruvian Bonds, Rear-Admiral Fairfax Moresby, the British commander in the Pacific, was dispatched to investigate the state of affairs on the Chinchas in 1853. He predicted that the deposits would be worked out in eight or nine years. He found 100 ships there, 65 of them American, and was not impressed by the methods of extraction and loading. The labourers were Chinese: 'They dig and wheel daily about 1,290 tons,' but only 1,100 tons arrived on board ship. 'A loss of 12 per cent occurs from the rude manner of its working and conveyance, daily observed in the dense cloud of pulverised guano blown seaward.'

The Chinchas were, in fact, soon exhausted, although fresh deposits made them workable again at the end of the century. They were replaced by other sources both in South America and on the south-west coast of Africa. But the growth of American participation in the guano trade, with the suggestion that the Peruvians were prepared to grant a virtual monopoly to the United States, was interpreted as a major threat to British pride and interest. The American President made the matter a point of congratulation in his Message to Congress, but in London 'The Guano Question' led to articles in *The Times* and discussions in Parliament. The Royal Navy was asked to search for other deposits, and the Royal Agricultural Society offered a prize of £1,000

Below: Advertisements in *Garden-Work*, 1889.

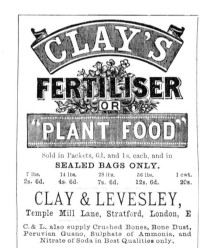

From *The Agricultural Gazette*, 1852: the cautionary style adopted by guano advertisers, and a patent india-rubber hose 'for watering gardens, distributing liquid manure, brewers' use, etc.'

I have tried experiments on about eight or ten various caterpillars, and some other insects, and have invariably found a solution of Guano kills them quickly, except when in an advanced state; then it took a longer time and a stronger solution... My last experiment was with the destructive grub *Melolontha*, so well known to subsist on the roots of grass, of which a friend kindly sent me a box. Six of these white grubs were placed in a saucer half full of water, in which a teaspoonful of African Guano had been put and well stirred. They immediately began to feel uneasy, and, in about two hours, the whole six were dead.

Gardening for the Million quoted in *The Annals of Horticulture.*

and a gold medal for the 'Discovery of a manure equal in fertilising properties to the Peruvian guano, and of which an unlimited supply can be furnished to the British farmer at a rate not exceeding £5 per ton.'

In spite of interruptions to the supply, constant adulteration and substitutes like 'Native Guano' (one of the names under which dried city sewage was sold), guano was a triumphant success. Some gardeners were so convinced of its virtue that they killed off their plants with massive overdoses; others found it a useful pesticide. But with the help of innumerable articles in the gardening press, and several books and pamphlets describing its proper application, it eventually came to be recognised as a valuable, though not all-powerful, aid to the grower. 'X.Y.Z.' observed in an 1853 number of *The Agricultural Gazette* that 'The old yeoman now likes guano.'

By the last decades of the nineteenth century, the effective use of fertilisers, together with an understanding of the structure of soils and the physiology of plants, had cleared the way for modern agriculture and gardening. Confessing in the 1840s that 'at present, in the science of the nutrition of vegetables, men, generally speaking, are merely empirics, —knowing almost nothing of the "mode of operation" of the food of plants,' *The Gardener and Practical Florist* had foreseen the change. 'It is, however, a gratifying fact, that rays of light are darting through the crevices of ignorance, and it cannot be doubted but that ere long, although we may not be walking in broad sun-shine, we shall be emancipated from the darkness which has so long invested this department of natural science. Liebig has risen as a star of the first magnitude, and promises, by his light, to guide us on our way to regions of comparative brightness.' Almost exactly forty years later the Sibthorpian Professor of Rural Economy at Oxford, the same Dr Gilbert who had worked with Liebig and Sir John Lawes, set out in his inaugural address (as reported by *The Gardeners' Chronicle*) a programme of lectures which 'will doubtless result in placing before the world the most compact, yet full statement, of the present condition of scientific principles applicable to the cultivation of plants and the nurture of animals for practical purposes that has yet been made, and the value of which will be, we may safely venture to say, beyond all precedent.'

The Pleasure Ground

Frontispiece of E. S. Delamer's *The Flower Garden* (1859 edition).

In the later years of the nineteenth century, gardeners watched with interest the long conflict between William Robinson and the upholders of more formal principles in design. Robinson was as skilful a propagandist as he was a gardener and his followers in the New Landscape School, notably Gertrude Jekyll, ensured that his opinions formed the basis of modern orthodoxy. Later writers have credited Robinson and his colleagues with restoring life and vigour in place of an outmoded and stultified tradition. In the words of Eleanour Sinclair Rohde, 'They retaught the almost lost art of gardening to a nation who were all eagerness to learn.' (*The Story of the Garden*, 1932).

This was a misleading over-simplification. Robinson's work was not a total revolution, but part of a continuous course of development. His major works, *The Wild Garden*, published in 1870, and *The English Flower Garden*, which originally appeared in 1883, both had a lasting influence. His campaign for a more 'Natural' approach was seen as a crusade against bedding-out—the system of filling flower beds with successive masses of plants raised in the greenhouse and discarded at the end of their season. It was a subject on which Robinson had definite views: 'The genius of cretinism itself could hardly delight in anything more tasteless or ignoble than the absurd daubs of colour that every summer flare in the neighbourhood of nearly every country-house in Western Europe.' Robinson's master plan for the natural garden also included the replacement of geometric beds with herbaceous borders of mixed hardy perennials. Terraces, arbours, clipped hedges, gravel walks and walls were to be dispensed with in favour of grass, rustic steps and shrubby clumps. Planning was acceptable, but 'lay-out', as in the formal gardens of Chatsworth and the Crystal Palace at Sydenham, was abhorrent.

The Gardeners' Chronicle gave a long and mainly favourable review of *The English Flower Garden* in the issue of 2nd February 1884, supporting Robinson's antipathy to excessive

117

formality: 'The "bedding-out" system, which led to the expulsion of hardy herbaceous plants from many English gardens, reached its climax about thirty years ago. The setting-up of the Crystal Palace on Sydenham Hill was the apotheosis of conventional formalism in laying-out pleasure-gardens, the sanction of a kind of Baal-worship under which all natural beauty was sacrificed.' Both the *Chronicle* and Robinson did, however, recognise the 'great varieties of style' in British gardens, 'for all of which something may be said,' but the periodical became a firm opponent of formalism and carried a series of articles on 'The Beauty of Appropriateness', which reflected the Robinson ideal. The magazine had changed its ideas since 1853, when it had been effusive in praising the Sydenham gardens and suggested that they successfully combined both formal and natural elements.

The New Landscape School of Robinson's followers shared many of the attributes of the Pre-Raphaelite Brotherhood and the Arts and Crafts Movement, as *The English Flower Garden* indicates: 'A beautiful house in a fair landscape is the most delightful scene of the cultivated earth, all the more so if there be an artistic garden. The union between the house beautiful and the ground near it—a happy marriage it should be—is worthy of more thought than it has had in the past, and the best way of effecting that union artistically should interest men more and more as our cities grow larger and our lovely English landscape shrinks back from them. We have never yet got from the garden and the home landscape half the beauty which we might get by

The Italian Garden at Wynyard Park, County Durham, photographed by the Marchioness of Londonderry, c.1890. An example of the late Victorian formal garden – the beds are planted with dahlias, yuccas and a variety of edgings. The wrought-iron gates in the background were brought from Ratisbon [Regensburg], Germany and erected in 1864.

As to "nature" and "art", Mr Robinson is often florid, never precise...
On the subject of clipt trees Mr Robinson becomes violent...
Mr Robinson has charged me with writing nonsense and attributing it to him...
It is sometimes difficult to see whether his perversions are wilful or merely stupid... Mr Robinson's irrational has betrayed him into unnecessary blunders as well as gratuitous discourtesy.

From Reginald Blomfield's preface to the 2nd edition of *The Formal Garden in England*, 1892.

The Italian Garden at Moor Park, Hertfordshire, in 1871. Beyond the formal parterre is the landscaped park.

abolishing the patterns which disfigure so many gardens. Formality is often essential to the plan of a garden but never to the arrangement of its flowers and shrubs, and to array these in rigid lines, circles or patterns can only be ugly wherever it may be.' The idea later put into practice by Sir Edwin Lutyens and Gertrude Jekyll that architecture and gardening should blend harmoniously conflicts with another passage in the same book, where Robinson castigates those who 'call themselves "landscape architects"—a stupid term of French origin implying the union of two absolutely distinct studies, one dealing with varied life in a thousand different kinds and the natural beauty of the earth, and the other with stones and bricks and their putting together.'

One designer who managed to combine the two studies was the ecclesiastical architect John Sedding, a founder of the Art Workers' Guild, whose church of The Holy Trinity in Sloane Street is described by Sir John Betjeman as 'the cathedral of the Arts and Crafts movement'. Sedding devoted himself with skill and passion to his own garden at West Wickham, and set out his ideas in *Garden-Craft Old and New*, published posthumously in 1891. The book contains much criticism of Robinson's theories, suggesting that art and artistry are as important in a garden as nature: 'To bring Nature up to the Window of your house, with a scorn of art-sweetness, is not only to betray your own deadness to form, but to cause a sense of unexpected blankness in the visitor's mind on leaving the well-appointed interior of an English home. As the house is an Art-production, so is the garden that surrounds it, and there is no code of taste that I know of which would prove that Art is more reprehensible in the garden than in the house.' This was a retort to an assertion by Robinson: 'There is no code of taste resting on any solid foundation which proves that garden or park should have any extensive stonework or geometrical arrangement.' Robinson, who was a master of the aggressive style in horticultural journalism, was for once a target for abuse: 'For the colonies,' Sedding wrote, 'I can imagine no

119

fitter doctrines than our author's, but not for an old land like ours.' Sedding also mocked him for pronouncing his opinions 'with the air of a Moses freshly come down from the Mount.'

Sedding was, of course, an elitist. He taunted Robinson with a remark of Hazlitt's that 'there is a pleasure in Art which none but artists feel', but in the last chapters of his book ('On the Other Side, a Plea for Savagery' and 'In Praise of Both'), he accepts the need for progress and for compromise: 'Those instincts of ours which seem to pull contrary ways—Art-wards or Nature-wards—and to drive our lopsided selves to the falsehood of extremes, are, after all, not incompatible.' Most important was his awareness that house and garden were a unity, and that different parts of the garden all had their value: 'The useful and the beautiful should be happily united, the kitchen and the flower-garden, the way to the stables and outbuildings, the orchard, the winter-garden, &c., all having a share of consideration and a sense of connectedness.'

The controversy of the 1880s and 1890s and the enthusiasm of 'modern' gardeners have combined to depict a world in which gardens could have one of only two characters—either the cheerful, wholesome innocence of the cottager's plot, or the sterile gloom of artificial parterres, with statuary, carpet-bedding and an edging of monotonous shrubberies and clipped hedges. Between these largely mythical extremes there was an entire range of types, and many authorities in addition to William Robinson urged moderation. 'In modern times, sure enough' wrote James Anderson in the 1870s, 'the geometric and gardenesque have been carried to an almost extreme interpretation, verging on absurdity.'

Gardening fashion changes as much in response to social and economic conditions as to theoretical prescriptions. No doubt, the nation's eagerness to learn from *The English Flower Garden* stemmed in part from the move towards small gardens in town or suburb and the increasing cost of trained professional help. Robinson had started his gardening career in the country estates of Northern Ireland, and there must have been many other professionals who were glad to abandon bedding-out and similar repetitive tasks for entirely unaesthetic reasons.

Garden planning and layout had been the subject of argument since the early 1800s, following the large-scale operations of the original 'Landscapers', William Kent and Lancelot 'Capability' Brown. They, too, had sought a natural appearance, which was often contrived with massive remodelling of the land surface and extensive replanting of woods and vistas. The inevitable rush by lesser designers to imitate the grand fashion meant that many ancient gardens were ruined by unimaginative landscaping. Loudon, writing of the early nineteenth century, noted that 'the modern style, as now degraded, had only three forms, a clump, a belt and a single tree.'

As Sedding well said, "Any garden whatsoever is but nature idealised." Mr. Robinson's answer to this is, "We cannot allow him (Mr Sedding) to bring the false and confusing art drivel of the day into the garden without showing the absurdity of his ideas." I do not observe that Mr Robinson has anywhere shown their absurdity, unless he supposes that his bare assertion that they are absurd, ought to convince any person of intelligence, for he drops the subject and proceeds to abuse the illustrations to Sedding's book and to call his opinions "childish." Mr Robinson is rather fond of calling people with whom he differs "childish."

Reginald Blomfield and F. Inigo Thomas, *The Formal Garden in England.*

Nature seems to have designed men for the culture of her works, and to have ordained that we should be born gardeners, since some of our earliest inclinations lead us to the cultivation of flowers. The infant can no sooner walk than its first employment is to plant a flower in the earth, removing it ten times in an hour to wherever the sun seems to shine more favourably. The school-boy, in the care of his little plot of ground, lessens the anxious thoughts of the home he has left. In manhood our attention is generally demanded by more active and imperious duties; but, as age obliges us to retire from public business, the love of gardening returns to soothe our declining years.

The Gardener's Weekly Magazine, April 1860.

Part of the pleasure gardens at Wynyard Park, c.1890. The posed figure is Fräulein Sturmfels, the household's governess.

Until the middle of the century, gardening writers dismissed flowers in favour of useful vegetable products. Sir Joseph Banks originally proposed to exclude decorative plants from the deliberations of the Horticultural Society. In the preamble to Book II of *An Encyclopaedia of Gardening*, Loudon explains: 'Floriculture is obviously of limited interest and utility, compared with horticulture; much less has accordingly been written on it, and our view of modern practice will, therefore, be proportionately brief'. However, he later concedes that 'there is no impropriety in having a large flower-garden to a small kitchen-garden or mansion, where the taste of the owner leads to such deviation from common rules.' As late as 1859, Eugene Delamer reflected on the ease of a flower gardener's life compared with those of colleagues in the kitchen garden: '*He* has only to keep up a goodly show, to maintain a fair outside, no matter with what materials; if one thing will not prove effective, let him try another...'

The 1834 edition of the *Encyclopaedia* describes the variety of flower-garden styles current at the time, their character partly determined by the circumstances of the owners. The labourer's cottage garden was entirely given over to vegetables and fruit, except for a rose and a honeysuckle over the porch. The artisan was allowed the luxury of a few flowers, while the tradesman and suburban dweller might have beds of perennials and annuals cared for by a jobbing

121

gardener. Later in the century, the labourer (or more often his wife) was encouraged to grow flowers—they gave a moral uplift to the poor.

Loudon in the *Encyclopaedia* and McIntosh in *The Practical Gardener* list five categories for the more affluent proprietor: '*The general or mingled flower-garden*, in which is displayed a mixture of flowers with or without flowering-shrubs, according to size... *the massed flower-garden*, in which the flowers are planted in masses of one kind, either in separate beds, or in separate divisions of the same bed... *the select flower-garden*, in which the object is limited to cultivation of particular kinds of plants... *the changeable flower-garden*, in which all the plants are kept in pots, and reared in a flower-nursery or reserve-ground... and *the botanic flower-garden*, in which the plants are arranged with reference to botanical study.'

This sums up fairly well the possibilies available to any flower gardener. The 'mingled' beds correspond very closely to the mixed herbaceous arrangements of the twentieth century. Indeed, it is hard to find much difference between some of the gardens described by Loudon and those recommended by Robinson's disciple Alice Martineau in her *Herbaceous Garden* (1913), where herbaceous perennials combined with bulbs and annuals to provide a spread of colour from early spring to the first autumn frosts. A correspondent to Loudon's periodical, *The Gardener's Magazine*, in 1829, sent a plan composed by 'a young lady, who, being fond of flowers, has directed her attention to the effects of arranging them in different manners.' Her beds include unspecified 'choice perennials' as well as collections of phlox and campanula. There are tulips, jonquils and other bulbs for spring, and pinks and carnations, salvias, clarkias and lobelias are among the summer flowers. The whole scheme is surrounded by roses and georginas (more familiar as dahlias).

...flower-gardening has progressed rapidly; and the amusement of floriculture has become the dominant passion of the ladies of Great Britain. It is a passion most blessed in its effects, considered as an amusement or a benefit. Nothing humanizes and adorns the female mind more surely than a taste for ornamental gardening. It compels the reason to act, and the judgement to observe; it is favourable to meditation of the most serious kind; it exercises the fancy in harmless and elegant occupation, and braces the system by its healthful tendency.

Louisa Johnson, *Every Lady her own Flower Gardener*, 1845.

Plan of a flower garden 'by a young lady' in *The Gardener's Magazine*, 1830. The beds were set in turf and surrounded by a border, or edging, of *Rosa semperflorens*, 'and within a row of georginas, about 100 sorts; every 12ft. a standard Noisette rose.' The garden opened off a gravelled area with a rustic seat, flanked by arcades covered with ivy.

Single dahlias of the mid-1880s: 'Magpie' and 'Freedom', from *The Illustrated Dictionary of Gardening*.

Below: A double variety of *Dahlia variabilis*, from *The Illustrated Dictionary of Gardening*. 'This is probably the first species introduced, and whence by far the majority of forms now very common, have originated.'

These had been introduced to Britain by Lady Bute in 1789, then lost. John Fraser of Chelsea brought a specimen from France in 1802, but it died after flowering. Another plant from Paris appeared in Woodford, Essex, in 1803, but the credit for their successful introduction was usually given to Lady Holland, who sent seeds from Madrid in 1804. More of them were imported after the end of the Napoleonic Wars, and the dahlia became fashionable. In the 1820s, however, it was thought that the name dahlia had previously been given to a South African plant genus—it was also confused with the unrelated dalea—and the alternative name, georgina (after the Russian botanist J.G. Georgi and not as sometimes suggested in honour of Lady Holland), was generally substituted. A few years later, the botanical authorities changed their minds again, restoring dahlia in Britain—though not in many parts of Europe.

Less ambitious gardeners than Loudon's young lady also favoured mixed beds and borders, if only because of their comparative ease of upkeep. Dr Nathaniel Paterson, of St Andrew's Church, Glasgow, writing for his fellow ministers in *The Manse Garden* (1838), observes that a five-foot border on either side of a gravel walk, 'for fibrous perennials and bulbous roots, with spaces here and there for the admission of annuals, deserves particular culture.' He gives only the broadest advice on filling the beds. 'It were needless to give a thousand names and descriptions; the mere name serves not the cause of botany: and no description on paper conveys an idea of a plant as it grows. The only rule, then, is to pick up at intervals, according to your fancy, and to stop when you have no more ground.' He does go so far as to provide a list of annuals which includes gourds and decorative runner beans as well as more predictable flowers.

For most of the first half of the century, garden planners used flowers as part of an overall design which included trees, shrubs, lawns and gravel walks—a recognisable English style had evolved. In a conscious break from the formalism practised in Europe, British gardeners adopted designs which reflected the mixture of elements in the countryside. McIntosh wrote in *The Flower-Garden* (1840): 'It is generally understood, that the style termed English in gardening consists in an artful imitation of nature, and is consequently much dependent on aspect and accessaries. In the true English style, accordingly, we have neither the Italian terrace, the French parterre, nor the Dutch clipt evergreens.' But he was quite well aware that care was needed to achieve the 'natural' look. 'The pretended adherence to nature is

Dahlia – a floral upstart, the whole course of whose rise to fame and fortune is within the memory of many persons now living. The original single-flowered plant, from Mexico, first claimed the attention of horticulturalists as an edible root, whose repulsive, nauseous, peppery taste inspires equal disgust to man and beast.

E. Delamer, *The Flower Garden*, 1859.

The Scarlet Runner is a favourite and useful summer vegetable. In England and Wales it is grown in nearly every cottage garden, but in Scotland it is not so well known; indeed, one may see hundreds of cottage gardens where this Bean was never grown, and those who do grow it generally do so for the beauty of the scarlet flowers and the value of the plant as a climber; but the pods are considered unfit for food.

Garden-Work, April 1888.

Examples of the Italian, the French
and the Dutch Garden illustrated by
Charles McIntosh in *The Flower
Garden*, 1838.

Left: The Yew Garden at Elvaston
Castle, Derbyshire: 'clipt
evergreens' on the grand scale.
From *The Illustrated Dictionary of
Gardening*.

'English Garden and Pleasure Ground' from McIntosh's *The Flower Garden*.

wholly a style of conventional artifice, not so stiff and formal, indeed...but still strictly artificial.' He gave warnings about the positioning of beds: 'Attention must be paid to avoid the spottiness which will result from placing a bed wherever room can be found for it; on the contrary, the beds should be treated on the same plan of arrangement as the shrubs which they are intended to accompany. The glades of lawn must not be destroyed by scattered beds of flowers, crossing them in all directions, though a bed may sometimes be advantageously introduced to break the continuity of the line of shrubs, and relieve by brilliancy of colour their more sober tone.'

At its best, the English style was a success. The gardener's aim was primarily to provide a space to be walked in and enjoyed throughout the year. Shrubberies, in spite of their relatively sober appearance, were places for agreeable relaxation when carefully laid out and imaginatively planted. 'The object of a shrubbery' said Mrs Loudon in 1841, 'is to produce as great an extent of interesting walk as the nature, extent, and other circumstances of the place will admit.' But in the wrong hands the English garden became a gloomy mess.

Murmurs of dissent began in the 1820s. In 1828, *The Gardener's Magazine* carried two articles by 'An Amateur' on 'The Present Style of Ornamental Gardening'. Though declaring himself a zealous admirer of the English style when applied to 'small country places', he complained that serpentine walks, shrubberies, and kidney-shaped flower-beds were

We recommend a rural walk from Whitechapel towards Mile-End; where, with a little sedulous examination, they may perceive many ingenious specimens of human art, in the variegated arrangement of broken slates, glass bottles, tobacco pipes, laths, brickbats, &c. in spots of eighteen feet by six; where effects are produced by civic genius in retirement, with the aid of daffodils and periwinkles, which would have been unthought of by a Capability Brown or a Repton!

A New System of Practical Domestic Economy, 1825.

not appropriate in gardens planned on a larger scale: 'The small walled-in gardens of the villas in the neighbourhood of London; the distribution of shrubs and flower-beds of the London squares; the college gardens of Oxford and Cambridge...the pleasure-gardens of our residences, both great and small, from those of Buckingham Palace and St James's Park to the humblest parsonage, are on precisely the same model.'

One reason for the failure of such gardens, according to 'An Amateur' was the climate: 'They hold forth every inducement to wander among their groves and lawns, and gaudy flower-beds; they are captivating at first sight; they are beautiful in fine weather... What are they for the greater part of the year? Do dripping shrubs, do wet grass, and swampy ground, and flower-beds, known only as beds for flowers by their dingy mould, contrasted with the yellow lawn, do all, or any one of these, invite us into the open air? Do we not rather turn our backs upon them, stir up our fire, resume our book, and sit at home? The first and chief object of a pleasure-garden being thus, throughout the greater portion of the year, denied to us.'

The suggested remedy was simple: 'We must condescend to borrow from our neighbours on the Continent some of that architectural taste in gardening in which many of them have so much excelled.' What the author recommended was, in effect, a complete break from the prevailing system: 'A plot of ground, of one acre only, attached to the mansion, laid out in the Italian manner, with its terrace, steps, balustrades, vases, fountain, and rectangular gravel walks, will add more to the cheerfulness of both the exterior and interior of that mansion...than five times the quantity of land laid out according to our present English style of gardening.'

Within a generation, the break had come about, and the English style was finished. In the 1840s, conservative authorities still adhered to it. According to *The Gardener and Practical Florist*, pleasure grounds usually consisted of 'lawn, shrubbery, flower borders, and beds of flowers, and sometimes rock work and architectural ornaments. Where there is sufficient extent, this is the most desirable style of garden.' As an introduction to an article on 'Flower Gardens and Shrubberies', the same periodical quoted from the *Florist's Manual*, claiming that it still applied 'although written some twenty years ago.' The same extracts had been used by Loudon and by McIntosh, and the *Manual* had in fact appeared in 1806. Even *The Gardener and Practical Florist*, though, included advice on making geometrical gardens in the Dutch fashion, and it is clear that interest in more formal designs was increasing. Mrs Loudon, in *The Lady's Country Companion* still approved of the shrubbery, but wrote of it only in visual terms, as a means of relating the garden to the general scenery beyond. Again, she favoured a formal plan for the flower-beds, with the emphasis on an arrangement to be looked at rather than walked about in: 'I think it should certainly be a regular geometric figure, and planted

The manor house 'in the improved state', from Mrs Loudon's *The Lady's Country Companion* (*see* page 21). The 'gloomy firs' have been cleared to make way for lawns and flower beds.
Below: The garden front of the house.

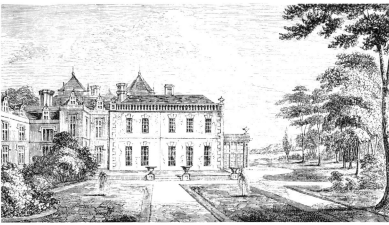

in masses, each bed containing flowers of one kind, so as to produce something of the effect of a Turkey carpet when looked down upon from the windows of the house.'

Formal, geometrical design, which became popular by 1850, featured in gardens such as Dropmore, where Lady Grenville had indulged her own rather individual tastes since the 1820s. Other examples mentioned with approval by 'An Amateur' in 1828 were on the estates of Earl Brownlow at Bolton, Lincolnshire, and the Earl of Plymouth at Hewell in Worcestershire. A major impetus to the fashion seems to have been given by the remodelling of the Chatsworth gardens, which Joseph Paxton carried out for the 6th Duke of Devonshire in the 1830s.

In Ireland, the philanthropist William Hickey, writing as 'Martin Doyle', reproduced the 'neat and simple plan' of a garden near Dublin, characterised by 'uniformity without stiffness', and wrote of the numerous fantastic shapes suggested 'by books old and new.' (*The Flower Garden*, 1845.)

As a greater proportion of the pleasure ground was given over to floral display, the 'bedding-out' system developed, where plants raised in nursery plots and glass-houses were set out to flower in prepared beds. This combined and extended features of the 'changeable' and 'massed' garden types, noted by Loudon and McIntosh: in particular, the

Below: Plan of a flower garden 'which I have recently seen near Dublin, at St. Helena, the rural residence of Dr. Hardy.' From Martin Doyle's *The Flower Garden*, 1845.

Design from *The Floricultural Cabinet*, 1836: 'The plan represents a Flower-Garden, which contains a little more than half an acre, having two alcoves at each end.

replacement of flowers as soon as they were past their best. Contributing to *The Gardener's Magazine* in 1831, Alexander Gordon, gardener to Sir Frederic Gustavus Fowke, Bart, at Lowesby Hall, reported: 'Last autumn...I was enabled to make a considerable addition to the already very extensive pleasure-grounds; a portion of which I have converted into two flower-gardens, where I principally adhere to the massing system in the different beds...and, although it does not exactly meet the approbation of my employer, he has generously allowed me to pursue it, in order that I may have a fair opportunity of displaying what I consider its intrinsic merits.' Whether this was true bedding-out or just group planting is not clear, but the baronet evidently gave the arrangement the thumbs down, as Mr Gordon is described in the next volume of the magazine as 'late gardener to Sir F.G. Fowke, Bart'.

Without the bedding system, the new style of flower-gardening would not have been possible. Bedding-out, in turn, was a response to the introduction of many plants, mainly half-hardy annuals, in the 1820s and 1830s. Writing in 1859, Robert Thompson explained: 'About the year 1830, in consequence of the many new annuals which the Horticultural Society introduced...chiefly from the west coast of America, a change began to take place.' (*The Gardener's Assistant.*) In a list of flower seeds advertised for 1836 in *The Floricultural Cabinet*, 74 out of 150 were recent introductions from the Americas—principally Chile, Mexico and California. Some, like *Penstemon campanulatum* and *Zinnia elegans* date from the 1790s, but 42 had been introduced between 1820 and 1829, and 22 between 1830 and 1834. They include many plants which were to become favourites: argemone, alstroemeria, clarkia, eschscholtzia, nemophila, oenothera, petunia, salpiglossis and schizanthus. Many professional and amateur collectors sent plants and seeds back to England, among them Douglas on the west coast of America, Tweedie in Buenos Aires, and Drummond (from whom *Phlox drummondii* gets its name) in Texas. There was considerable competition among seedsmen to obtain and market the latest varieties. Apart from botanical ambition, there was a strong commercial incentive in plant-hunting, and firms thought it worth while to send their representatives all over the world. Lowe's nursery in Clapham sent a collector, Anderson, through South America to the Straits of Magellan, while Backhouse travelled to Tasmania for his family firm in York.

Most of the new annuals were only half hardy in the British climate. They were ideally suited to short-term planting, and their availability was probably, as Thompson suggests, the main reason for the popularity of the bedding-out system. However, even hardy plants were raised in seed beds and transplanted in groups or patches to their flowering position: 'As soon as the patches have been removed, fresh earth should be spread on the hard ground, and fresh seeds sown in it, the plants springing from which will be ready to

The comparatively short-lived display is one of the arguments which has been often urged against composing our flower-gardens entirely of half-hardy plants. It would be much less objectionable could the season of full bloom be greatly protracted. It is to my mind questionable whether this be either a well-founded or philosophical ground of objection. True, a vacant bare bed can be pointed to as an eyesore for half the year. But such an objection need not necessarily exist. The beds can be filled up at once with abundant material for an early spring display, or even with a variety of beautifully-ornamented shrubs where families are resident in winter.

David Thomson, *The Gardener*, January 1867.

be transferred to the beds as soon as the first series have done flowering; and in this way a succession of flowers may be kept up nearly all the year.' (Mrs Loudon, *Gardening for Ladies*, 1841.) *The Annals of Horticulture* described the system as 'now deservedly common' in 1847, suggesting that plants should be put out as early as the end of April, so long as the beds were covered every night. In this, as in other aspects of bedding-out, an abundance of labour was essential.

As well as the huge numbers of annuals which were raised and planted out each year, many tender perennial subjects were found to be appropriate for bedding. Some, like the dahlia, were lifted at the end of the season and the tubers replanted in the spring; most—including the pelargoniums, calceolarias, salvias and verbenas—were overwintered as cuttings in frames and greenhouses. Even on a small scale, the labour was considerable. In September 1852, *The Gardeners' Chronicle* described Mr Bellenden Ker's 'little flower garden' at his cottage near Cheshunt: 'Among bedding plants the following are still gay, viz:- Tom Thumb, Ivy-

It must be recollected that bedding-out has entailed an amount of labour in general gardening that few but the thoroughly practical man can estimate. The desire to rival or excel a neighbour famed for his designs is very natural; and, moreover, every man who is taught to handle a spade is not an artist, any more than every one who handles a brush is a painter. To lay down a truly artistic garden is about as difficult as arranging the materials for forming or heightening the effect of a landscape. But notwithstanding all this the idea of bedding-out is good, and is capable of being brought out in such a way as not to displease even those that are eternally carping about an imitation of nature.

J. Anderson *The New Practical Gardener*, c.1875.

Title page of a book of designs published in 1853: 'This work contains designs of a size and character suitable for gardens generally, and will enable those who may be unacquainted with the science of gardening, by referring to the diagrams, to make them without difficulty, and, at the same time, to give the flower-beds style and proportion pleasing, symmetrical, and durable.'

leaved, Ayres' Gem, Huntsman, Lady Mary Fox, Mangles' variegated, and Compactum Pelargoniums; Kentish Hero, Amplexicaulis, and Kayii Calceolarias; a semi-double purple Petunia; Robinson's Defiance and other Verbenas, Lantana delicatissima, Bouvardia triphylla, Salvia patens, Cuphea platycentra, the white-flowered variegated Alyssum, and Isotoma axillaris, which is the only annual Mr Wooley (the gardener) has retained.' A large garden was thought to need up to seventy thousand individual bedding plants.

The wholesale removal of plants in the autumn meant that there was nothing left to look at but earth. For gardeners on large country estates, it was generally not a problem, since their owners moved to London at about the same time as the beds were cleared. Even so, there was a solution, if required, in winter bedding, a reversal of the summer process, in which the spaces could be filled with dwarf conifers and other evergreens.

The bedding-out system was an indispensable part of the high Victorian style of gardening which became firmly established in the 1850s. The 'architectural' elements found

in the most highly developed examples of the style varied from plain stone or brick terracing to elaborate buildings and collections of statuary. Summer-houses, monuments and temples in the antique manner had been used often enough in the landscaped grounds of the eighteenth century, and the shaded walks of the 1800s were punctuated by rustic seats and hidden cottages for rest and meditation. But the full exuberance of nineteenth-century garden architecture was first expressed in the grounds of the Earl of

Winter bedding at Heckfield, Hampshire in 1884, from *The Gardeners' Chronicle*. The shrubs and heaths were planted out in October; 'In a few days the gay pompadour dress of the garden has given way to the sombre but more seasonable velvet attire, and the garden stands arrayed in fitness, but still in exceeding beauty for the winter months.'

Even in large gardens, ornaments are best avoided, unless appropriately chosen: for we have seen many structures, of high pretension, but ill-suited to the genius of the places. It is true that our real ecclesiastical and military ruins are highly beautiful and impressive, but all effect is lost when they are imitated upon a small scale. In our moist climate, too, particularly in the marshy and fenny districts, grottos and hermitages are worse than absurd – they become too often but the vestibule of the grave!

A New System of Practical Domestic Economy, 1825.

Left: Alton Towers, from John Loudon's *An Encyclopaedia of Gardening*.

A view of part of the park at Alton Towers, near Cheadle, Staffordshire, from J. Loudon's *An Encyclopaedia of Gardening*: 'Proceeding a little farther towards the dry bridge, Stonehenge appears in the foreground, and the tops of the seven gilt glass domes of the main range of conservatories below... It fills the mind with astonishment and delight, to find so much of the magnificence of art, and the appearance of refined enjoyment, amidst so much of the wildness and solitary grandeur of nature.'

Shrewsbury at Alton Towers, laid out between 1814 and 1827. This Staffordshire estate was described by Loudon as 'one of the most singular anomalies to be met with among the country residences of Britain, or, perhaps, of any part of the world.' The earl consulted every available expert, including Loudon himself, then ignored all the advice he was given and himself devised the plans for 'an immense pile of building in the way of a house, with a magnificent conservatory and chapel, but with scarcely a habitable room; a lofty prospect tower, not built on the highest part of the ground; bridges without water underneath; ponds and lakes on the tops of hills; a quadrangular pile of stabling in the midst of the pleasure-ground; and, what may be said to have eclipsed, and still to eclipse, every thing else, a valley, naturally in a high degree romantic with woods, water, and rocks, filled with works of the highest degree of art in architecture and gardening.' (*An Encyclopaedia of Gardening*.) The grounds contained an imitation of Stonehenge, a Gothic tower, a Greek temple, a Chinese pagoda 95 feet high and grottoes carved in the rock, as well as terraces, arbours, waterfalls, statues, railings, walls and other relatively prosaic features. There was also a cottage for a blind harper: whether it was inhabited is unclear, but such additions to romantic scenery were not unknown. A few years earlier, 700 guineas had been offered to anyone who could live for seven years as a hermit in the gardens of Pains Hill near Leatherhead. One applicant lasted for three weeks.

Even in 1867, Alton Towers was listed as first in the list of famous English gardens. (Chas. McDonald in *The Gardener*.) Its flamboyant style was much imitated on a smaller scale, but not often with success, and its fame was mainly as a curiosity: 'There is an imposing grandeur about Alton Towers, but its beauty is not that of a flower-garden.' The

true fusion of the floral and architectural elements was achieved in the 1850s, and found confident expression in the parks and gardens of the Crystal Palace at Sydenham.

The Palace and its surroundings were intended as a place of public entertainment and instruction, but Paxton's design for the Sydenham gardens embodied all the fashions of the time, even if their scale was far beyond the aspirations of the ordinary gardener. A thousand labourers were employed at the end of 1852 to prepare the ground for the terraces and to dig out the fountain basins, which were lined with burnt clay produced in huge, smouldering bonfires. The terrace garden was divided in two by a walk one hundred feet wide and three thousand feet long between vases, urns and statues as well as the flower beds themselves. *The Gardeners' Chronicle* reported that '50,000 scarlet Pelargoniums have been contracted for,' while in 1854 *The Cottage Gardener*, reviewing the palace's first year in operation and commenting 'on what was done there this season, confessedly, in a very great hurry,' mentioned in addition calceolarias, lobelias, petunias, verbenas, gaultherias, alyssums, nemophilas, salvias and heliotropes, interspersed with plantings of dwarf rhododendrons and azaleas. Below the 'kept ground', an area of woodland held a pair of glass and iron water-temples, and a lake dotted with islands, on which the celebrated concrete dinosaurs were displayed in lifelike poses.

The gardens were an immediate success and attracted tens of thousands of visitors every year. The Palace complex certainly had a considerable influence on popular taste, although there was always some difficulty in defining its exact role. Largely intended for the benefit of the people, it was nevertheless closed on Sunday, presumably the one day when the people were free to go. Parliament received a petition from Wiltshire parishes against Sunday opening, and Dr Vaughan, Headmaster of Harrow School, devoted a pamphlet to the question of whether the public should be allowed to frequent the place on the Sabbath. After observing that 'whatever tends to refresh the mind and body without the stimulus of an undue excitement, will be, in itself, a desirable occupation for the Christian Sunday,' he rather confusingly concludes that it should be closed.

Paxton's successors at Sydenham maintained the high standards which he had set. A writer in the 1871 *Journal of Horticulture and Cottage Gardener* (as the magazine had by then become) remarks: 'I am inclined to think that the Crystal Palace gardens do more to encourage a taste for gardening and a love of flowers among the lower classes than even the London parks.' One advantage which they had in this respect was clean air. City gardeners had to contend with a heavily polluted atmosphere—'Very soon London air and London smoke make the flowers fade, the bright-foliaged plants grow dirty, and the dark ones

View along the nave of the Crystal Palace after it had been rebuilt at Sydenham. The arrangement of trees and climbers was an 'artist's impression' to show the intended appearance. From *The Cottage Gardener*, 24th October 1854.

dingy.' Although the general layout of the terraces stayed the same, the planting schemes were varied from year to year, and the plans were carefully noted by visiting gardeners: 'It may not have been the aim of the Crystal Palace Company, but it is none the less the case, that these gardens give their character not only to others in the neighbourhood of London, but also to others in distant parts of the country. I know one garden nearly two hundred miles from London where year after year the most effective arrangements of the previous year at the Crystal Palace have been adopted.'

The company met with financial trouble in the 1880s, and the Crystal Palace never properly recovered its early magnificence. In 1887, *Punch* included an ode 'In Reduced Circumstances':

> Please to remember the Crystal Palace! Only once in
>   fifty years!
> Am I alone to be out in the cold, gentle Sirs, as Her
>   Majesty's Jubilee nears?
> Everyone now is a-touting for everything, Church
>   Houses, Institutes, Hospitals, Towers.
> Has no one a good word for me and my gardens, my
>   fun and my fireworks, my fountains and flowers?
> Am I to become as Extinct as my Animals? Pass, like
>   my Mammoth and Ichthyosaurus?
> Go, like the ghosts in my Courts and my Temples,
>   vanish like RAMESES, hook it like HORUS?
> ALBERT the Good and the year 'Fifty-one, the great
>   Cosmopolitan era of Progress?
> Have they no spell, Sirs, to rescue me yet from
>   Oblivion's maw, the edacious old Ogress?
> Truly the spirit of PAXTON might plead for me, say
> that   the thought of my death is a scandal.
> Would not Her MAJESTY—bless her!—object, for the
>   sake of her Consort? And how about HANDEL?...
>
> How they've allowed me to get impecunious. Think
> of my Rose-Shows! And what are you going
> To do with your Shahs and your Emperors in
> future?   for when *I* am gone there'll be *nothing* worth
> showing.
> Say, must I pass like old KUBLAI-KHAN's Pleasure-
> Dome
>   —fade like the Looking-Glass World of sweet *Alice?*
> Nay, I am sure, from the Court to the Cot, all will aid
> a   "whip-round" for the poor Crystal Palace!

After putting Lord Shrewsbury first on the list of 'great names in the progress of British gardening', McDonald, in his series of articles in *The Gardener* ('Beauty in a Flower-Garden'), mentions as especially influential the Duke of Devonshire, Sir William Middleton and Harriet, Duchess of Sutherland, who were responsible for the gardens at Chatsworth in Derbyshire, at Shrublands Park, near

I have another thing to mention, upon which I cannot speak without feeling grieved. On the last day but one of the old year, the Crystal Palace at Sydenham narrowly escaped destruction by fire. As it was, £250,000 worth of property was lost, and that too in what was to gardeners the most interesting and instructive part of the edifice – the Tropical Department. We, as gardeners, may look with peculiar pride upon the fairy-like structure, for it was produced by the genius of one of our own craft. It was the one feature which we could, with any degree of national pleasure, point out to the foreigner. We have but few imposing streets – our public edifices are nothing to boast of – in works of art we are dreadfully poor – our national wealth is only shown by the enormous masses of ugliness into which our towns have most of them grown – our extended commerce has to be inferred from the numbers of dirty vessels huddled together in every port; but the one thing which our visitor could never have seen before, the only unique object we could call his attention to, is that marvellously light and beautiful palace which crowns the heights of Sydenham. We can hardly think now what we could have done without it, had the Crystal Palace been entirely destroyed. As it is, its fair proportions are marred – only temporarily, we hope. No expense was spared to stock that building with the rarest of plants, when it was originally erected. The magnificent collection of Palms belonging to Messrs. Loddiges, which had long previously obtained a world-wide fame, was bought as a whole. Some of these specimens were of such a size that more than a dozen horses were required to transport them singly from Hackney to Sydenham. Date-palms were imported direct from Egypt, and of a size to give a character to the Egyptian antiquities with which they were associated. Tree-ferns from Australia, rare orchids, majestic bananas – nothing seemed too rich or rare to be bought by the Palace Company. Most of these tropical rarities are gone; some of them can never be replaced.

The Gardener, February 1867.

'The Mother of the Forest' – sections of the bark of a Wellingtonia tree reconstructed inside the Sydenham Crystal Palace. From *Beauties and Wonders of Vegetable Life*, c.1860.

Ipswich, and at Trentham in Staffordshire. By this time (1867), Chatsworth had lost some of its splendour, but the other two were acknowledged show-places among the great estates of Victorian England. In 1856, the floral expert of *The Cottage Gardener*, Donald Beaton, who had been gardener at Shrublands, reported on a visit to the grounds in the company of the then head man, Mr Foggo. The flower gardens were designed to be looked at from the drawing-rooms of the house, and were invisible from the front entrance. The terrace, 'one blaze, in one line, of Scarlet Geraniums', was divided by a broad walk, flanked with laurels, which ended at a temple of the winds. Below this was a grand flight of steps to 'the best picture of flower-gardening I ever saw.' Complicated patterns were filled with every kind of bedding plant—many varieties were bred on the estate. 'There is, without exception,' wrote Beaton, 'the very best and richest style of making beds on a gravel terrace, the edges being nine or ten inches higher than the gravel. There are grass and sand patterns with architectural accessories, and rare trees and shrubs at each end of the terrace, the tree which Prince Albert planted in 1851 being one of them (*Libocedrus Chilensis*).' One of the features of Shrublands was the planting of ribbon borders—bands of massed flowers set out to form interlocking designs of contrasting colours:

'The plain ribbon system was originated here by Lady Middleton...more than twenty years back. If the Crystal Palace authorities had seen how this pattern is bound round with the blue and yellow ribbon, their own chain pattern in the two centre panels might have been in better taste.'

The Duchess of Sutherland, an influential figure in court circles, engaged Sir Charles Barry to draw up plans for a new terraced flower garden at Trentham in his favourite Italianate style. The task of putting them into effect was given to George Fleming when he was appointed head gardener in 1841. Later work was done under the direction of William Nesfield, an ex-army officer who gave up a distinguished career as a water-colourist to take up garden design. His greatest achievement was the layout of the Horticultural Society's gardens at South Kensington. Barry and Nesfield approached their commissions as architect and decorative artists, leaving most of the horticultural practicalities to others. At Trentham, of which McDonald observed that 'a more unsuitable site for a great garden could hardly be imagined,' Fleming was initially, according to a profile of him in *The Cottage Gardener*, 'often on the verge of despair, but hope sustained him amid all his trials.' He embarked on a massive drainage programme to dry out the waterlogged soil, eventually, in 1853, diverting the Trent into a new channel to prevent the build-up of river mud in the lake. The ornamental garden was a rectangle covering about eleven acres, the flower beds combined with pavilions, statues, vases, plant boxes and walks laid with gravel in different colours. The statuary was particularly remarked on: '...we see reflected in indescribable beauty the beds around the fountain, with an Eve watching, and in majestic calmness Atalanta smiling on opening rose-beds: this is beautiful indeed! This terrace is divided from

Design for a scroll-border from David Thomson's *Handy Book of the Flower-Garden* , 1868. He recommends planting in primary colours: yellow (*Calceolaria canariensis*) in the central circles, blue (*Lobelia speciosa*) in the scrolls and scarlet verbena in the outer border. Neutral gravel was laid in the unshaded areas.

As for the landscape about Trentham, in its own native character it is neither picturesque nor beautiful; almost everything has to be created. Indeed, were it not for the noble masses of timber, which crown or flank the sides of the higher grounds by which it is surrounded, the locality would wear but a barren aspect; but much has been done by art to give expression to the scenery. After wandering through the intricacies produced by the different levels, descending from the terrace, and after descending sundry massive flights of steps, the flower-gardens burst upon you in refulgent beauty; the atmosphere all the while teeming with sweets.

The Cottage Gardener, 1855.

The ribbon-border that became so fashionable after 1851, interrupted the higher objects of flower-gardening, and reduced the *art* of imagination to the lowest ebb. The minute beauties of flowers were no more than a line of purple-leaved beetroot – even the "aromatic odours" were at a discount; lucky trifles that give pleasure by novelty, were uncared for; and this *mechanical* style of planting had often but one stand-point from which to look at it, and so tame was it in some cases that one look sufficed for the season. I do not speak condemnatory of ribbon-borders, where such borders are planted as an aid to the flower-garden; I have spoken of ribbon-borders when put forward as a substitute for a flower-garden, where we look for the highest beauty in variety and permanent effect and succession of pleasure – far above the transient display of hard lines of mere colour.

Chas. McDonald, *The Gardener*, 1867.

The geometrical style...may be carried on through a series of terraces, sloping banks, flights of steps of turf or stone, retaining walls, &c., until it occupies the whole of the inclosed lawn. Scroll-work patterns of box on gravel, the interstices filled with broken red or white brick, Derbyshire spar, blue slate, coal, silver, yellow, or red sand, may also be introduced, as has been very successfully done in the Horticultural Society's Gardens at South Kensington.

Beeton's Book of Garden Management.

the great parterre by a fine stone balustrade; at the angles are two temples, in which stand mythological statues; from the temple on the left a fine walk leads along the "window trellis" which is 15 feet high, and a masterpiece in the design of the garden; along the sides of this trellis are marble figures of a classic age, which animate the scene, and in themselves possess an unfading interest; this walk commands views of the fruit and kitchen gardens, and runs onto the broad walk by a balustrade screening the lake.' (Chas. McDonald in *The Gardener*.)

Nesfield's gardens at South Kensington were constructed on land bought out of the profits of the 1851 Exhibition, and leased to the Horticultural Society. They occupied 23 acres between Exhibition Road and Prince Albert Road, now Queen's Gate, and extended northwards to where the Albert Hall was later built. The Prince himself took an interest in the project, suggesting ideas and helping the Society, which was in a poor financial state, to raise the £100,000 needed. The area was divided into three sections: an 'ante-garden' of fairly simple design, with a maze and a shrubbery, was followed by the elaborate principal garden, laid out in geometric flower beds and 'box embroidery', gravel walks, basins and cascades. This led up to the highest part of the site, a terrace with two band-stands and a conservatory. Corridors, or walkways, ran round the outside, passing through arcades in a variety of architectural styles. An article written in 1861 and included in *Beeton's Book of Garden Management* describes the grounds as they were on their first opening. The trees and shrubs were not yet fully established and the buildings seemed initially rather stark—'The dazzling newness of the architecture leaves the eye with no repose.' The overall appearance, however, was applauded: 'The general effect of these gardens cannot fail to exercise a beneficial influence on the art of laying out ornamental flower-gardens. While the terraces and arcades are felt to be oppressive from their freshness, the reverse is the case with the arrangement of the beds; the tracery of some of these is of the most brilliant colouring, but the elegant lines of the clumps, and the presence of occasional patches of dwarf box, in the design, agreeably subdue the blaze of colour.'

These great gardens, and others that were formed in a similar fashion during the third quarter of the century, embodied in their floral and architectural elements everything which a later generation found objectionable. But there is no real reason why we should now think them, if we could see them as they were in their prime, any less splendid than they appeared to the thousands of people who knew and enjoyed them. To dismiss them as freakish deviations

Right: The gardens at South Kensington in the 1880s, not long before they were removed. Behind the conservatory is the Albert Hall, begun in 1867. The monument towards the left commemorated the Great Exhibition.
Below right: The interior of the conservatory at South Kensington. The central group included an Abyssinian banana and a pair of American aloes. From *The Journal of Horticulture,* 1872.

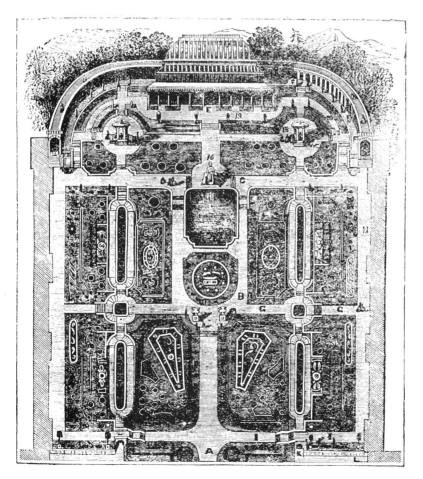

Schematic drawing of the South Kensington gardens from *Beeton's Book of Garden Management.*

Carpet bedding, or mosaiculture, as it is called in America, is comparatively a modern idea, and one which has many points that render its adoption to a moderate extent desirable. Practically it may be defined as a system of bedding in which neat and dwarf-growing foliage plants alone, are used in the form of mosaic, geometrical, or other designs, the beds being either flat or more or less raised from the level. In some cases, indeed, very dwarf-growing flowering plants, as dwarf lobelias, are used, but as a rule the best and most permanently effective carpet-like designs are those formed of brightly coloured foliage plants alone.

Robert Thompson, *The Gardener's Assistant,* 1881 edition.

from a supposed true line of development in British gardening required arrogance of the kind that until comparatively recently dismissed even the best art and architecture of the Victorian period. Bedding-out, and especially the development (from about 1870) of carpet-bedding, using low-growing or closely cropped flowers mixed with foliage plants and succulents such as sempervivums, came in for repeated vilification; yet, at the 1983 Chelsea Flower Show a piece of carpet-bedding as outrageous as anything a hundred years before—a cottage faced entirely with echeverias and thatched with heather—won general acclamation and a gold medal.

It has been maintained that bedding, with its emphasis on annuals and a limited number of perennials, caused gardeners to disregard old-established plants, bringing some of them close to extinction. Even Trentham, however, had 'masses of fine flowering shrubs, with old-fashioned tall flowering herbaceous plants merging into the open park,' and by no means all gardens followed the geometric style. Mr Weaver, gardener to the Warden of Winchester College, described his herbaceous borders in *The Journal of Horticulture* of 1871, and an anonymous correspondent a few weeks later submitted 'Notes on My Herbaceous Garden'. As a decided opponent of current fashion, the writer prefaced them with the hope that 'if they only add the smallest particle of assistance in putting down the present system of bedding, I shall deem myself abundantly rewarded.' The Editors replied: 'We do not comprehend why he wages a

The Terrace Garden at Windsor Castle, from *Garden-Work*, 1889: 'A long, narrow border contains old-fashioned plants – garden Roses, Antirrhinums, Phloxes, Mignonette, &c. The flower beds are of considerable size, and appropriately plain in shape; they are extremely attractive. Most of the beds contain shrubs and Conifers, Yews in variety, Retinosporas, Thujas, Euonymuses, &c. Between the shrubs are planted such rather tall-growing plants as Ageratums, Pentstemons, and Petunias, surrounded with Geraniums and edged with dwarfer plants of contrasting colours.'

Right: 'A Prize-winning Cottage Garden' – the top exhibit in a cottagers' show at Roehampton in 1887, reproduced in *Garden-Work*. The pattern was formed from bands of coleus, fuchsia, calceolaria and pelargonium, with echeveria and box in front – not the conventional idea of 'cottage' planting. The top half of the illustration shows the winning window-box, planted with fuchsias, lobelias and pelargoniums of various kinds.

142

war of extermination against the bedding system. He reminds us of the crusty old gentleman who preferred a grey poney to one of any other colour, and wishes especially that all blacks and chestnuts should be exterminated. Now, though our correspondent likes his hobby above all others, why cannot he let others ride theirs in peace and quietude, though of quite a different colour?'

Of course, plenty of badly designed and ugly gardens arose from attempts to adapt methods developed in great estates and public parks to a smaller scale. Many writers, like Elizabeth Watts (*Flowers and the Flower Garden*, 1869) encouraged ordinary gardeners to be moderate in their ambitions: 'The plain flower garden, with its border round, its beds of just any convenient shape, its lawn, if there be room for one, and the ease with which its work can be done, is especially suitable...' But it was inevitable that people who had marvelled at the beds and terraces at Sydenham should try to copy their effects at home. Private gardens, too, were often accessible to the public. In 1867, the editor of *The Gardener* noted on a visit to Chatsworth that 'the park and

No doubt the nature of gnomes, as of other such phenomena is in our present state of knowledge or ignorance, very incomprehensible, but it is difficult to see why these useful though occult agencies should be disregarded at the present period of research, especially as it is now acknowledged by many that seeing such things does not indicate mental delusion, but EXTENSION OF FACULTY.

Sir Charles Isham, Bart., *Remarks on Rock Gardens, also Notes on Gnomes*, c.1890.

grounds were swarming with holiday-makers, for it was one of England's great holidays, Whit-Monday. Here were little pale-faced men and women from the cotton factories of Manchester, dark denizens of the Staffordshire potteries, and the sharp, active-looking mechanics of Leeds, Bradford, and Halifax, all brought hither in special trains, and, in the full heyday of an English holiday, rushing through the gorgeously-fitted-up rooms of the ducal mansion—admiring the conservatories, rockeries and fountains...'

Sometimes a property-owner's generosity in opening gardens to the public produced farther-reaching effects than could have been imagined. At Lamport Hall, Northamptonshire, in the 1880s, the colourful Sir Charles Isham, Bart, innocently introduced the garden gnome. When *The Cottage Gardener* described the grounds in 1859, the gardens were mostly typical of the time, but included the already-famous Lamport Rockery, 'grouped and studded with next-to-endless varieties of rock and alpine plants.' Then, to increase the rockery's appeal, and to amuse and edify his visitors, Sir Charles added the revolutionary element: 'The most distinctive feature of the Lamport Rockery is its miniature population: to some this even seems to be the chief attraction... That energetic horticulturist, the late Mr. Loudon having been impressed with the value of such an adjunct

Below and right: The Gnomes of Lamport in about 1890, from Sir Charles Isham's *Remarks on Rock Gardens, also Notes on Gnomes*.

when tastefully introduced, idealised, forty or fifty years since in one of his ponderous volumes, a group of children under some specimens of Pinus nanus, adding remarks on the beauty and interest such a treatment might add gardens. What delight would the realisation of the idea have afforded him, especially the Gnomes.' (*Remarks on Rock Gardens, also Notes on Gnomes.*)

Isham believed that his rockery was the first garden outside Japan to be decorated with figures. Lamport Gnomes were adapted from imported German drawing-room novelties intended for holding matchboxes (and so known as 'Men on Strike'). He positioned them among the miniature boulders and dwarf trees of the rockery to represent the 'mine fairies' and earth spirits of folklore, in which he was a firm believer.

Rock-work had a place in many gardens, either in the form of a romantic 'ferny grot' or as a setting for alpine plants. Its decorative use echoed the *chinoiseries* and rococo ornament that had become popular in the 18th century. The proper style was a matter of controversy, since attempts to reproduce mountain scenery in miniature usually produced ludicrous effects. In 1830 McIntosh wrote: 'Where an imitation at natural rocks is not attempted (and this we would not recommend unless natural circumstances are very favourable, and great taste employed in the erection),

a rock or Alpine garden may be made very pleasing by merely elevating the borders to a convenient height, and covering them with rude stones, blocks or over-burnt bricks, flints, &c, interspersed with a few specimens of mineral substances that may be most conveniently procured, between which the most curious and rare Alpine plants will succeed, if planted in a stratum of soil congenial to their several natures.' Martin Doyle, too, suggests 'the erection of a rude piece of rock-work, which, when raised with taste and judgment, presents a pleasing contrast to the formal and trim parterre. Besides it may be rendered really useful as well as ornamental, by affording a position for those dwarf shrubs and plants which would be overwhelmed amidst the luxuriant vegetation of the flower-borders.' McIntosh's *Flower Garden*, in the edition of 1844, lists fifteen annuals, seventeen biennials, and 104 perennials suitable for rock-planting, some native to Britain, but including many from the Alps, the Pyrenees and America.

Two estates which were particularly noted for their ambitious rock structures were the gardens at Hoole, near Chester, where Lady Boughton designed a model of the mountains of Savoy 'with the valley of Chamouni', and Syon House, where the Duke of Northumberland ordered a reproduction of the wilds of Scotland. Mrs Loudon was not too impressed with this: 'The rock-work at Syon has been compared to the scenery of a highland glen; but I must confess there does not appear to me the slightest resemblance.' (*Gardening for Ladies*.) She complained that its beauties were apt to pass unnoticed beside the conservatory and geometric flower gardens close by.

A renewal of interest in rock-gardening followed the publication of William Robinson's *Alpine Flowers for English Gardens* in 1870. 'In a handsome book...Mr Robinson gives us a valuable work on Alpine flowers,' commented *The Gardener*. 'Such a book was greatly needed, and it appears at an opportune time, just when so many of the lovely flowers, of which the book treats, are surely rising into a most deserved

A dark cave, penetrating into the thickest part of the erection, is not very difficult to construct, and, when encircled with ivy, and inhibited by a pair of horned owls, which may be easily procured, it will form a most interesting object.

C. McIntosh *The Flower Garden*.

Rockwork is a very favourite decoration for gardens and pleasure grounds. Some people may call it a Cockney fancy to pretend to bring wild nature into trim gardens, by building up stones, and planting ferns, trees, sedums, and appropriate vegetation among them, but what matter if the owner likes it, he may do what he likes with his own; and it might be better for us if we were contented to admire all that is good and admirable in our neighbour's garden, aye! and in his character too, without ultra criticism.

Elizabeth Watts, *Flowers and the Flower Garden*, 1869.

Above right: 'Aquarium and Rock-Work in the Gardens of E. Hartford, Esq. From *The Annals of Horticulture*, 1847.
Right: The Dripping Pool' at Glencormac, County Wicklow. From *The Gardeners' Chronicle*, 1884.

popularity. One thing is quite certain, that in the future of popular gardening, Alpine flowers will play an important part, to the great advantage of practical horticulture.' The book was partly a descriptive list of alpines suitable for cultivation in Britain and partly an account of Robinson's 'Little Tour in the Alps' in 1868, with a general outline of rockwork and fernery construction. Many of the illustrations were engraved from photographs of the Lamport rockery. Robinson argued reasonably enough for a style avoiding excess and allowing the plants themselves to be seen at their best. The theme of moderation was repeated by various contributors to Robinson's *Gardening Illustrated* ten years later: 'Avoid shells, quartz, or anything that will lead the mind away from the real object in view, viz., giving each plant the position it most delights in, that is the use of a rockery', and, 'the whole effect should tend to the "rustic". The monstrosities known as "burrs" and "clinkers" should be avoided; gorgeous shells, corals, plaster casts, should be banished from a rockery having any artistic pretensions.'

Robinson's ideas were also influential in the specific area of subtropical bedding and, as Eleanour Sinclair Rohde mentions, he did much to popularise the subtropical garden. In *Gleanings from French Gardens* (1868), *The Parks, Promenades and Gardens of Paris* (1869) and *The Subtropical Garden* (1871), he lent his weight to an already fashionable trend. Since the early 1860s, gardeners had used many of the foliage plants which had previously been treated as stove or greenhouse subjects to add a contrasting element to floral bedding during the summer. David Thomson notes in his *Handy Book of the Flower-Garden*, also published in 1868, that 'It is now

Rockwork. The desire for a Rockery of some kind is now generally evident in most gardens – but unfortunately, from want of attention to the necessities of the plants, and the manner in which they are found in their native state, it often finds issue in the construction of something, which, albeit, is frequently very costly, is neither suitable to the plants, nor satisfactory to true taste. In the first place, a heap of stones is not rockwork, neither will plants thrive in dry dusty soil loosely spread between such – although we have seen numberless cases of the attempt having been made.

Hooper's Gardening Guide, 1883.

Battersea Park, illustrated in Nathan Cole's *The Royal Parks and Gardens of London*, 1887.

several years since, in the pages of *The Scottish Gardener*, I advocated the use of many of the gracefully-foliaged plants which can be wintered in a greenhouse temperature, and that will therefore bear exposure outdoors all summer and autumn with impunity.' The gardens of Battersea Park, which had been enlarged and improved in 1860, were well-known for this type of planting, but Robinson took exception to the way the plans were carried out. Although he had mentioned the 'superb results' produced by 'the able Superintendent' of Battersea in *Gleanings*, a review of *The Subtropical Garden* complained: 'We do not admire the sneering way in which the author speaks of Mr Gibson's labours at Battersea in this particular department of gardening. Mr Gibson has done more by example to inculcate the best manner of subtropical decorations in a few years, than a mere writer on the subject is likely to do in a lifetime.' (*The Gardener*.)

British gardeners were used to treating yuccas, aloes and other tender, bold-foliaged plants as single specimens in favoured situations, but the example of the French encouraged them to experiment more widely. In France—where the style had originated, according to a writer in *The Gardener*, with 'the wealthy nobles like Prince Demidoff'—a prominent feature of the streets and squares was 'the immense quantity of handsome and beautifully-leaved plants used in giving effect to flowers in beds and borders during the summer and autumn months.' Not all the habits of the French, however, were approved of: 'In all cases the beds are elevated, and in many instances most ridiculously, as in those at the Champs Elysées; but this is considered a necessary evil, in order to hide the singing restaurants, so plentiful in these gardens.'

Robinson lists as indispensable to the subtropical enthusiast ricinus (castor-oil plant), canna, polymnia, colocasia, uhdea, wigandia, ferdinanda, yucca, dracaena and palms. Despite a claim in a recent biography that, as a result of his efforts, 'so vanished the preposterous *Musa ensete*, the Abyssinian Banana, and other horrors, he was too much of a gardener to think of any plant as preposterous although he always campaigned against what he saw as the use of a plant in the wrong place. Indeed, he recommends *Musa ensete* as 'one of the most noble plants used in what is termed the subtropical garden', and devotes to it the leading feature in 1879 issue of his weekly *Gardening Illustrated*. The species still merited an entry in the 1909 edition of *The English Flower Garden*. The aralias also became popular, as well as crotons, phormiums, rubber plants *Ficus elastica*) and some annuals grown for their tall habit and showy foliage, notably the Indian hemp (*Cannabis sativa*).

The subtropicals continued in use for many years, usually mixed in with the now-traditional bedding plants. The poet laureate, Alfred Austin, here writing mercifully in prose, described part of a garden in 1897: '...in two of the largest beds I have this year planted three rows of cannae, two rows of white-flowering marguerites, and an edging of the dwarf,

This is, as far as we are aware, the first work devoted to the Wild Garden in which we are happy to meet with Mr Robinson, for he is well versed in all that pertains to the plants by the introduction of which he wishes to enhance the beauty of wild unkept grounds, and to weed from highly-kept gardens such subjects as he justly characterises as too coarse for such positions... There can be little difference of opinion of the desirability of adding the charms of many hardy exotics to our natural grounds and woods; and to those who are desirous of making the effort we say, purchase Mr Robinson's book; it cannot fail to be an efficient aid; and it is, moreover, pleasantly written and handsomely got up.

Review in *The Gardener*, April 1871.

shrubby, never-failing yellow zinnia. In another bed, an oval one, there is a centre of cannae; round these are yellow-flowing marguerites and dwarf bronze-leaved castor-oil plants, placed alternately; and the whole is carpeted with the dark-coloured heliotrope.' (*In Veronica's Garden.*)

The movement away from the true Victorian style during the last decades of the century reflected in, and partly brought about by Robinson's other works, was inevitable. The new generation of gardeners and garden owners who formed his readership were looking for change, and the men whose inventiveness had created the great gardens were gone, their ideas converted into stereotypes. Paxton had died in 1865, Nesfield, one of the last survivors of the Duke of Wellington's army in the Peninsular Wars, in 1881. Six years later, Nesfield's Horticultural Gardens in South Kensington were dismantled. Robinson himself redesigned the flower garden at Shrublands Park, replacing the beds with 'picturesque groups' planted to stay, and substituting lawn for gravel walks. Flamboyant display went out and discreet charm came in.

Robinson was as skilful a propagandist as he was a gardener, and his condemnation of much that had previously been in favour makes persuasive reading. It is easy to forget that he was presenting only one side of an argument. The ideas expressed in *The Wild Garden* and *The English Flower Garden* certainly did plenty to reinvigorate the horticultural scene. But millions had taken pleasure in the style of gardening that he condemned, and, if he inspired the 'modern' gardener, he just as effectively destroyed the reputation of his predecessors.

Charles Kingsley's rectory at Eversley. The garden was commended by William Robinson as modest, simple and charming. From *Gardening Illustrated*, 1879.

Floramania

The conventional picture of the Victorian young lady suggests that her floral interests were not very practical. Many publications encouraged a sentimental attitude, which was characterised by the 'language of flowers'. The fashion for assigning verbal meanings to particular plants and flowers was said to have been started by Lady Mary Wortley Montague in the eighteenth century and based on Turkish traditions, and there were plenty of precedents in folk-customs, as well as in the sixteenth-century 'emblematic' use of flowers with heraldic and religious associations. The 'language' developed to an elaborate degree in the years around 1850, following the appearance in France and Belgium of works such as Martin's *Le Langage des Fleurs*. The many books published in Britain include the Revd Robert Tyas's *Sentiment of Flowers* and *Language and Poetry of Flowers* from Marcus Ward & Co. In his *History of the Christmas Card* (1954), George Buday refers to more than sixty editions of various books produced between the 1820s and 1890s, and notes, 'It may be taken for granted...that amongst the people who exchanged greetings cards at Christmas the emblematic significance of plants and flowers was a known and understood convention, just as the rules of etiquette and contemporary "observances of the best society" were known.' This aspect of floriculture was more the province of general authors like Anne Pratt, who joined with Thomas Miller in compiling *The Language, Associations and Tales of Flowers*, than of horticultural writers, although articles on ancient customs and beliefs sometimes appeared in the periodicals for historical interest. In 1843, *The Gardener and Practical Florist* quoted as a curiosity a seventeenth-century recipe for gilding rosemary—a plant with lasting associations in folklore.

The vocabulary of flower language was necessarily standardised in order that the receiver of a carefully assembled posy could decipher the sentiments of the sender. The origin of most meanings is plain enough—'egotism' for the narcissus, 'sympathy' for the balm and so forth—but there seems no obvious reason why the zinnia should convey 'thoughts

Gilding the leaves of flowers.
A branch of box or rosemary will carry their *leaves gilded a long time faire*, notwithstanding the violence of rain, if you first moisten the leaves with the gumme of Mastick, first dissolved in a hard egg according to art, and leafe gold presently laid thereon. Do this on a summer day, when all the dew is ascended, and when the sun being hot, may presently harden the Masticke, and so bind down the gold fast upon it.

Quoted in *The Gardener and Practical Florist*, 1843.

Left: 'The Lily', engraved from a watercolour by J.J. Jenkins. From *The Illustrated London News*, 1851. *Above:* A later and more prosaic view – Mr James McIntosh pictured with specimens of *Lilium auratum* in *Garden-Work*, 1888.

of absent friends'. Charity is aptly represented by a turnip. Sweet basil is translated in one list both as 'good wishes' and as 'hatred', which might have led to a number of misunderstandings. Sometimes, however, ambiguities could be cleared up by putting a flower in different positions: 'Place a marigold on the head, and it signifies "Mental anguish"; on the bosom, "Indifference".' (Ward's *Language and Poetry of Flowers*). Sending a message was quite a test of ingenuity. Anyone wanting to say 'My fortitude forsook me on your refusal to be mine' had to collect *Dipteracanthus spectabilis*, laburnum, a striped carnation and some four-leaved clover. The urge to reply to 'Our unexpected meeting (lemon geranium) left but transient impressions (a withered white rose)' with the retort 'Vulgar minds soon forget' could be indulged only if an African marigold and some moonwort were to hand.

These notions, better suited to the salon and the parlour than to the garden, represent a convention that is common enough in art and literature: 'The poet and the painter are both indebted to the flower-garden. What simple, yet what elegant and striking metaphors, similes and apostrophes, has not the poet drawn from the Rose, the Tulip, and the Lily!' (Thomas Hogg, *Treatise on the Carnation*.) At the other extreme was the totally unsentimental philosophy of the dedicated florist.

The art of floristry, originally the ·cultivation and improvement of individual flowers, is generally held to have been introduced into Britain by immigrant workers, particularly Flemish weavers escaping religious persecution in the Low Countries. It was already well established in the eighteenth century, but reached its peak in the 1830s. Florists were traditionally of the artisan class—the plants in which they specialised are sometimes described as 'mechanic's flowers'—but, as with other supposedly lower-class pastimes, a good many practitioners could be found in the upper levels of society. *The Young Man's Best Companion* of 1824, a work definitely aimed at the bourgeoisie, gave in a brief gardening section directions for growing many of the florists' flowers, and it would be a mistake to assume that they were never to be found in the pleasure-grounds of the rich. Workers in the industrial towns, however, took to floristry as about the only form of gardening open to them in the restricted spaces of urban living.

The florist was the ultimate 'artificial' gardener, working with a limited number of plants to perfect existing strains and to introduce new and better varieties in the pursuit of agreed standards. In the early 1800s, the list of flowers acceptable to the true enthusiast comprised only the auricula, the pink, the carnation, the tulip, the ranunculus, the hyacinth and the polyanthus. George Glenny maintained in an article written for *The Gardener's Gazette*, 'There are some particular points belonging to all of these, which constitute their claim to distinction. First, they can be raised from seed, and the seedlings produce new varieties; second, they can be propagated so as to perpetuate a new variety when it is produced.' The same applied to other plants which were later admitted, among them the pansy, the dahlia and the calceolaria.

The definition of excellence was arbitrary. 'Who then is to decide the taste by which the floral world is to be governed?' asks Glenny, since there is 'no means of trying a flower as there is a horse, which you may race; a pigeon, that you may fly; a dog, that you may fight; or a bullock, that you may weigh.' The answer, for many years, was Glenny himself, who had started writing in 1832 and regarded himself ever afterwards as the supreme judge of the floral world: 'In Miller's day, it was Miller; in Curtis's day, it was Curtis; and, reader, we can afford to be taunted with a charge of egotism; for no man living can deny the fact, that

153

in our day it is *ourselves. We* have for ten years been prime minister at the court of Flora.'

The system demanded a precise code of 'properties' by which a flower was to be judged. Above all, it was to be regular, with a circular form prescribed as the ideal. Flowers like the rudbeckia, however showy they might be in the border, were anathema to the florist. *The Gardener and Practical Florist*, which carried many contributions from Glenny, illustrated this American introduction, a 'coarse, weedy-looking plant', only in order 'to show the kind of flower that botanists delight in...the florist is for improving; while the botanist does all he can to keep things in a state of uncultivated nature.' Many of the plant varieties produced by intensive breeding shared little in appearance with their original species, and Glenny, in particular, believed that the aim should be, first, to decide on what constituted perfection and, secondly, to develop a flower to match the ideal: 'Now, the difference between the authorities that preceded us, and ourselves, is this—our predecessors looked at the nature of a flower, and estimated the best as perfection...

Ideal forms of florists' flowers from *The Gardener and Practical Florist*, 1843. *Top left*, the pink, with, *top right*, a side view; between them is a perfect petal, which 'should be thick, broad, smooth at the edges, without notch or serrature'. *Centre and bottom left*, side and front views of a ranunculus. *Bottom right*, the polyanthus. *Bottom centre*, a petal which would disqualify a pink, with a rough edge and broken markings.

Properties of flowers
This important subject has been appropriated by one person to himself, and subsequent attempts to supersede him have failed.

The Annals of Horticulture, 1846.

The Ranunculus:
The shape of this admired flower is as attractive as its hues, and on an extensive scale of plantation it is, perhaps, the most gratifying object in the flower garden or pleasure ground. A considerable portion of garden was allotted by the late Lord Downes to this beautiful flower, and a similar gratification was to be found, though on a smaller scale, in the garden of the late Mr Cave, whose collection was sold at auction by his executor for £150.

Martin Doyle, *The Flower Garden*, 1845.

The Rudbeckia, the opposite of the florist's ideal.

we, on the contrary, simply consider what would look the best if we could produce it.'

The properties in each case were listed in detail, covering size, form and colour. The auricula, a plant with a long history in floristry, and one which was especially associated with the Lancashire weavers (as the pink was with the workers of Paisley) is described by *The Gardener and Practical Florist* as having ten 'Properties which constitute Perfection', five relating to the 'pip', or individual floret, and four to the plant as a whole, with the final requirement that a pair put in for exhibition should be as nearly identical as possible. Rival publications put forward their own lists, but all were broadly similar. The editor of *The Gardener and Practical Florist* complained self-righteously in 1843 that a writer in the *The Gardeners' Chronicle* had filched Glenny's prescriptions: 'While he pays us, unwittingly, the compliment of preferring our rules to any body else's, it is only like the pickpocket in the crowd, who preferred taking a particular silk hankerchief which he knew to be the best.'

Development of florists' flowers was so intense that there were vast numbers of named types, some with such minute differences between them that they were distinguishable

155

only by an expert. The ranunculus, bred to achieve its ideal form of 'two thirds of a ball', had more than a thousand varieties. At the height of the fashion for dahlias in 1836, the Young & Penny nursery advertised 493 different named seedlings, from the scarlet Abelard to the buff Zero, at prices between a shilling and 10s. 6d.

The plant which perhaps attracted more attention than any other, the carnation, had been popular in Britain since the early seventeenth century, when it had already become distinct from its original species, *Dianthus caryophyllus*, the clove-scented pink or clove-gillyflower. The gillyflower (its name derived from the French *girofle*, clove, and not from a conjectured corruption of 'July-flower') had been introduced from southern Europe in the middle ages, rather earlier than the pink proper, descendant of another *Dianthus* species, which also became a florists' flower. In a lecture given to the Vale of Evesham Horticultural Society in 1828 and printed later in *The Gardener's Magazine*, Edward Rudge noted that there were 360 'good sorts' listed in Rea's *Flora* of 1676, while in his own day a single Evesham grower had raised over 2,000 seedlings. In his *Treatise* (1820) on the carnation and other flowers, Thomas Hogg gave over 300 different types, all of which he had in cultivation, and in the fifth edition (1832) there are nearly 400. Each was known by its own, usually heroic-sounding name, and that of its raiser—a necessary convention to identify, for example, Colcutt's Emperor, Strong's Emperor and Snook's Emperor. There was a strong line of patriotism, with ten Lord Nelsons (plus a Hero of Trafalgar); nine were named after the Duke of Wellington and three after his wife.

Florists admitted three main types of carnation: the flake and the bizarre, in which the petals were marked with radial stripes, and the picotee, with the colour 'disposed on the outer edges of the petals.' A fourth form, the Painted Lady, with petals coloured red or purple on top and white underneath, never became popular. Purists insisted that the background should be snow-white, and Glenny ruled that 'If the colours run into the white and tinge it, or the white is not pure, the fault is very great, and pouncy spots or specks are highly objectionable.' An exception was made for the yellow picotee, which Hogg describes as difficult to cultivate and more favoured in Europe than in England. But it was, he says, 'constantly imported by the families of the nobility and gentry, in their excursions thither... The late Queen Charlotte and the Princesses, a few years ago, had a very superb collection of yellow Picotees at Frogmore, which were obtained principally from Germany; they were the delight of all who saw them.'

The highly developed carnations and picotees produced flowers of a considerable, and often unwieldy, size. A diameter of two-and-a-half inches was the minimum acceptable, but many were larger. An Irish lady wrote to *The Floricultural Cabinet* in 1835, claiming to have flowered a mulberry-coloured picotee twelve inches in circumference—nearly

Properties of a good Picotée. – It is divided into seven classes. 1. Red, heavy-edged. 2. Red, light-edged. 3. Rose, heavy-edged. 4. Rose, light-edged. 5. Purple, heavy-edged. 6. Purple, light-edged. 7. Yellow grounds, without any distinction as to the breadth of the edge colour.

The characteristics of good *form* are the same as for the Carnation, but with regard to *colour* – 1. It should be clear, distinct, confined exclusively to the edge of the petals, of equal breadth and uniform colour on each, and not running down (called sometimes *feathering* or *barring*), neither should the white ground run through the coloured border to the edge of any one of the petals. 2. The ground must be pure white, without the slightest spot (This rule renders the name, still retained by florists, inappropriate, for *Picote* is the French for spotted).

Disqualification of a Carnation or Picotée. – 1. there be any petal dead or mutilated. – 2. If there be any one petal in which there is no colour – 3. If there be any one petal in which there is no white – 4. If a pod be split down to the sub-calyx. – 5. If a guard petal be badly split. – 6. Notched edges are glaring faults, for which no excellence in other respects compensates.

Florists' Flowers for the Many, c.1860.

Opposite: The carnation and picotee, from *The Gardener and Practical Florist*, 1843. *Left:* Picotee, with, *centre*, a theoretically perfect flower with a circular rise: 'We may be asked where we shall find such a flower, we answer no where; but we hope to find some one day or other, and the nearer any one can approach it the better it will be.'
Top left, two examples of 'correct' picotee petals; *top right*, two 'incorrect' petals.
Right: A bizarre carnation, with white ground and two distinct colours.
Centre, below: Bizarre petals, 'very fine' and 'very bad' specimens.

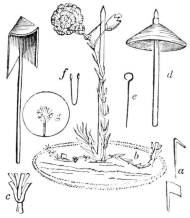

four inches across, and a white and purple form almost as big. Flowers like these inevitably tended to burst their buds, and had to be given artificial help: 'As the buds swell, they must be tied around the middle with a bit of bass-matting, or coarse worsted, and the tips of the calyx, or case of the bud, may be torn down to the bass-matting at each division; it enables the flower to open even instead of its bursting out on one side, and secures a more uniform bloom.' (G. Glenny, *The Culture of Flowers and Plants,* 1861.)

The emerging petals needed almost constant attention, and a sequence of operations was laid down for 'dressing' the perfect flower. A collar of card, supported by a wire loop, was placed round the bud, and the petals arranged for the best effect: 'The lower or large petals, as they open, are brought down on the card to form the outer row, which should be circular. The petals of the next size are brought down over each place where the others join, and form a second row', and so on until the smallest were set upright in the centre to form a crown. Any petals which were deformed or badly marked were pulled out with the pair of tweezers, which, with a small bodkin, constituted the florist's *étui.*

Like the carnation, the tulip had many dedicated admirers. In the same way, distinct types were recognised according to ground colour and marking—rose, byblomen and bizarre,

157

One of the reasons why a tulip assumes so many names, is innocent enough, but it is impossible to deny that it is a very great evil. The breeders from which many standard flowers have been "broke" have got spread among many growers. Each, when he breaks a flower, gives it a name, and thus is the identical variety named in half-a-dozen places at once. In this way has Davey's Trafalgar been called twenty names already, and stands a very good chance of twenty more.

The Gardener and Practical Florist, 1843.

or bizard—the first two patterned with shades of pink or purple on white, the third variously striped on a yellow ground. Dutch growers had other categories, including the brown-and-white Baguettes and the cherry-coloured Incomparable Verports, but these were not much taken up by the English florists, nor were the early-flowering Van Thol varieties. All were derived from the 'Gesnerian' tulips introduced to Europe in the sixteenth century and described by Conrad Gesner, and from *Tulipa suaveolens*, native to eastern Europe. There was little interest in other tulip species, and as late as 1876 F.W. Burbidge complained: 'The Dutch florists raise hundreds of seedling Tulips annually, but, singularly enough, they keep plodding on with the forms of *T. Gesneriana* and *T. suaveolens*, instead of cross-breeding with some of the other distinct species, so as to originate new and more beautiful races.' (*Cultivated Plants, their Propagation and Improvement*.) Unlike carnations, though, tulips acquired markings not from genetic variation but from virus effects. Although they were ignorant of the cause, the nineteenth-century growers were aware that a seedling would produce plain, 'self' flowers for up to eight years before breaking into a patterned form.

The need to wait for long periods to see how 'breeding' or 'mother' tulips would break was one reason for the high prices of bulbs. None approached the enormous sums paid during the Dutch tulip craze two centuries earlier, but a hundred pounds and more could have changed hands for a prize-winning bulb in the 1840s. Glenny mentions a Bethnal Green weaver who bought a tulip for ten pounds, paid

One Christopher Nunn, of Enfield, Middlesex, a noted florist in his day, was eminent for his skill and dexterity in dressing Pinks and Carnations for Prize exhibitions; some will even tell you, that Kit was the father of the art. Upon such occasions he had as many applications to dress flowers, as he had to dress wigs; for he was a barber and friseur by trade, and withal a good-natured, facetious, prating barber, and could both shave and lay Carnation with the greatest nicety. The novices of that day, who, being unacquainted with his secret art, trusted to Dame Nature to open, expand, and perfect their flowers, were no match for Nunez: for he began where she left off, and perfected what she had left imperfect. – His arrangement and disposition of the petals were admirable, and astonished those novices. Kit's art of dressing is still an enviable art, and attainable only by few.

Hogg, *Treatise on the Growth and Culture of the Carnation, etc.*, 1832 (fifth edition).

158

Above: Hyacinth illustrated in *The Gardener and Practical Florist*, 1843. George Glenny accused Dr Lindley of pirating the engraving for an article in *The Gardeners' Chronicle*, until it was pointed out that the *Chronicle* piece had first appeared two years before his own.

in weekly instalments: 'Although this man's family were almost wanting common necessaries, he never missed payment of the three shillings until the debt was satisfied.' An 'Old Florist' tells the same story in *The Annals of Horticulture* a few years later as a caution against buying on credit; this time it is a five-pound tulip, five shillings at a time—'the facilities afforded him of indulging in his fancy, without first getting the money, was his ruin.' Clearly, tulips were grown by working men only with considerable sacrifice, and Thomas Hogg included a fairly short account of them in his *Treatise*: 'A moderate collection of choice Tulips,—of those beautiful, those exquisitely beautiful flowers, which are the pride and boast of every amateur who grows them, could not be purchased for a sum much less than one thousand pounds, at the usual catalogue prices, nor obtained and got together till after years of patient search and unwearied labour.' In 1834, Loudon suggested that tulips were becoming more widely grown and quoted Hogg's view that a hundred pounds then would buy what would have cost £250 ten or twelve years before.

The tulip-fancier flowered his bulbs in a specially prepared bed. They were set out, normally in rows of seven, and graded according to size—'first-row' varieties on the outside, 'fourth-rows' in the middle. A standard six inches between plants brought the width to just over four feet, so that a bed twenty-five feet long, 'quite enough for a private first-rate collection', held 350 individual specimens. This represented a fair investment even if they were established types costing a few shillings each.

Bulbs were arranged along the rows to produce a regular sequence of colours, successive rows beginning with a rose, a byblomen or a bizarre, giving a mixture that was 'perfectly surprising'. Correct identification was essential to the system, so suppliers were expected to label each one precisely, as: 'Claudiana, 4th row, rose' or 'Duke of Clarence, 4th row, bizard'. At the end of the flowering season, the bulbs were lifted and stored for replanting in November, and again had to be marked. One answer to the storage problem was the tulip-case recommended by Mr Groom, Florist, of Walworth, to readers of *The Gardener's Magazine* in 1827: 'It having been frequently remarked to me by gentlemen purchasing tulips, and indeed all named flowers, that they had great difficulty in keeping them in order under their different names, I shall feel obliged by your inserting the annexed plan of my tulip-case in your valuable Magazine.' The arrangement of shallow, compartmented drawers meant that up to 700 bulbs could be kept without risk of confusion in a chest measuring less than four feet by three, and two feet deep.

Florists were fond of ingenious contrivances. In the pursuit of their particular kind of excellence it was not the overall effect that mattered, as in the general flower-garden, but the individual specimen, and anything which helped to bring it to perfection was welcome. Protection against the

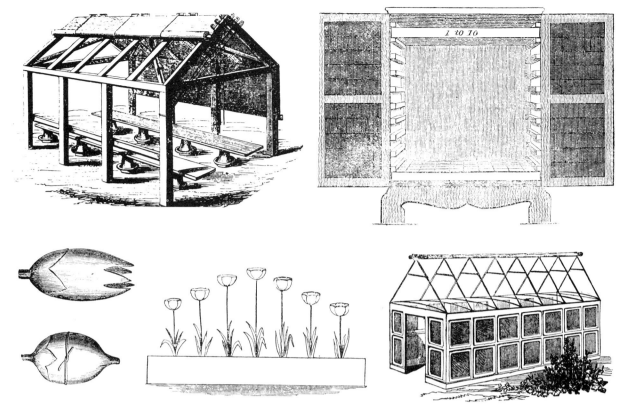

weather was a preoccupation, and hand-lights, frames, mats and blankets were essential equipment for the poorest enthusiasts, while the more affluent erected all sorts of structures over their beds or pots, from a row of iron hoops driven into the ground and covered when necessary with lengths of cloth, to wooden-framed 'tulip-houses' fitted with roller blinds to keep out the rain and hail or to shade the developing flowers from too much sun. The most elaborate frames were large enough to allow for a path around the bed and a row of seats at the end for admiring visitors.

The devotion of amateur growers to their plants was legendary. The 'Old Florist' of the *Annals* described the progress of a young man whom he had rescued from debt and set upon the proper course of the art. An unscrupulous dealer, Gabel, had 'inveigled the boy' into buying a bed of inferior tulips for twenty pounds, these were returned and better ones found at half the price. Afterwards, 'The tulip bloom came round, and he had a pretty good one; but as to a night's rest, there was hardly such a thing for himself or anybody else. He was out at twelve or one o'clock to see that all was right; and if there was the least indication of wind or frost, for weeks before they opened, he would get up and cover them in the night with a second layer of mats. He often walked to Mr Austin's, at Clapham, to see his flowers, and back to breakfast, though it was five miles from his own flowers, and a bad time of the day... One severe week, just before they had begun to show their shapes, he had actually taken both blankets off the bed, and laid

Above left: Covered blooming-stage for carnations, from Charles McIntosh's *The Flower Garden*, 1838. The supports rest in pans of water to keep out earwigs.
Above right: Mr H. Groom's design for a tulip-case, submitted to *The Gardener's Magazine*, 1827; there is space for ten drawers, each holding 70 individual bulbs.
Below left: A carnation bud cut to avoid bursting, and one tied with thread. From McIntosh's *The Flower Garden*.
Below centre: Section of a tulip bed, from *The Gardener and Practical Florist*, 1843.
Below right: Shelter for a tulip bed from *The Gardener and Practical Florist*, 1843; the framework could be covered with canvas or matting.

Right: Florists' flowers from Thomas Hogg's *Treatise on the Growth and Culture of the Carnation, etc.*, 1832 edition. *Above*, yellow picotee and polyanthus; *below*, tulip and bizarre carnation.

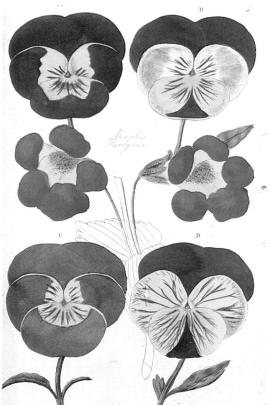

Viola Banksiana

1. *Passiflora Loudoniana* — 2. *Adesmia Loudonia*.
3. *Isopogon Loudoni* — 4. *Loudonia aurea*.

An unwelcome visitor to the tulip-bed, by Robert Seymour (1800-36) from *Sketches by Seymour*, Volume IV, c.1835.

Opposite page, above: The rockery in the Horticultural Society's gardens at Chiswick in the 1850s.
Below left: A plate from *The Floricultural Cabinet,* 1836: 'The panseys in the plate of the present number are seedlings raised by Mr. Barratt, Nurseryman, Wakefield.' The mimulus in the centre was a variety *'Ranbyana'* raised by the Dowager Duchess of Newcastle's gardener at Ranby Hall, Lincolnshire.
Below right: The frontispiece of Mrs Loudon's *The Ladies' Companion to the Flower Garden,* 1841: 'As this was the only one of my works in which any assistance was given to me by my late deeply lamented husband, it has afforded me some consolation to collect in the frontispiece all the plants that have been named in honour of him.'

The high prices that have for many years been affixed to Tulips in the printed catalogues of our florists are so deterring and repulsive of the fancy, that persons with a taste and fondness for this flower are afraid to indulge and enter into it.

T. Hogg *Treatise on the Growth and Culture of the Carnation, etc.,* 1832(fifth edition).

Protecting a dahlia: 'it is quite certain that a few hours' hot sun, or a cold gusty wind, distresses the blooms of a Dahlia very much.' From *The Gardener and Practical Florist,* 1843.

Have you seen the hounds this way, my good man? Hounds? Dogs, I mean, you know what a pack of hounds are, don't you?

without any.' The young protégé's early death, though unconnected with this exploit, perhaps inspired the many tales of florists dying of cold while their budding auriculas snuggled under the bedclothes.

A later writer recalled old times when the florist passed 'whole days, ardent as a young lover watching the changing emotions of his mistress, in admiring the colours of a ranunculus, the beauty and fragrance of a hyacinth, or trembling like the aforesaid lover lest a rival should injure the bloom of a favoured auricula,' and told how a retired tradesman 'infected with the floramania' suffered a severe attack of rheumatic gout after rushing about in his nightshirt to protect his flowers from a 'pitiless pelting storm.' (*Beeton's Book of Garden Management.*)

Competition was the essence of floristry, and the spring and summer months were filled with shows held all over the country. Some were arranged by dealers, the 'floricultural foxes' like Gabel, but most were organised by the local

161

florists' clubs which had developed during the eighteenth century. The clubs, often based in public houses, held regular meetings where members could eat and drink while trading plants and information, discussing activities in the floral world or listening to lectures. *The Gardener's Magazine* for 1826 contains an account of the Islington Florists' Society, which claimed to be 'the parent Society of all others that have of late been established in the vicinity of the metropolis,' having started about fifty years before. Meetings were first held at the Barley Mow in Troy Lane, then at the Britannia, which became a famous venue for shows. Later the society moved to the Canonbury Tavern, and to the King's Head in what is now Upper Street. 'The shows of flowers at this Society' wrote the Secretary, Mr Greig, 'consist of auriculas and carnations, and the prizes are adjudged under the regulations...the first prize being a silver cup, of the value of five guineas. The Society has always been supported by many amateur growers, and, generally speaking, (their enthusiastic fondness for the flowers inducing the greatest care in the growth of them), they have borne away the prize from the regular dealer.'

Prizes were modest—a cup, a medal, a silver spoon or a few pounds—and bore no relation to the time and money spent on bringing a flower to the show bench. Entries came from amateurs with a handful of plants, and from professionals with their selected best out of a stock of thousands. Both were keen to be noticed; apart from the prestige of winning, there was the chance that a new strain would become a valuable property. The North was more generous, in quantity at least, than the rest of the country. At the Lancaster show in 1827, there were 32 prizes for auriculas, while Manchester gave 40 for carnations, compared with only five offered at Windsor. As well as competing among themselves, members clubbed together to challenge rival groups for much higher stakes. The Islington Society proposed 'That each member will, on a day in July next, to be agreed upon, shew a pan of carnations, consisting of twelve blooms, the produce of their own gardens, (and according with the rules of the Islington Society), against the same number of gentlemen from any part of the kingdom, for any sum not exceeding £100.' In 1836, the East London Ranuncula Society at the Salmon and Ball in Cambridge Heath Road issued a similar challenge to ranunculus growers for twenty pounds or upwards.

Since success or failure might depend on the position of a single petal, exhibitors devised cases for carrying the flowers to the shows and stands for displaying them at their best. To avoid unfair comparisons, many societies insisted that they should be shown in standard trays or boxes. At the shows themselves there were inevitably accusations of cheating and of unfair judging, although the rules, at any rate those of the Islington Society as quoted by Hogg, were strict enough. Each member had to take his seat after he had brought in his exhibit, and not leave it 'until the flowers have

The rising buds confirm the grower's hopes and fears; the particular hue of the green, then the indication of stripes – and lastly, the opening flowers crown his labours... His friends now begin to call on him; he is as great among his flowers as an emperor in the midst of his court; he feeds upon their admiration. No woman more susceptible of flattery; yet there is little of flattery in a tulip-bed: the gentleman and the clown are equally pleased with the scene before them and all the admiration of the splendid bed comes from the heart. In short we know of hardly any but the tulip fancy that occupies so much time so agreeably, we admit that floriculture, in all its branches, has its charms, and that we have felt their influence; but they who do not grow tulips know nothing of the best and brightest hours of a florist's life.

'The Tulip Fancier', *The Gardener and Practical Florist*, 1843.

Tulips are not generally gathered and shown in competition in the neighbourhood of London, though they are in Lancashire, and other parts of the country, and have been occasionally so near the metropolis. The practice of florists with respect to this flower, is to appoint particular days to visit celebrated collections. A number of connoisseurs then assemble, compare, criticise, exchange and purchase, and afterwards dine together &c.

The Gardener's Magazine ,1826.

Auriculas were favourites with him, and he was successful with them; and he has walked to the Greyhound, at Dulwich, with two boxes formed to hold one pot each, and shut up in front, and carried them the whole distance with a yoke, like a milkman carries his pails – we never dreamed of Dulwich omnibuses at the time – twice he did this before he was successful; but, nothing daunted, he succeeded.

'The Floricultural Enthusiast' by An Old Florist, in *The Annals of Horticulture* 1847.

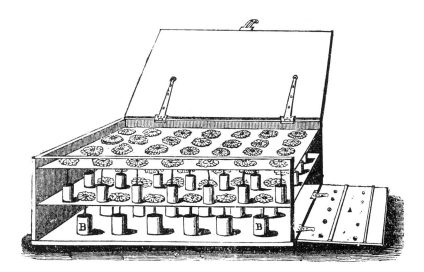

Carrying case for flowers from *The Floricultural Cabinet*, 1836: 'The box is of deal and can be made by any village carpenter... This mode of conveyance has given general satisfaction to those acquainted with it.' The cylinders of tin (B) were filled with moist sand.

been brought into the dining-room, and have passed round the table, beginning on the president's right hand, and returning to his left, in order that each person may distinctly view them.' Anyone questioning the decisions of the judges was liable to a fine of a guinea; improper handling of the blossoms cost a pound.

The rigid tables of points laid down by George Glenny and other authorities, if they were adhered to, at least meant that competitors knew what they had to aim for. *The Gardener and Practical Florist* thought that some societies were so vague in their conditions that 'winning exhibitors know not why they win, and losing candidates for the honours are as ignorant of the reasons why they lose,' and commended the example of the Ipswich Cucumber Society, where almost the only criterion was the length of the exhibit: 'The judges at the Ipswich Society have no right to be in doubt an instant.' Gooseberry-growers in the North and the Midlands, whose clubs and shows were closely linked to those of the florists, similarly avoided problems by judging prize exhibits solely on the weight of the fruit. The Metropolitan Society of Florists and Amateurs in which Glenny was a leading figure, 'published for each flower a standard of perfection. An exhibitor knew as well as the judge who had to decide, whether he would lose or win, and unless a man had overlooked some blemish, which the judge discovered, he was not often disappointed.'

Floristry seems to have been exclusively a man's business. In 1831 *The Suffolk Chronicle* complained of horticultural societies in general: 'Ladies were excluded from the dinner and dessert provided for the male subscribers... Why are we not permitted to obtain the benefit of their judgement on the horticulturist's labours?' But women were occasionally credited with achievements in plant-breeding. Lady Mary Bennet, a daughter of Lord Tankerville who became the second wife of Sir Charles Monck, was instrumental in the development of the pansy as a florists' flower after a Hammersmith nurseryman, James Lee, admired a bed of the annual heartsease, *Viola tricolor*, in her garden at Walton-on-

Our English florists have also raised Tulips for which high prices have been obtained, and now rival the Dutch in this fascinating class of flowers. They have for some years paid much attention to raising them from seed, and it may not be uninteresting to state a few of the earliest and most celebrated English raisers. A Rev. Mr Wood, of City Gardens, City-road, who died about the year 1805, left behind him a very fine collection of Tulips. They were sold in the first instance to Mr Wm. Gabel, and by him returned in a very disordered state, and sold to Mr Drinkwater and Mr Davis, who had gardens in the same vicinity. It is supposed that the Tulip called Strong's King, so celebrated in the south, was broken from one of his breeders. Mr Pearson, of Chilwell near Nottingham, also stood high for a short time; but other varieties were raised which threw him in the background. Mr Austin, of Clapton, raised breeders, but none of much note. Mr Holmes raised some fine varieties, one of which, Louis XVIII, was sold to John Goldham, Esq., of Pentonville, for £42; and the whole of the stock is in that gentleman's possession.

John Slater *The Amateur Florists' Guide*, 1859.

Thames. In 1813 or 1814, Lady Mary's gardener, Richardson, and Lee's foreman were encouraged to experiment by crossing the heartsease with the perennial form, *Viola lutea*, and a large blue variety brought from Holland. This story is given by many writers, including the Loudons, and by McIntosh, who grew pansies from 1826 and 'obtained a very considerable number of new varieties.'

An alternative version attributes the early development of the show pansy to Lord Gambier's gardener, Thompson. His claim to have originated the breed rests mainly on an article in *The Floricultural Cabinet* of 1841, and an account in *Flora's World* a couple of years later. According to a writer in the 1843 *Gardener and Practical Florist*, who seems to suggest that Thompson was not entirely reliable, 'he talks about his ever to be lamented master having requested him, eight and twenty years ago, to cultivate heartsease, and of his dutiful undertaking to comply with the request. He informs us that he collected all he could; saved seed, raised plants, and the first that pleased his master he named "Lady Gambier".' Certainly, if Thompson shared the attributes of his employer, he would have been an unsatisfactory source—Admiral Lord Gambier, described by Lord Cochrane as 'a canting and hypocritical Methodist', was a naval officer more at home on land, who survived an accusation of incompetence by insisting on a court-martial, at which, as the *Dictionary of National Biography* puts it, he was acquitted 'after a grossly partial trial.' He arranged for one of his closest friends to preside over the court, and for all the prosecution witnesses to be absent on foreign service; hence his exploits 'have given his name a distinction not altogether glorious.'

Even if he was not the first to see its potential, Thompson was mainly responsible for the popularity of the pansy among florists by passing on his best varieties to other growers. Glenny called him the 'father of the fancy'. Pansies were widely grown for some years—Mrs Loudon mentions a mania from 1835 to 1838—but dealers tried to promote too many inferior strains at high prices. After a few seasons when 'respectable raisers and dealers' had been 'doing nothing but wait for better times', the market settled down. The 1845 edition of McIntosh's *Flower Garden* gives a list of 354 recommended sorts, and most of them could be bought for between one and five shillings. The pansy was an ideal example of a florist's flower. The original heartsease species were small, discreetly coloured and irregular, but they hybridised freely and were easily propagated, providing show blooms that were satisfyingly large, bright and, in theory, perfectly shaped.

Exploitation by dealers was one of the main reasons for the decline of floriculture in general in the 1840s. The intention of the founders of large, centralised societies had been to benefit both commercial and amateur interests, but, although they succeeded for a time in dispelling the unnecessary mystique of floristry and exposing the malpractices associated with it, the professionals resented the autocratic

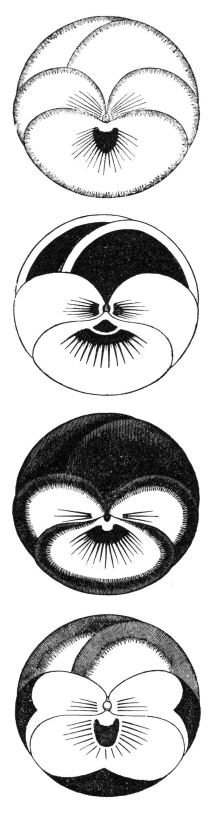

'Varieties of style in the Pansey' as observed by *The Gardener and Practical Florist*, 1843.

'A representation of a show-room of the most perfect construction' in *The Gardener and Practical Florist*, 1843.

When I, said the lecturer, first knew Heartsease, this was the character, (handing about at the time a diagram of the original form,) and when I ventured to say that flower should be round, I was laughed at; nevertheless, it was not many years before I produced one myself, and the laugh went the other way.

George Glenny, lecturing to the Royal Western Literary Society in 1843.

manner in which the societies were governed and felt that they raised too many obstacles in their business dealings. The Metropolitan was particularly severe in its testing of new varieties, and tended to exclude as 'mere novelties' many of the strains which dealers hoped would be most profitable, and Glenny's argumentative nature contributed to the ill-feeling. Even *The Gardener and Practical Florist* seems to have been embarrassed: 'We consider Mr Glenny's papers among the most valuable we have, when he confines himself to Floriculture, or, indeed, to any practical subject; and, were it not for the difficulty of getting him to write without censuring somebody else, we should have a good deal more of his writing than we have.' There were similar problems at the Friendly Society of Florists, founded like the Metropolitan in 1832, whose president, John Goldham, 'king of florists', had earlier been described by Loudon: 'This gentleman is actively engaged a great part of the day, and we may say night, in effecting the most useful reforms in the fish-market at Billingsgate, and the remainder of his time he devotes to the carrying on of what we cannot better designate, than by calling a tulip manufactory, at Pentonville.' (*The Gardener's Magazine*, 1827.)

165

The degeneration of floristry was inevitable once it became more than a private obsession shared by small groups of enthusiasts. The feeling of brotherhood which had been an essential feature of the original florists' clubs was gradually lost, and the elders of the fancy grumbled at its increasing commercialisation and looked back nostalgically over the past. The societies lost much of their membership not only because the dealers found that the pickings were less rich than they had anticipated, but because aspiring amateurs became frustrated and disillusioned as they saw the same small circle of growers take the prizes at show after show.

The Gardener and Practical Florist was keen to bring back the spirit of the early 1830s: 'The necessity of making some effort to rouse the dormant energies of Florists would be at once apparent, if we could refer our readers back to the manner in which it was revived in 1832, and we doubt not, that were the means that were then so successful applied now, they would produce the same results.' But the circumstances were no longer favourable in the 1840s. Apart from the disagreements in the narrow world of floriculture, the wider economic climate, which had improved after the wartime slump at the beginning of the century, had worsened again. *The Gardener and Practical Florist* itself admitted that there was a 'general depression that affects the trade in luxuries'. The nursery business suffered more than other trades, and many firms collapsed: 'Several of the most respectable concerns have been consigned to the hammer this autumn [1842], and more yet are destined to undergo spoliation under the influence of the same knock down fiats.'

In spite of various attempts to re-invigorate the fancy, which included the proposed setting-up of a Central Board of Florists, the dedicated passion of earlier years had been dissipated, and the gradual spread of urban building deprived the city gardeners of the space to practise their art.

But let me ask the numerous exhibitors in this country, how many societies are there got up by men for their own benefit? Have your readers never observed a gardener or a nurseryman in some village, begging of the public all around him for subscriptions in aid of a floral show? a list of prizes offered to suit his own garden? a town hall, or a school room, spread all over with his nursery stock? the majority of prizes awarded for his own plants? the quality of the prizes made to suit his own book – and the quantity nicely adjusted to balance the receipts? In such cases there is little done for morals – nothing for science.

Again, have not some of your readers observed the workings of societies at public-houses, where the established florists' flowers are shown, by all the members who grow them? There have been known many strange doings at such; the begging, borrowing, or stealing of flowers to help out a stand; the disguising of a bloom gone by, or even the making of one flower of the fragments of several; the contriving that some friend who knows the flowers shall be accidentally there, and shaking hands as if he had not been seen for a twelve months, congratulating the meeting upon his fortunate visit, because he's an excellent judge, and thus making sure of the prize! These and fifty more things, are too familiar, and I fear that they engender an increasing laxity of morals.

'A Country Clergyman' in *The Gardener and Practical Florist*.

Fuchsia macrantha, sent to Veitch and Son of Exeter by their collector in South America, Mr W. Lobb, in 1846. From *The Annals of Horticulture*, which remarked: 'Florists have attempted to bring the Fuchsia under cognizance of their rigid rules, but with such a variety of original forms, it is no wonder that they have been less successful in moulding this flower to a "standard" than most others to which their attention has been directed.'

Illustration to 'Florists' Flowers' in
The Annals of Horticulture, 1847:
calceolaria, picotee, dahlia, pansies,
tulip and auricula.

The Hollyhock is not, and never
can be a florists' flower, any
more than a horse can be a lap
dog. It is essentially an out-door
plant. Its properties are almost
limited to the form of the plant.
A lady would as soon think of
having a pig in a parlour, as a
ramping spike of Hollyhock in a
bouquet; and even a coachman,
who on state days is expected to
wear a nosegay as large as a
cauliflower, would look
awkward with six feet of
Hollyhock stuck in his button
hole.

The Gardener and Practical Florist,
1843.

The flowers themselves never lost their popularity—descriptions of florists' flowers were included in books and periodicals all through the nineteenth century, while Glenny's 'Properties', collected together in *The Culture of Flowers and Plants*, still provided a standard of reference many years later. The list, however, expanded to cover plants which the rigorous florist would never have admitted. *The Cottage Gardener* of 1856 mentions the antirrhinum, geranium, fuchsia, petunia, lobelia and verbena, as well as the traditional flowers, adding the hollyhock, scorned by purists not long before. The line between floristry and flower-gardening became blurred, most of the specialist societies and shows disappeared, and their function was absorbed into the more broadly-based organisations. Some, such as the Scottish Pansy Society, founded in 1845, survived independently, and there was something of a revival around 1860. *The Cottage Gardener* in 1861, campaigning for a national exhibition of auriculas, began: 'Unmistakeable signs are manifesting themselves in various quarters that my old friends and favourites, florists' flowers, are about to raise their heads once more, and that there will be found shortly many who will not begrudge the time and trouble necessary for their proper cultivation.' The author of this article, the Revd H.H. Dombrain, was responsible for starting a new Metropolitan Floral Society in 1870, with the express purpose of encouraging interest in old-style floristry. The Society's first show was staged at the Crystal Palace in September, and the Committee reported at the beginning of 1871 that 'their movements for the ensuing year must depend greatly on the amount of support they obtain; it is their wish not only to hold the Autumn Show at the Crystal Palace, but also to offer prizes for the other flowers named in their prospectus at some of the metropolitan exhibitions.' They sponsored awards for auriculas at the Royal Horticultural Society in April, and later for pansies, tulips, ranunculuses, carnations,

pinks and picotees. David Thomson noted in his magazine *The Gardener*: 'We gladly give these remarks and lists a place in our pages, as we desire to aid in reviving a taste for these now rather neglected beauties.'

A general flower show – The Horticultural and Floral Exhibition at the Royal Old Wells, Cheltenham in 1851. From *The Illustrated London News*.

The practice of combining specialist and general shows was increasingly common. The National Tulip Society, which met in a different place each year, held a notably successful exhibition in 1870 in conjunction with the first ever Cambridge Horticultural Show. Four years later, there was a move to establish a Pelargonium Society, again under Royal Horticultural auspices. Many of the most active figures in the revivalist tendency seem to have been ministers of the church. The best remembered was the Revd S. Reynolds Hole of Caunton in Nottinghamshire, later Dean of Rochester, who was ready to encourage gardening in any form, in the belief that it contributed even more to human happiness than art, music or hunting, and was an admirer of florists' flowers though not a grower of them. He remarked that 'The carnation requires the skill of an expert, and the patient devotion of "a man who would sit up all night with a sick cactus".' He was, however, fanatical about roses, which he grew, exhibited and wrote about with passionate conviction. His books and articles, a mixture of expert advice and anecdote, attracted a wide readership and gave him the reputation, according to *The Gardener*, of 'a true cosmopolitan —a man with a genial loving heart, and broad, generous sympathies: such men are at once the glory and the boast of Floriculture.'

Hole began his book on the rose, serialised in *The Gardener* in 1868, with the claim that over a period of twenty years he had won 'more than thirty cups "open to all England", with a multiplicity of money prizes', had originated the first show devoted to roses only, and had 'attended since that time

'To change white roses into red ones – a piece of parlour magic transferred to the garden. Sprinkle the petals with aniline crystals and amaze the audience by spraying the rose with eau-de-Cologne from a vaporiser: 'those connected with a finger-ring enable the performance to be most mysteriously accomplished – the delicate white petals can be promptly suffused with a rich crimson blush.' From *Scientific Mysteries*, 1891.

Those who look upon the thousands of houses which now cover the space that used to boast of the gaudy Tulip-beds of hundreds of working men, would scarcely think it possible to have made so great a change; but there are many small gardens, even now, in the Mile-end-road, with their canvass houses, which, in the season, look like an encampment, but which are doomed to give place to brick and mortar dwellings, and its present occupants must be scattered far and wide, or give up the innocent and healthful pursuit of gardening. The distribution of the occupants of small gardens has been large, and for some years gradual; first, one giving place, then another, to the new buildings, which cover almost every once vacant place; and unless something be done to provide the mechanic with the means of indulging the practice of Floriculture, he will have recourse to the public-house and the skittle-ground, for less healthy amusements.

The Annals of Horticulture, 1846.

Left:
Pot-grown rose from *The Gardener and Practical Florist*, 1843. In *The Rose Amateur's Guide* (1872) Thomas Rivers wrote: 'it is now the fashion for Horticultural Societies to offer prizes for "roses in pots"... I must here caution the reader that occasional disappointment must be expected in growing them in pots for exhibition, as roses, like facts, are stubborn things.' Roses were usually shown as cut flowers.

nearly all the great Rose shows, either as judge or as an exhibitor.' The first Grand National Exhibition of Roses was held at St James's Hall, London on 1st July 1858, with the Revd S.R. Hole as Honorary Secretary. For a reviewer in *The Cottage Gardener*, recalled by Hole years later as 'dear, quaint, old Donald Beaton,' the gaiety of the proceedings proved too much: 'The Hall was crowded, and ladies were industriously noting the names; but I was compelled to leave the Hall early in the afternoon, being almost stunned with the horrid noise and jingling of the band, which had no sort of business there, but to satisfy a cockneyfied taste for outlandish noises.'

The rose show moved to the Crystal Palace in 1860, where Beaton found conditions slightly easier, despite the pressure of 16,312 visitors in the day. He complained only that some of the exhibits were in 'nasty, dirty, slimy pots'. The Revd Hole won a second prize and a third. He was a member of the committee which met in 1862 to set up the Birmingham Rose Show, and a regular competitor at the other provincial shows which followed London's example. He scored two firsts at the inaugural Manchester event in 1871, shortly after a narrow success over a fellow cleric, the Revd Pochin, on his home ground at Newark. His display there was reported as not quite up to his usual mark, because of the weather. He appears to have missed out Hereford, where it was left to the Revds Arkwright, Camm and Smythe to uphold the honour of the church.

Part of the appeal of the rose was that, however intensively it was bred, it never acquired the apparent artificiality of a florists' flower. Reynolds Hole observed that his 'Queen of all Flowers and Empress of all the Gardens...indignantly declines to be "improved".' The prevailing horticultural feeling in the last decades of the century was unsympathetic to ideas of improvement and artificiality, though, paradoxically, one of the least natural-looking of popular flowers, the amaryllis, was being hybridised from various *Hippeastrum* species at the same time as it became fashionable to disparage the florists. A regular contributor to *The Gardeners' Chronicle* wrote in 1884: 'It seems to me rude and unthankful in the highest degree to speak or write of the florist as one who has abused or spoiled, rather than aided Nature in improving her own handiwork,' and quoted one of the critics of the art on the subject of exhibition chrysanthemums: 'They are altogether repellent, rather than attractive, to tasteful and artistic people.'

In time, the name florist was transferred to shop-keepers and flower-arrangers, while the 'florist proper' was dismissed as a man 'good for nothing else but pottering over a few fanciful flowers.' But florists' windows and flower gardens would be the poorer without the work of the old enthusiasts and their philosophy of combining Nature and Art.

> I've been to all the flower shows, north, south, and
>   east, and west,
> By rails and roads, with huge van loads of plants I
>   love the best;
> From dusk to dawn, through night to morn, I've
>   dozed 'mid clank and din,
> And woke with cramp in both my legs, and bristles on
>   my chin.
> I'm a poor, used up exhibitor,
> Knocked out of present time.
>
> Here comes my wife! Now, on my life, of Hebes she
>   is queen;
> My big prize cup she's filling up with "Bass" of
>   golden sheen—
> Delicious! I'm myself once more; and all I want
>   to know,
> Is where and when we show again? hurrah for that
>   next show!
> I'm a fine, revived exhibitor,
> Quite up to present times.

Two verses from Dean Hole's 'Song of the Exhibitor'.

Cast-iron plant-stage made by Boulton & Co., Norwich. From Shirley Hibberd's *The Amateur's Greenhouse and Conservatory*, 1873.

The Garden Indoors

Palmerston's government passed the Smoke Nuisance Act in 1853. The spread of industrialisation, with thousands of coal-powered factories and foundries powered by coal, and the growth of densely-populated towns using coal for domestic heating had caused an uncontrollable pollution problem. The British economy depended on coal, already consuming fifteen million tons a year in the early 1830s, and the rate of use increased rapidly throughout the middle years of the century. In 1866, the geologist Joseph Holdsworth saw the hand of the Almighty not just in the way that the deposits were laid down in the Carboniferous epoch for the future service of mankind, but in the fact that He had chosen to lay down so many of them in His favoured land: 'Whilst we ourselves are intently occupied in the extraction of our 100 million tons of coal in a year from the dark recesses of the land, we become the unconscious agents of Providential designs. England herself is evidently destined by nature long to perform a great, if not leading, part in the sublime and gracious scheme of the Divine mind...' (*On the Extension of English Coalfields.*)

The Palmerston Act attempted to impose controls on the emission of smoke from industrial premises, but, though it led to better-designed and more economical furnaces, its effect in reducing the fogs that hung over British cities for many days in the year was only partial. The atmosphere in London, Birmingham, Glasgow, Manchester and other centres continued to poison their inhabitants, and the sulphurous fumes affected plants as well as people. Londoners found that they had to escape to Sydenham to enjoy clean air and healthy plants, and gardeners in the Midlands and the North suffered increasingly appalling conditions. The fog and smoke of the manufacturing towns was yet another factor which brought about the decline of floristry in the 1840s and 1850s.

One solution for the urban plant-lover was the closed glass 'Wardian' case. In 1829, Nathaniel Bagshaw Ward, a doctor and accomplished amateur botanist, discovered the

Many years ago, we accepted an invitation to visit a gentleman living in the very centre of the densest part of London, – a square, only second in its smoky atmosphere to the celebrated square in which Mr Dickens has placed the Cherrible Brothers, and their factotum, Tim Linkinwater. We were ushered into a room well enough as to size, but in which darkness was nearly visible. Here we found every window occupied by a glass case, in which plants were growing in a manner which astonished us; ferns of the greenest and freshest hue; orchids, such as we have rarely seen surpassed, were growing there, redolent of health and vigour; and we were told, to our great surprise, that the cases were hermetically sealed, and that no water had been administered for many months. This was the first we had seen of the Wardian cases, since so celebrated.

Beeton's Book of Garden Management

Wardian case illustrated by Louisa Johnson in *Every Lady Her Own Flower Gardener*, 1845 edition.

principle of what would now be called a micro-climate when stray fern spores germinated and grew for four years in a sealed bottle which had contained a pupating moth. He experimented with larger glass boxes and found that the plants inside them thrived, while unprotected specimens soon succumbed to the London atmosphere. The cases created an environment of constant humidity and temperature. Outdoors, the cases kept out the worst of the smoke-filled air, and (more often) indoors they excluded fumes from coal fires and gas-jets.

As a trial of the system, Ward sent two cases to Australia and back. The contents survived a rigorous voyage round Cape Horn and through the tropics. Salty air, lack of fresh water, and rough handling usually killed a high proportion of plants carried on board ship, but the introduction of Wardian-type containers dramatically lowered the general mortality. Robert Fortune sent twenty thousand tea seedlings from China to India, and plants of the banana *Musa cavendishii* travelled safely from Chatsworth to the islands of the South Pacific. In 1851 *The Illustrated London News* noted: 'Some years ago we remember to have seen the vessel about to start to survey the settlement of Adelaide, in Australia, and we were much delighted to see two or three of these cases filled with small gooseberry and currant trees, in order that the emigrants might enjoy those delicious fruits which we have in such perfection in this country; and now not a

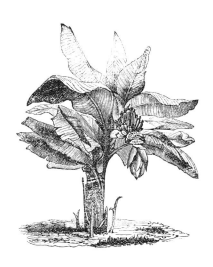

Orange orchard at Parramatta, New South Wales, in the 1870s. Gardens were established here by the colonial administration at the end of the eighteenth century, and it was the home of Australia's first Agricultural and Horticultural Society. The use of Wardian cases greatly simplified the exchange of plants between Britain and her colonies. The Horticultural Society in London received regular consignments of new species from New South Wales and from Western Australia.

Left: The 'Dwarf Sugar Banana', *Musa cavendishii*, described in *The Gardener and Practical Florist* (1843) as one of the best of the whole genus, though 'there are many spurious varieties sold for it'. This specimen, 3ft 5in high to the top of the stem, was in an Exeter nursery in 1836. Joseph Paxton had 100 plants at Chatsworth in 1837, 'part of which I shall have to distribute'.

week passes but that ships arrive bringing plants from the remotest habitable regions in these Wardian cases, which have thus conferred upon us a power of procuring exotic vegetable productions, which before their introduction was never possessed.'

Ward's cases were quickly accepted as valuable aids, particularly by botanical enthusiasts and growers of tender plants in difficult circumstances. They were initially purely functional, but as they came into wider use in the 1840s some makers began to produce them as decorative objects. The publishers of Louisa Johnson's *Every Lady Her Own Flower Gardener* added to the 1845 edition a chapter on 'Domestic Greenhouses', which had evidently become fairly common in better-off households at that time. The design recommended in this little manual has a mahogany stand and planting-box with brass fittings, and a brass-framed cover with a door on one side. The cover is lodged in a groove round the top of the box, and notches encouraged water that had condensed on the inside of the glass to drain back into the soil.

Several cases were shown in the Great Exhibition, including the first rather basic ones made by Ward himself. 'Though, at the present time, their design has been much improved,' commented *The Illustrated London News*, 'yet it is interesting to have the first example of the invention.' They were still sufficiently unfamiliar to need explanation: 'In various parts of the Building the visitor may observe live plants, growing, in some instances, under handsome glass shades, and in other

173

cases in glass frames, of so unprepossessing an appearance that he might naturally be at a loss to account for the reason why so uninteresting an object has been sent to the World's Fair. These contrivances are called Wardian cases...'

'In London but very few plants will thrive,' the article continues, adding that, apart from the Oriental Plane and the Lime it was practically impossible to grow any 'flower and vegetable structures' at all. The writer was obviously a keen Wardian convert, with cases of his own containing *Hoya carnosa*, *Hoya bella* and *Franciscea hopeana* as well as lycopodiums, ferns and foliage plants. Better still, 'By simply preventing the access of the London smoke to injure the leaves, we have this year succeeded in growing cucumbers in the very centre of the metropolis, showing what may be effected when the deleterious gases which emanate from the combustion of coal are prevented from exercising their baneful influence.'

The excitement generated by the Crystal Palace meant that almost anything made from glass was bound to appeal to the public of the 1850s. Ward's own book *On the Growth of Plants in Closely Glazed Cases*, first produced in 1842, was expanded and reissued in 1852, and interest was further encouraged by the attention given to the cases in works like Shirley Hibberd's *Rustic Adornments for Homes of Taste* of 1856. Above all, they were essential equipment for fern collectors in years when the craze for ferns, stimulated by a number of specialist works, was at its height. *The Gardeners' Chronicle* reviewed J.E. Sowerby's *The Ferns of Great Britain* and its companion, *The Fern Allies*, in 1856, but used the space mainly to castigate the Society for Promoting Christian Knowledge for publishing Anne Pratt's rival *Ferns of Great Britain and their Allies*. The complaint was not simply that they had rushed an oppo-

Those who remember the philanthropic wish of poor Suttum, uttered to Mr Layard as he waded his mare through a sea of bright blossoms on the plain of Nineveh, – "Ya! what do the dwellers in cities know of true happiness? GOD have pity on them. They have never seen grass or flowers! What delight has GOD given us equal to this It is the only thing worth living for!" – will hail the publication of Mr Hibberd's work as a practical commentary on Suttum's kindly sentiment, which every one who loves the country for the country's sake will share with him towards those who have the misfortune to be dwellers in towns.

Review of *Rustic Adornments* in the *Naturalist*, 1856.

Wardian cases for ferns and selaginellas, from J. Mollison's *The New Practical Window Gardener*, 1894.

'A Plant Case for a Room' from *Garden-Work*, 1887.

The ultimate destination of the Crystal Palace is, I think, becoming the main subject of the town and table talk of the day... The agitation in favour of upholding the structure is certainly more lukewarm than might have been anticipated, while the party whose war-cry is "The Park, the whole Park, and nothing but the Park!" is indefatigable in its exertions... Connected more or less with the Crystal Palace have been the several suggestions which have been circulated for throwing glass roofs over several of the principal thoroughfares, turning them, in fact, into vast arcades; and the still bolder scheme hinted at of arching a square or two with the same tranparent covering. Lincoln's Inn-fields, for example, converted into a vast glazed flower and winter garden, would hold, at all events, a central position, forming, as it does, almost the very heart of London. The smoke, however, would be the great drawback. A fortnight's muggy weather would strew the whole surface of the glass with more "blacks" than there are in Africa, while nothing like the fine fresh air, which ought to breathe among the fruits and flowers of any garden, winter or summer, could, we fear, be entrapped beneath the glass athwart the roofs and chimney-pots.

The Illustrated London News, 2nd August, 1853.

sition volume into print—'We do not presume to enquire whether an application of funds subscribed for religious purposes to the publication of works having no bearing upon religion is proper'—but that Miss Pratt had pinched Mr Sowerby's illustrations. 'It is obvious that they have been in several cases purloined from that gentleman, without the slightest acknowledgement, and as we have reason to believe without any permission having been granted.' According to the *Chronicle* writer, the note in Anne Pratt's book that her artist had purchased permission 'to copy certain details' was included only when 'legal proceedings had been threatened, and even then was conceded with the worst possible grace.' No such controversy seems to have been attached to Thomas Moore, whose *Ferns of Great Britain, Nature-printed* was produced by the technique of pressing specimens of the plants into soft metal to make the printing plates. He dedicated his *Popular History of the British Ferns* to 'N.B. Ward Esq., F.R.S., F.L.S., whose invention of close glazed cases has extended the cultivation of plants, and of ferns especially, to the parlour, the window-sill, and the city courtyard, and rendered their preservation in smoke-polluted localities possible, as well as enriched our gardens with the fruits and flowers of other lands.'

The cases were not always successful. Some of them became the fashionable toys of owners who failed to understand their use. In 1847, Ward had explained to the British Association that plants would stay healthy only if they were

given plenty of light and the right amount of moisture, and other experimenters pointed out that the system needed a certain amount of ventilation. Because of the difficulty of making completely tight joints, the first models had luckily allowed a slow circulation of air, but professional makers struggled to achieve a hermetic seal, with fatal results. A contributor to the *Chronicle* exclaimed in 1856: 'Can any reader of this Paper recollect a Wardian case in which the imprisoned plants were in good health?' People had come to believe that the increasingly ornamental 'domestic green-house' had an almost magical effect on the plants inside, though practical gardeners did their best to disabuse them: 'It has been urged times out of number...that the interior of a Wardian case, having the welfare of its inmates in view, must **not** be wholly cut off from the outside air... Throw away all ideas of any talismanic power existing in such a plant receptacle with respect to plant developments, and consider the total exclusion of the air as a popular fallacy.'

As the fad spread, glazed cases diverged more and more from Ward's original conception. The Waltonian, sold by the Winchester ironmonger, West, for about fifty shillings, had a heating boiler fired by a gas-jet or oil lamp. The precursor of the heated propagator, it was developed from a small frame for striking cuttings with a tank of hot water and an oil lamp in the base, which had been made up by Mr W. Walton, 'a gentleman of Surbiton', in 1855. An article in *The Cottage Gardener* seems to have caused Mr Walton considerable trouble. He was 'persecuted, almost every day for the last six months' by people wanting more details of the frame, many of whom doubted his estimate of the running cost. Donald Beaton wrote in the following year, 'All I can do now is to repeat, that Mr Walton's own Case costs him no more than twopence for the four-and-twenty hours,

Plate 4.

W. H. Fitch, del.

G. Severeyns Brussels.

LAPAGERIA. 1. Rosea. 2. Rosea Albeflora.

IN-DOOR PLANTS.

Day & Son, Lith. to the Queen.

1. FINE LEAVED GYMNOGRAMMA
Gymnogramma leptophylla

2. PARSLEY FERN.
Allosorus crispus

'Ornamental Plant Case with
Fountain and Hanging Basket'
from *The New Practical Window
Gardener*.

Opposite page, above: 'Garden Scene'
appropriate to the Victorian villa: a
plate from Shirley Hibberd's *Rustic
Adornments for Homes of Taste*, also used
as the frontispiece of his 1878 *The
Amateur's Flower Garden*.
Below left: Frontispiece for Miss E.A.
Maling's *In-door Plants*, 1862.
Below right: 'Fine Leaved
Gymnogramma and Parsley Fern': a
plate from Anne Pratt's *The Ferns of
Great Britain*, 1856, which was alleged
to have been copied from J.B.
Sowerby.

Unless you are a good hand at
growing Ferns *in the open air*, take
our word for it, you will kill
many of them before you learn
their culture in a Wardian case.
There is no ornamental piece of
drawing-room furniture which
we prefer before a Wardian case,
when under the management of
good gardeners; but there is not
one in a thousand who can
manage a case to our liking. We
have seen a dozen of them in
London, made up by the best
gardeners in the world, and then
were handed over to some one
or other who soon made a
regular Balaclava of them...

We are sorry to cast a damp
upon your Wardian Case
culture, but are compelled to
state facts that we know to be
true from our own experience.
Like every other gardening
operation, the plants in a
Wardian Case require constant
attention, and the plants
frequently renewed as they
perish, and they (the plants)
require a preparation and
course of culture on the starving
system (*a la Chinois*) to give them
a woody, dry texture, in order to
bear such a close confinement.
We can truly advise you not to
expect too much, and to be
content with partial success.

You are quite mistaken in saying
that we generally condemn
Wardian-cases. On the contrary,
we think them very interesting
and even useful in rooms,
especially as affording a
recreation and amusement to
many a suffering invalid.

from answers to correspondents
in the *The Cottage Gardener*, 1854,
1855 and 1856.

taking the average of the propagating season. Mr Walton's
butler, who gives out the oil declared this to me last week.'

E.A. Maling's *In-door Plants*, 'chiefly intended for the use
of those ladies who, while they are very fond of plants and
flowers, are yet obliged either to live in town or to spend
many months of every year in London,' describes a similar
design with a concealed tank which was simply refilled with
hot water once or twice a day—'The stands are perfectly
clean and unobjectionable; while their light construction
renders them very ornamental in a drawing-room window.'
This pattern, which was supplied at two guineas and upwards by Pickard & Co. of King's Cross, was highly recommended in the 1862 edition of the book, not surprisingly,
since the author had taken out a patent on it. A previous
maker had failed to give satisfaction: 'The carpenter, mentioned in the earlier editions of this little book as having
made an experimental case, is no longer employed by me;
nor is he at liberty to make the cases for others.'

Miss Maling makes it clear that not all drawing-room gardeners expected to fill their cases once for all and leave them
untended year after year. She suggests a form of 'bedding-
in' for each season, mixing ferns and dwarf evergreens with
a variety of small flowering shrubs and plants. 'As a general
rule,' she writes, 'I may observe that, while the brighter
flowers are better in the winter and spring months, in summer the darker and brighter the foliage is, the more really
refreshing to the eye will the plant-case appear.'

Variations of the basic form were produced from the
1860s to the 1890s, some built as miniature palaces, many
decorated in the height of late Victorian fantasy. The Warrington type combined fern-case with aquarium, while

Left: A Warrington plant case and aquarium, with filmy ferns, and, *above*, ornamental window layout, from *The New Practical Window Gardener.*

others had ornamental centrepieces and fountains. Yet another way of creating the closed environment was to glaze over an entire window recess or, if the window was flush with the wall, to construct a sealed case projecting outwards. An example is described in *Gardening Illustrated* for 1879, fitted with 'green cathedral glass' and incorporating a fish tank, a fountain, some rock-work and a fernery. It is hard to believe the claim that it did not 'unduly lessen' the light entering the room.

Window gardening was fairly common long before Ward produced his invention, and continued to be popular, where conditions allowed, independently of the fashion for closed cases. The window garden ranged from a few pots on the sill to complicated arrangements of troughs, vases, trellises and pillars. These were acknowledged to have been inspired by French and Belgian models, and the style was always associated more closely with continental Europe than with Britain: 'In Brussels the balconies are turned into greenhouses and miniature stoves, gay with the brightest and greenest foliage; and in Paris there are many contrivances in use by means of which the rarest and most beautiful plants are produced. Passifloras cling to columns in the upper floors; water-plants start into blossom, in tiny basins, curiously contrived in solid brickwork; and limpid water flows down a miniature rockery, from whose crevices start up ferns and lycopodiums.' (*Beeton's Book of Garden Management.*)

Opposite, above: A balcony garden from *The Journal of Horticulture*, 1872.
Below left: Window conservatory advertised by Ewart & Son in *Hooper's Gardening Guide:* 'Window Conservatories increase the size of the apartment, provide delicious ventilation in summer, and keep out the cold in winter. At the back of the house they are useful to hide a bad look out, and in the front improve the elevation.'
Right: A balcony garden from *The New Practical Window Gardener.*

The fountains which figured in many of these window arrangements were often of the 'self-acting' kind originally designed by Hero of Alexandria in the second century BC and described from time to time in the nineteenth-century gardening press. Larger versions were also made for use outdoors. All of them consisted of two interconnecting closed reservoirs, the pressure of air created by filling them

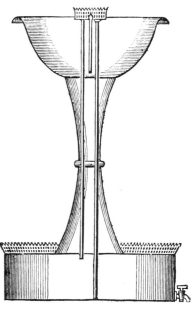

Self-acting fountains of the 1870s, with, *right*, a section of a home-made version. From *The Journal of Horticulture*.

with water forcing a jet out of the top. The water passed through the system in half-an-hour or so, according to the size, and the process was repeated as required. In the early 1870s, *The Journal of Horticulture* gave instructions, taken from *English Mechanic*, for making a fountain out of a fourteen-inch galvanised iron basin, some sheet zinc, a length of gas piping and the nozzle from a carpenter's oil can. A tray of ferns round the base hid any imperfections. Another design has a gravity-fed fountain between two ornamental cisterns which can be reversed like an hour glass, the nozzle being switched from one to the other: 'The whole operation can be performed in half a minute without spilling one drop.'

While richer householders experimented with intricate constructions and exotic displays, simpler styles were encouraged among the poor. In the suburbs and the town, where successive legislation and improved technology were beginning at least to reduce the smoke menace, window gardening to some extent took the place of the earlier tradition of floristry. When Thomas Moore brought out a revised edition of Thompson's *The Gardener's Assistant* in 1881, he commissioned J.C. Niven, the curator of Hull Botanic Garden, to add a chapter on window gardening—'The numerous societies that have been established throughout the country for the purpose of stimulating by means of exhibitions and prizes a taste for the growth of window plants amongst artisans and cottagers, point to the necessity of devoting some space to this special subject.' As ever, the poorer classes were felt to be safely occupied when they were gardening; Niven urged his readers 'to give material assistance towards the development of a taste which not only contributes to the adornment and beauty of our towns and villages, but to the moral elevation of the dwellers therein...

There are numerous small town gardens in Paris, and many houses have gardens of pots on their roofs. In a work entitled *Le Jardinier des Fenêtres*, the author directs how a considerable collection of plants may be grown on the roofs of houses. Not only botany, he says, but many of the operations of gardening, such as planting, sowing, grafting, striking by cuttings, pruning, training, &c., may be thus taught, so as to give persons who pass their youth in towns in acquiring an independency, such a knowledge of country matters as may lead them to retire there, when the objects of their industry have been obtained.

J. Loudon, *An Encyclopaedia of Gardening*, 1834.

'Arrangement of Plants and Fountain in Window' from *The New Practical Window Gardener*.

> ...till your flower-garden is made, I would advise you to have a few plants in pots in the east window. Remember, though, you must have only a few plants, as more than five or six would give the window the appearance of being a substitute for a greenhouse, a most unpleasant idea at any time, and particularly so in the country.
>
> Mrs Loudon, *The Lady's Country Companion*.

> The very ring of the name of window gardening is pleasant, and suggests hosts of beautiful parlour gardens, with the Ivy twining around the edges of the window sash; or on a stand in front of the pane is a pot of Geraniums, and over all hangs a basket filled with drooping plants. We are glad to see a growth of taste for plants; a genuine love for flowers promotes the love of home.
>
> *The Journal of Horticulture*, 1872.

If flora reigns on the window-sill, order, neatness, and tidiness will pervade all the internal arrangements of the cottage.' The moral improvement, however, was not taken entirely on trust. To make sure that all the exhibits were *bona fide* window plants, competition organisers were recommended to visit the homes of entrants two or three months before the show, and attach registration labels firmly to the flower stems.

Few Victorian houses were without plants for room decoration. Large London establishments entered into contracts with professional gardeners for the supply and regular replacement of house-plants, and special displays of plants and small trees were brought in for parties, balls and 'routs'. Ordinary homes were brightened up by a wide range of flowers and foliage, and benefited, like the gardens, from

the continuous introduction of new species and improved varieties, George Glenny remarked in an 1843 lecture: 'Those who have not a garden, I should like to see cultivate plants in pots; they are elegant ornaments in a drawing-room, and may be easily kept in perfection.' He went on to criticise the way they were treated, usually (according to him) by women: 'If ladies are ever concerned in the man-agement of plants, they kill them with kindness; lest they may be thirsty, they drown them in saucers of water.'

In the early part of the century, house-plants were usually grouped together on flower-stands or in open cases. For a long time wire was the most common material for stands, but later containers were made from wood or sheet metal. Miss Maling was firmly opposed to wire, which she thought was untidy and tended to rust, preferring wooden boxes of rustic pattern, or, best of all, basketwork trays lined with zinc. 'The basket-stands are an American contrivance, I believe, and I do not know of any English place where they may be met with; but at the London Asylum for the Blind all such work is undertaken, and, as the blind make so neatly the pretty plant-baskets for hanging from the roof, I doubt

Impression of a hallway decorated with pyramid-trained pelargoniums, suggested by a house in Paris: 'By this means the odour, the freshness, and the floral beauty of the plants accompanied the visitor to the very door of the principal saloon.' From 'A Plea for Pyramidal Pelargoniums' by the late Mr George McEwen, of the Horticultural Society's Garden at Chiswick, in *The Journal of Horticulture*, 1862.

THE SUPPLY OF HOUSE PLANTS
There are many ways of doing this; but to those who have the opportunity, and choose to be at the expense, there is, perhaps, none better than that of contracting for the year with some skilful and respectable nurseryman; in this case the plants will be attended by the contractor, and kept in the best condition. Much pleasure, is, however, sacrificed by those who adopt this mode, inasmuch as the chief enjoyment of plants arises from the feeling that they are the nurslings of our own care; and it is astonishing how strongly the judicious treatment of plants leads to judicious management in all other matters.

Charles McIntosh in Louis Johnson's *Every Lady Her Own Flower Gardener*, 1845(eighth edition).

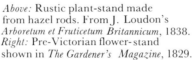

Above: Rustic plant-stand made from hazel rods. From J. Loudon's *Arboretum et Fruticetum Britannicum*, 1838.
Right: Pre-Victorian flower-stand shown in *The Gardener's Magazine*, 1829.

Then, taking any common moss that can most easily be obtained (the men who sell primroses, &c., in the streets, can often procure luxuriant specimens from the woods), a canful of boiling water should be thrown upon it, to destroy the insects and eggs of insects that may be in it: this process makes the moss particularly dry and clean, only the moss should be spread out in the sun first, or washed, to make the living insects go away. With this moss the spaces between the plants are to be filled.
E.A. Maling, *In-door Plants*, 1862.

not that they would immediately, and beautifully, execute orders for basket-stands.' She also liked to convert old oak chests and coffers: 'The plants look so exquisitely fresh, contrasted with the almost blackness that age has given to the oak: many persons possess such beautiful pieces of oak carving, which they would be quite glad to find a use for.' To keep the pots from drying out, they were plunged in silver sand and hidden with moss.

Later still, individual pots and vases appeared as decoration on tables, sideboards and shelves. Plants were chosen for bold foliage effects, the favourites being dracaenas, palms, agaves, crotons, rubber-plants and others which would stand a dimly-lit position. Common ivy, a useful climber for indoor trellises, was even trained over wire-netting frames to form screens in front of fireplaces in the summer. Centrepieces of plants mixed with cut flowers and fruit became essential parts of the setting for fashionable dinner tables. Their construction was something of a specialised art, and again merited an addition in *The Gardener's Assistant* in 1881. Arrangers were advised to use a measuring-stick to make sure that the diners' view was not obstructed: 'If there is to be any speech-making after dinner any decoration higher than 15 inches should be avoided.'

Classes for table arrangements were included in exhibitions. The Royal Horticultural Society's show in May 1872 had two long tents devoted exclusively to them, with prizes

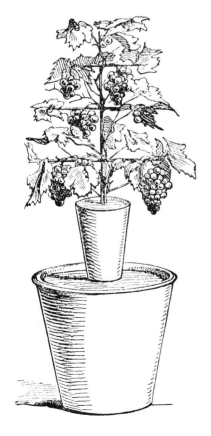

amounting to £84. Entries were received from glass and china dealers as well as gardeners, but first place went to an amateur entry. According to the Revd Dombrain's notice in *The Journal of Horticulture*, 'it consisted of two large ferns let into the table, and surrounded by fern leaves, so as to hide all appearance of their being so done. The centrepiece was singularly elegant—a tall glass, with Cacti blooms at the base of it; the vase itself containing Lily of the Valley, salmon-coloured Geraniums, and light Grasses. On either side were two recumbent figures surrounded by moss...' The also-rans included an exhibit topped with miniature flags, and another built round two huge blocks of Wenham Lake ice. In another class, economy of cost was considered by the judges, and the reviewer commented: 'I am glad to find a more simple taste encouraged, and hope it augurs better things in table decorations than the vulgarities we have been treated to.'

The Society was attacked for offering a substantial prize for 'mere matters of taste and ornament where no horticultural skill is called into requisition', and correspondents to the *Journal* complained about the absurdity of cutting holes in valuable mahogany tables and damask cloths to hide plant pots. 'I feel that the ornamentation of the dining-table is drifting into the wrong direction,' wrote one, 'and hope the table will at least be respected, if not the comfort of the guests.' It was perfectly possible to provide effective displays without vandalising the furniture. William Thomson devised an ingenious way of growing vines for the Duke of Buccleuch's table at Dalkeith which avoided large, unsightly containers. When he started the shoots into growth, he passed them through a second pot on top of the main one: 'The small pot gets filled with roots by the time the grapes are ripe, when it may be detached from the large pot, and can be set in a small vase on the table, where the tree-like plant with fine pendulous bunches of grapes looks all that can be desired.' (*Cultivation of the Grape Vine.*)

The taste for filling rooms with plants revived the controversy about their 'poisonous emanations'. *The Dictionary of Daily Wants* of 1860 warns: 'It must be borne in mind that the odours of flowers are very injurious to health, if the plants are confined with us in closed rooms. During the night, plants generally give out a gas, which is especially hurtful to human beings in a sleeping apartment of which the door and window are closed. The effluvium, also, which sometimes arises from our bodies during sleep, has an unhealthy effect on the plants.' In his *New Practical Window Gardener*, however, John Mollison included a chapter, 'Plants in our Dwellings; are they Beneficial or Not?', where he tried to show that the idea was 'to a great extent chimerical' and to explain to his readers that the small quantities of carbon dioxide given off were hardly likely to do them any harm, especially if they opened the bedroom window a little—'You should do this in any case during summer, for it is very beneficial to the health of sleepers.' If anything, it was the plants that suffered: 'When night comes on we draw down the blinds, shut our doors and windows, stir up the fire and crowd round the cheerful hearth all unconscious that by keeping out the cold and raising the temperature of the room several degrees we are keeping the poor plants in a state of unhealthy excitement, keeping them feverishly awake when they should be at rest... Window gardening at best is plant growing under difficulties; the more therefore you can assimilate their existence to the life of the same plants in their natural homes the more successful you will be.'

Cast-iron plant-stand and fountain from *American Gardeners' Monthly*, reproduced in *The Cottage Gardener*, 1860.

Book List

Books on Gardening, Garden Design and Garden History

Abercrombie, John *Every Man His Own Gardener*. 1767; 20th ed. J. Rivington and others, London, 1813; 26th ed. with notes and additions by James Main and George Glenny, Longman & Co., and others, 1857.

Abercrombie, John *The Practical Gardener*. T. Cadell, London, 1834.

Anderson, James *The New Practical Gardener and Modern Horticulturist*. William Mackenzie, London, c.1880.

Baines, Thomas *Greenhouse & Stove Plants*. John Murray, London 1885; revised ed. 1894.

Beeton's Book of Garden Management. Ward Lock & Co. London, 1872.

Blomfield, Sir Reginald, and Thomas, F. Inigo. *The Formal Garden in England*. Macmillan & Co. London, 1892.

Boyle, Hon. Mrs E.V. ('E.V.B.') *Days and Hours in a Garden* Elliot Stock. London, 1884.

Bradley, Richard *A General Treatise of Husbandry and Gardening*. 1726.

Bridgeman, Thomas *The Young Gardener's Assistant*. New York, 1829; 12th ed. 1847.

Burbidge, F.W. *Cultivated Plants, Their Propagation and Improvement*. William Blackwood, Edinburgh, 1877.

Cobbett, William *The English Gardener*. London, 1833; reissued by Oxford University Press, 1980.

Cole, Nathan *The Royal Parks and Gardens of London*. Journal of Horticulture, London, 1877.

Delamer, E.S. *The Flower Garden*. George Routledge & Sons, London, c.1860.

Delamer, E.S. *The Kitchen Garden*. George Routledge & Sons, London, c.1860.

Don, James *Hortus Cantabrigiensis*. Cambridge, 1796; 13th ed. revised by P.N. Don, 1845.

Doyle, Martin [pseudonym of William Hickey] *The Flower Garden*. William Curry & Co., 1845 ed.

Florists' Flowers for the Many The Cottage Gardener, London, c.1855.

Glenny, George *The Culture of Flowers and Plants*. Houlston and Wright, London, 1861.

Glenny, George *The Hand-Book of Gardening*. Cassell, Peter and Galpin, London, 1865.

Glenny, George *Glenny's Hand-Book of Practical Gardening*. C. Cox, London, c.1855.

Glenny, George *Hand-Book to the Flower-Garden & Greenhouse*. C. Cox, London, 1851.

Harrison, Charles *A Treatise on the Culture and Management of Fruit Trees*. 1823; 2nd ed. London, 1825.

Hazlitt, William Carew *Gleanings in Old Garden Literature*. Elliot Stock, London, 1887.

Hibberd, Shirley *The Amateur's Flower Garden*. Groombridge and Sons, London, 1878.

Hibberd, Shirley *The Amateur's Greenhouse and Conservatory*. Groombridge and Sons, London, 1873.

Hibberd, Shirley *The Amateur's Kitchen Garden*. Groombridge and Sons, London, 1877.

Hibberd, Shirley *Brambles and Bay Leaves*. Groombridge and Sons, London, 1855; 2nd ed. 1862.

Hibberd, Shirley *The Fern Garden*. Groombridge and Sons, London, 5th ed. 1875.

Hibberd, Shirley *Profitable Gardening*. Groombridge and Sons, London, c.1860.

Hibberd, Shirley *Familiar Garden Flowers*. Cassell, Petter, Galpin & Co., London, c.1875.

Hobday, Edward *Villa Gardening*. Macmillan and Co., London, 1887.

Hole, S. Reynolds *A Book about the Garden*. Thomas Nelson & Sons, London, 1892.

Hooper's Gardening Guide. 3rd ed. 1883.

Hogg, Thomas *A Concise and Practical Treatise on the Growth and Culture of the Carnation* etc. Whittaker, Treacher and Co., London, 5th ed. 1832.

Johnson, George W. *The Gardeners' Dictionary*. 1856; revised ed., George Bell and Sons, London, 1877.

Johnson, Louisa *Every Lady Her Own Flower Gardener*. 8th ed. William Orr and Co., London, 1845.

Keane, William *Out-Door Gardening*. Journal of Horticulture, London, 1865.

Kingsley, Rose G. *Eversley Gardens and Others*. George Allen & Sons, London, 1907.

Loudon, Jane *The Amateur Gardener's Calendar.*
Longmans, Green and Co., London, 1867.

Loudon, Jane *The Lady's Country Companion, or How to Enjoy a Country Life Rationally.* London, 1845.

Loudon, Jane *The Ladies' Companion to the Flower-Garden.* 1841; 4th ed. William Smith, London, 1846.

Loudon, Jane *Practical Instructions in Gardening for Ladies.* 1840; 2nd ed. John Murray, London, 1841.

Loudon, John Claudius *Arboretum et Fruticetum Britannicum.* Longman, Orme, Brown, Green, and Longmans, London, 1838.

Loudon, John Claudius *The Cottager's Manual.* Baldwin and Cradock, London, 1840.

Loudon, John Claudius *An Encyclopaedia of Gardening.* 1822; new ed. Longman, Orme, Brown, Green, and Longmans, London, 1834.

Loudon, John Claudius *An Encyclopaedia of Plants.* Longman, Orme, Brown, Green, and Longmans, London, 1829.

Loudon, John Claudius *An Encyclopaedia of Trees and Shrubs* (abridged from the *Arboretum*). Longman, Brown, Green and Longmans, London, 1842.

Loudon, John Claudius (anonymously) *The Green-House Companion.* Harding, Triphook, and Lepard, London, 1825.

Loudon, John Claudius *Hortus Britannicus.* 1830; new ed. Longman, Brown, Green, and Longmans, London, 1832.

Loudon, John Claudius, edited and revised by W. Robinson, *The Horticulturist.* Frederick Warne and Co., London, 1871.

Maling, E.A. *In-Door Plants and How to Grow Them.* Smith Elder & Co., London, 1862.

Martineau, Alice *The Herbaceous Garden.* Williams & Norgate, London, 1913.

McIntosh, Charles *The Flower Garden.* 1838; new ed. William S. Orr & Co., London, 1844.

McIntosh, Charles *The Practical Gardener and Modern Horticulturist.* Thomas Kelly, London, 1830.

Miller, Philip *The Gardeners Kalendar.* J.& J. Rivington, London, 1757.

Mollison, John R. *The New Practical Window Gardener.* Groombridge and Sons, London, c.1875; new ed. Henry J. Drane, London, 1894.

Moore, Thomas *A Popular History of British Ferns.* Lovell Reeve, London, 2nd ed. 1855.

Nicholson, George *The Illustrated Dictionary of Gardening, a Practical and Scientific Encyclopaedia of Horticulture.* L. Upcott Gill, London, 1887.

Outline of Flemish Husbandry. Baldwin and Cradock, London, 1840.

Paterson, Nathaniel *The Manse Garden.* 1838 ed. William Collins, Glasgow.

Paxton, Joseph *A Pocket Botanical Dictionary.* J. Andrews, London, 1840.

Pratt, Anne *The Ferns of Great Britain.* S.P.C.K. and Frederick Warne and Co., London, 1856.

Prior, W.D. *Hardy Shrubs.* George Routledge and Sons, London, 1881.

Rivers, Thomas *The Rose-Amateur's Guide.* Longmans, Green, and Co., London, 10th ed. 1872.

Robinson, William *Alpine Flowers for English Gardens.* John Murray, London, 1870.

Robinson, William *The English Flower Garden.* John Murray, London 1883.

Robinson, William *Gleanings from French Gardens.* Frederick Warne and Co., London, 1868.

Robinson, William *The Wild Garden.* John Murray, London, 1870.

Robinson, William with Barnes, James *Asparagus Culture.* George Routledge and Sons, London, 1881.

Rohde, Eleanour Sinclair *The Story of the Garden.* The Medici Society, London, 1932.

Sedding, John *Garden-Craft Old and New.* Kegan Paul, Trench, Trübner & Co., London, 1891; 2nd ed. 1892.

Shaw, C.W. *The London Market Gardens.* The Garden, London, 2nd ed. 1880.

Slater, John *The Amateur Florists' Guide.* John Heywood, Manchester, c.1859.

Smith, John *A Treatise on the Growth of Cucumbers and Melons.* J.M. Burton, Ipswich, 1839.

Sweet, Robert *The Botanical Cultivator.* James Ridgway, London, 1821.

Thomson, David *Handy Book of the Flower-Garden.* William Blackwood & Son, Edinburgh, 1868.

Thomson, David *Handy Book of Fruit Culture under Glass.* William Blackwood & Son, Edinburgh, 1881.

Thomson, William *A Practical Treatise on the Cultivation of the Grape Vine.* William Blackwood & Son, 6th ed. 1869.

Thompson, Robert *The Gardener's Assistant.* Blackie and Son, Glasgow, 1859; revised and extended by Thomas Moore, 1881.

Towers, John *The Domestic Gardener's Manual.* John W. Parker, London, 1839.

Watts, Elizabeth *Flowers and the Flower Garden.* Frederick Warne and Co., London, 1869.

William, B.S. *Choice Stove and Greenhouse Flowering Plants.* 3rd ed. pub. by author 1883.

Wood, Samuel *The Bulb Garden.* Crosby Lockwood & Co., London, 1878.

Wood, Samuel *The Ladies' Multum-in-Parvo Flower Garden.* Crosby Lockwood & Co., London, 1881.

General Books

Austin, Alfred *In Veronica's Garden.* Macmillan and Co., London, 1897 ed.

Ball, T.F. *Queen Victoria.* S.W. Partridge & Co., London, Jubilee ed. 1886-87.

Beauties and Wonders of Vegetable Life. The Religious Tract Society, London, c.1860.

Copley, Esther *The Complete Cottage Cookery.* Groombridge and Sons, London, 10th ed. 1858.

The Dictionary of Daily Wants. Houlston & Wright, London, 1858.

Dodd, George *British Manufactures.* Charles Knight & Co., London, 1844-46.

Friend, Rev. Hilderic *Flowers and Flower Lore.* Swan Sonnenschein and Co., London, 1883.

Griffiths, A.B. *Manures and their Uses.* George Bell & Sons, London, 1889.

Hall, Sir A.D. *The Book of the Rothamsted Experiments.* John Murray, London, 1905.

Hall, Sir A.D. *Fertilisers and Manures.* John Murray, London, 1909.

Hall, Sir A.D. *The Soil.* John Murray, London, 1903.

Holdsworth, Joseph *On the Extension of the English Coal-fields*. R. Middleton, London, 1866.

Jones, William. *The Book of Nature*. S.P.C.K., London, 1846.

The Juvenile Rambler, or Sketches and Anecdotes of the People of Various Countries. John Harris, London, 1838.

The Language and Poetry of Flowers. Marcus Ward & Co., London, 1831 ed.

Liebig, Justus *Chemistry in its Application to Agriculture and Physiology*. Taylor and Walton, London, 1846.

'Martha Careful' *Household Hints to Young Housewives*. Dean & Son, London, 12th ed. 1859.

McLeod, John *Voyage of H.M.S. Alceste*. John Murray, London, 2nd ed. 1818.

Mortimer, Thomas *A General Commercial Dictionary*. Rees, Orme, Brown, and Green, London, 4th ed. 1827.

Murray, L. *The Young Man's Best Companion*. Thomas Kelly, London, 1824.

Peter Parley's Tales about Plants. Edited by Mrs Loudon. Thomas Tegg, London 1839.

Phillips, Sir Richard *A Dictionary of the Arts of Life and Civilization*. Sherwood, Gilbert & Piper, London, 1833.

Pratt, Anne and Miller, Thomas *The Language, Associations and Popular Tales of Flowers*. Simpkin, Marshall, Hamilton, Kent & Co., London, 1897 ed.

Rundell, Mrs. ('A Lady') *A New System of Domestic Cookery*. John Murray, London, 2nd ed. 1807.

Scarth, John *Twelve Years in China*. Thomas Constable and Co., Edinburgh, 1840.

Schnebbelie, Jacob *The Housekeeper's Instructor*. J. Stratford, London, 1808.

Scientific Mysteries. The Chemist and Druggist, London, 1891.

Smiles, Samuel *Self-Help*. John Murray, London, 1862 ed.

Thompson, Flora *Lark Rise*. Oxford University Press, 1939.

Tonna, C.E. 'Charlotte Elizabeth' *Chapters on Flowers*. R.B. Seeley & W. Burnside, London, 2nd ed. 1838.

Vegetable Substances used for the Food of Man. Charles Knight, London, 1832.

Wilson, John *Our Farm Crops*. Blackie & Son, London, 1859.

The Young Woman's Companion or Female Instructor. Allman & Son, London, c.1830.

I have also drawn on various issues of the following periodicals:

The Gardener's Magazine 'and Register of Rural & Domestic Improvement'.

The Gardener and Practical Florist.

The Annals of Horticulture, 'and Year-Book of Information on Practical Gardening' (the annual compilation of *The Horticultural Magazine*).

The Gardeners' Chronicle and Agricultural Gazette.

The Floricultural Cabinet and Florist's Magazine.

The Floral World and Garden Guide.

The Naturalist; 'a Popular Monthly Magazine Illustrative of the Animal, Vegetable, and Mineral Kingdoms'.

The Cottage Gardener, and Country Gentleman's Companion. (From 1861, *The Journal of Horticulture, Cottage Gardener and Country Gentleman*).

The Gardener's Weekly Magazine and Floricultural Cabinet.

Gardening Illustrated.

The Gardener, 'a Magazine of Horticulture and Floriculture'.

Garden-Work, 'for Suburban, Town and Cottage Gardens'.

Chambers' Edinburgh Journal.

The Illustrated London News.

Index